John Smith

Waldeinsamkeit
Films from the 21st Century

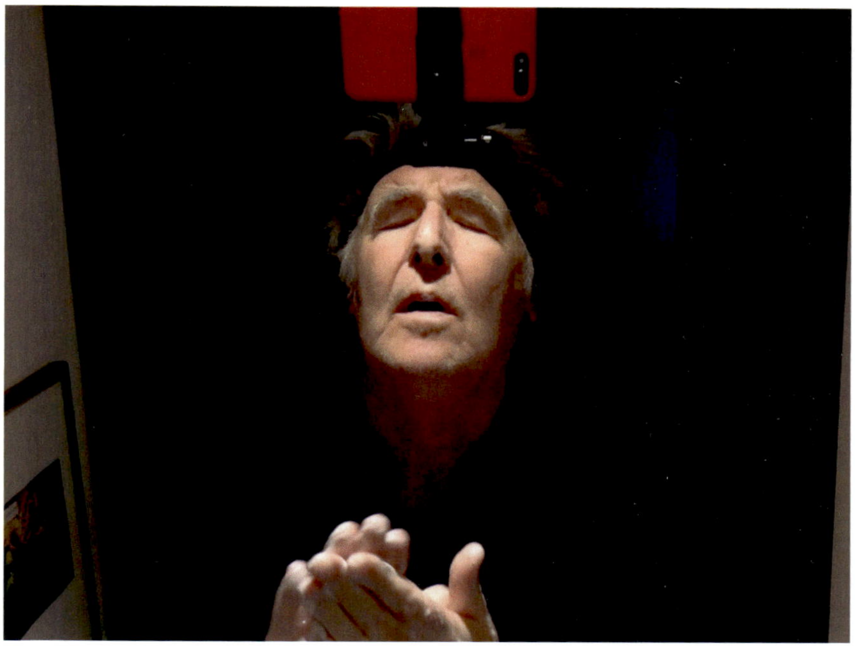

Covid Messages, 2020, HD video, 22 minutes

John Smith films himself in the mirror, washing his hands while singing *Happy Birthday* twice to the tune of Chopin's funeral march.

Covid Messages, 2020, HD-Video, 22 Minuten

John Smith filmt sich selbst im Spiegel, während er, sich die Hände waschend, zweimal *Happy Birthday* zu der Melodie von Chopins Trauermarsch singt.

Verlag für moderne Kunst

KUNSTMUSEUM MAGDEBURG KLOSTER UNSER LIEBEN FRAUEN KMd

Thanks / Dank

This publication has been kindly supported by the State of Saxony-Anhalt and Kloster Bergesche Stiftung

Die Publikation wird unterstützt durch das Land Sachsen-Anhalt und die Kloster Bergesche Stiftung.

Waldeinsamkeit

Annegret Laabs

In 1790 the British satirist Horace Walpole (1717–97) mocked his fellow countrymen: 'One would think the English are ducks, they are forever waddling to the waters.'[1] Though it may seem quite irrelevant, knowledge of the Britons' relationship with their sea is not insignificant in the context of John Smith's suggestion that his exhibition in Magdeburg be titled 'Waldeinsamkeit' – a proposal that caught us by surprise. The beauty and terror of nature: this pair of opposites has always been destined to captivate people, and the nostalgic role that the sea plays for the maritime nation of England is played by the existential metaphor of *Waldeinsamkeit* for the Germans.

Great Britain's history as a trading nation and sea power is still alive today in Britons' relationship with their almost 12,500 km of coastline. Like a national ritual (and increasingly since the outbreak of Corona), families from every part of the island set out on traditional excursions to the seaside. The British have learned everything from the sea: the love of freedom, the courage to take risks and a faith in the power of the moment. The roots of the island and its people lie in the sea: Daniel Defoe's (d.1731) *Robinson Crusoe* is the best literary example of this. Each day, the title character faces the terror of the sea as a force of nature, and he finally tames it. In his film *Horizon*, Smith has also taken up Crusoe's point of view – but also that of J. M.W. Turner. Like the British Romantic, Smith has looked out across the sea from the coast at Margate and captured the forces of nature in an image for all those who would prefer not to expose themselves to a dangerous sea storm from this vantage point.

While an increasing number of Britons have been drawn to the seaside during the last few months of the pandemic, Germans have directed their attention more and more to 'their' forest. Reflecting a kind of 'Fernstenliebe' – a love of getting as far away as possible – 87% of Germans of all ages surveyed in a recently published study said that they regularly go to the forest.[2] Two thirds of Germany are covered by forest, and it has the most forest of any country in the European Union. It still has 1,420 square metres of forest per capita, and the Germans' interest in the forest has remained unbroken in the new millennium.[3] And there is a reason for this: in *Germania* Tacitus (*c.* AD 58–120) had already begun telling ancient Roman readers about the gigantic old-growth forests in the Germanic north and its inhabitants' fear of entering them. The origin myth of the Germanic Forest and

1. Cited in David Hodgkins, 'How they did like to be beside the seaside', in *The Property Chronicle 2017*, www.propertychronicle.com, accessed 12.11.2021.

2. n-tv.de, jaz/dpa, 21.03.2021, https://www.n-tv.de/wissen/Die-Deutschen-lieben-ihren-Wald-article22440587.html, accessed 08.11.2021.

3. See the results of a research project on 'forest knowledge' by the Institut für Volkskunde Hamburg: Albrecht Lehmann, 'Mythos Deutscher Wald: Waldbewußtsein und Waldwissen in Deutschland', in *Der Deutsche Wald*, ed. by Landeszentrale für politische Bildung Baden-Württemberg, no. 1 (2001), 4–9.

Waldeinsamkeit

Annegret Laabs

„Man könnte meinen, dass die Engländer Enten seien, weil sie ständig zum Wasser watschelten",[1] spottete 1790 der britische Satiriker Horace Walpole (1717–97) über seine Landsleute. So abwegig es scheint, doch ebendieses Wissen um die Beziehung der Brit*innen zu ihrem Meer ist nicht unbedeutend mit Blick auf den Begriff „Waldeinsamkeit", den John Smith als Titel für seine Magdeburger Ausstellung zu unserer Überraschung vorgeschlagen hat. Schönheit und Schrecken der Natur, von jeher ist dieses Gegensatzpaar dafür bestimmt, die Menschen in ihren Bann zu ziehen, und was für die Seenation der Brit*innen das von Nostalgie getragene Meer ist, ist für die Deutschen die Daseinsmetapher *Waldeinsamkeit*.

Die Geschichte Großbritanniens als Handelsnation und Seemacht lebt noch heute in der Beziehung der Brit*innen zu ihrer fast 12.500 Kilometer langen Küste fort. Traditionelle Familienausflüge werden, einem nationalen Ritus gleich, und seit Corona Zeiten wieder verstärkt, von jedem Ort der Insel aus ans Meer unternommen. Alles haben die Brit*innen vom Meer gelernt: die Liebe zur Freiheit, den Mut zum Risiko und das Vertrauen in die Macht des Augenblicks. Die Wurzeln des Kontinents und seiner Bevölkerung liegen im Meer, *Robinson Crusoe* von Daniel Defoe (gest. 1731) ist das literarische Beispiel hierfür. Jeden Tag von neuem steht Robinson dem Schrecken der Naturgewalt Meer gegenüber, um es schließlich zu bezwingen. Auch John Smith hat mit seinem Film *Horizon* die Betrachterperspektive Crusoes eingenommen, aber auch jene eines William Turner. Wie der britische Romantiker, so hat auch John Smith an der Küste von Margate über das Meer geschaut und die Naturgewalten im Bild für all jene festgehalten, die sich selbst dem Standpunkt im gefährlichen Sturm am Meer nicht aussetzen möchten.

Während es die Brit*innen in der Pandemiezeit der letzten Monate verstärkt an die Meeresküste zog, gilt die Aufmerksamkeit der Deutschen mehr denn je „ihrem" Wald. In einer Art „Fernstenliebe" geben in einer kürzlich veröffentlichten Studie 87 Prozent der Deutschen jedes Alters an, regelmäßig in den Wald zu gehen.[2] Deutschland, zu zwei Dritteln von Wald bedeckt, ist das waldreichste Land der Europäischen Union. Noch sind es 1420 Quadratmeter Waldbestand pro Einwohner, und das Interesse der Deutschen am Wald ist auch im neuen Jahrtausend ungebrochen.[3] Und das nicht ohne Grund: Bereits Tacitus (ca. 58–120 n. Chr.) erzählte seinen römischen

1. Zitiert nach David Hodgkins, „How they did like to be beside the seaside", in: *The Property Chronicle 2017*, www.propertychronicle.com, abgerufen am 12.11.2021.

2. n-tv.de, jaz/dpa, 21.03.2021, https://www.n-tv.de/wissen/Die-Deutschen-lieben-ihren-Wald-article22440587.html, abgerufen am 08.11.2021.

3. Vergleiche die Ergebnisse eines Forschungsprojektes zum „Waldwissen" am Institut für Volkskunde Hamburg: Albrecht Lehmann, „Mythos Deutscher Wald. Waldbewusstsein und Waldwissen in Deutschland", in: *Der Deutsche Wald*, hrsg. von der Landeszentrale für politische Bildung Baden-Württemberg, Heft 1 (2001), 4–9.

the people devoted to it had been born, and the various research work conducted by Romantics like Jacob Grimm, scholars of German language and literature, teachers and anthropologists continued to render this myth directly manifest until well into the first half of the 20th century.

On the other hand, the term *Waldeinsamkeit*, which refers to the solitude of the forest and which genuinely has no parallel in any other language, strikes today's Germans as strange. It thus seems all the more difficult to understand why several English-language blogs have placed the term among the '10 words in German' that are untranslatable and that everyone definitely ought to know – alongside words like 'Fernweh', 'Weltschmerz' and 'Torschlusspanik'.

After all, the Romantic existential metaphor of *Waldeinsamkeit* had almost completely vanished from Germans' vocabulary for many years.[4] Only in recent years has the term occasionally found its way back into everyday language. The sole reason for this may perhaps be found in German newspaper reports about people spending more time in nature during the current Corona pandemic and the temporary lockdowns connected with it. The situation is very different in numerous essays published in languages other than German: since the spring of 2021 these have increasingly conveyed the impression that *Waldeinsamkeit* is an important term in everyday communication among Germans and described it as an 'essential component in the German psyche'.[5] In addition to the Italian *Metropolitan Magazine*,[6] the English-language online magazine *The Local*, for example, has presented multiple articles on the term *Waldeinsamkeit* since April 2021 in its section 'Germany's news in English'.[7] It has been declared the 'German word of the day' and, in the article *Waldeinsamkeit: Five of the best forest walks around Berlin*, it is used to promote walking in the Plänterwald and Treptower Park during the pandemic, thus definitively ensuring that 'being alone in the woods' can become a mass phenomenon.

An article about cross-country skiing in the Black Forest that was published by the *Rhein-Neckar-Zeitung* in the winter of 2021 at least suggests every reader can make sense of the term: 'And

4. Word-frequency chart for 'Waldeseinsamkeit', generated through the *Digitale Wörterbuch der deutschen Sprache*, https://www.dwds.de/r/plot/?view=1&corpus=zeitungen&norm=-date%2Bclass&smooth=spline&genres=0&grand=1&slice=1&prune=0&win-dow=3&wbase=0&logavg=0&logscale=0&xrange=1946%3-A2021&q1=%7B'Waldeinsamkeit'%2C'Waldeseinsamkeit'%7D, accessed 26.10.2021.

5. Tom Burson, *Wellness Through Waldeinsamkeit. Why Germans go into Forests Alone to Cure Stress*, 18.09.2018, https://amuse.vice.com/en_us/article/5984vb/waldeinsamkeit-ger-man-cure-stress, accessed 17.11.2021.

6. Stella Grillo, *Waldeinsamkeit, parole dal mondo: contemplare la natura in solitudine*, 07.10.2021, https://metropolitanmagazine.it/waldeinsamkeit-parole-dal-mondo-contemplare-la-nat-ura-in-solitudine, accessed 19.11.2021.

7. Charlotte Hall, *German word of the day: Die Waldeinsamkeit*, 06.04.2021, https://www.thelocal.de/20210406/german-word-of-the-day-die-waldeinsamkeit; Sophie Shanahan, *Waldeinsamkeit: Five of the best forest walks around Berlin*, 07.05.2021, https://www.thelocal.de/20210507/waldeinsamkeit-five-of-the-best-forest-walks-around-berlin, accessed 16.11.2021.

Leser*innen in der *Germania* von den riesigen Urwäldern im germanischen Norden und von der Furcht der Bewohner*innen, diese zu betreten. Der Ursprungsmythos des germanischen Waldes und des ihm zugetanen Volkes war geboren und wurde durch Romantiker*innen wie Jacob Grimm von Germanist*innen, Lehrer*innen und Volkskundler*innen bis in die erste Hälfte des 20. Jahrhunderts durch diverse Forschungen geradezu manifestiert.

Der Begriff *Waldeinsamkeit*, für den es tatsächlich keine Entsprechung in einer anderen Sprache gibt, mutet uns hingegen heute fremd an. Umso unverständlicher scheint, dass einige englischsprachige Blogs den Begriff neben „Fernweh", „Weltschmerz" und „Torschlusspanik" unter die „10 Wörter der deutschen Sprache" einreihen, die nicht übersetzbar sind und die man doch unbedingt kennen sollte.

Dabei war die romantische Daseinsmetapher *Waldeinsamkeit* für viele Jahre aus dem deutschen Wortschatz fast vollständig verschwunden.[4] Erst die letzten Jahre brachten den Begriff hier und da in den Sprachalltag zurück. Der Grund hierfür mag allein in der Berichterstattung der Feuilletons über den vermehrten Aufenthalt der Menschen in der Natur während der aktuellen Corona-Pandemie und des damit verbundenen zeitweiligen Lockdowns zu suchen sein. Ganz anders hingegen in zahlreichen nicht deutschsprachigen Essays, in denen seit dem Frühjahr 2021 vermehrt der Eindruck erweckt wird, dass die *Waldeinsamkeit* ein wichtiger Kommunikationsbegriff im deutschen Alltag sei und dieser einen wesentlichen Bestandteil der deutschen Psyche beschreiben würde.[5] Neben dem italienischen *Metropolitan Magazine*[6] präsentierte zum Beispiel das englischsprachige Onlinemagazin *The Local* unter der Rubrik „Germany's news in English" ab April 2021 gleich mehrere Artikel zum Begriff *Waldeinsamkeit*,[7] die diesen zum „German word of the day" küren oder unter *Waldeinsamkeit: Five of the best forest walks around Berlin* für Spaziergänge während der Corona-Pandemie im Plänterwald oder im Treptower Park werben und somit das „Einsamsein im Wald" ganz sicher zu einem Massenerlebnis werden lassen.

4. Statistische Auswertung der Wortverlaufskurve für „Waldeseinsamkeit", erstellt durch das *Digitale Wörterbuch der deutschen Sprache*, https://www.dwds.de/r/plot/?view=1&corpus=zeitungen&norm=date%2Bclass&smooth=spline&genres=0&grand=1&slice=1&prune=0&window=3&wbase=0&logavg=0&logscale=0&xrange=1946%3A2021&q1=%7B'Waldeinsamkeit'%2C'Waldeseinsamkeit'%7D, abgerufen am 26.10.2021.

5. Tom Burson, *Wellness Through Waldeinsamkeit. Why Germans go into Forests Alone to Cure Stress*, 18.09.2018, https://amuse.vice.com/en_us/article/5984vb/wald, einsamkeit-german-cure-stress, abgerufen am 17.11.2021.

6. Stella Grillo, *Waldeinsamkeit, parole dal mondo: contemplare la natura in solitudine*, 07.10.2021, https://metropolitanmagazine.it/waldeinsamkeit-parole-dal-mondo-contemplare-la-natura-in-solitudine/, abgerufen am 19.11.2021.

7. Charlotte Hall, *German word of the day: Die Waldeinsamkeit*, 06.04.2021, https://www.thelocal.de/20210406/german-word-of-the-day-die-waldeinsamkeit; Sophie Shanahan, *Waldeinsamkeit: Five of the best forest walks around Berlin*, 07.05.2021, https://www.thelocal.de/20210507/waldeinsamkeit-five-of-the-best-forest-walks-around-berlin/, abgerufen am 16.11.2021.

you can glide through these fairy-tale boughs – which do not seem so sombre at all because of the abundant snow – letting yourself be carried away and 'feeling Waldeinsamkeit', without any pressure at all.'[8] Alone in the woods, no one is there except the protagonist and a feeling defined by physical distance from the events of the world and the certainty of being in the right place at this precise moment. Joseph von Eichendorff (1788–1857) writes: 'How far it lies, / The world, from here!'[9] The tranquil forest – which Eichendorff still experienced as a site of the divine in nature and associated with the beautiful metaphor of Mary Mother of God's starry robe – has a long tradition in literature and visual art. The motif of the dark and impenetrable forest, in which the lone wanderer, rambler or knight is all alone, can already be found in the luxuriant forest pieces that the Flemish painter Gillis van Coninxloo (1544–1607) began creating in 1588, but these works remained unique and without followers.[10] Was the overwhelming impression that the forest regions of the Palatinate made on this painter from Antwerp during his exile in Frankenthal what inspired him to create these pictures? We do not know. The composed forest pieces, easily recognised as artful interventions, convey the mythical transfiguration of the forest, its symbolic significance. It was not until 200 years later that this solitude in the forest would be verbally articulated through the neologism *Waldeinsamkeit*. In 1797 Ludwig Tieck (1773–1853), an early Romantic from Berlin who was only 23 years old and already painfully experienced with regard to solitude,[11] laid the song of *Waldeinsamkeit* in the beak of a bird in his literary fairy tale *Der blonde Eckbert* (Blond Eckbert). It was astonishingly successful. Over the course of the 19th century, the neologism *Waldeinsamkeit* quickly became German Romanticism's best-known metaphor for solitude. Not just in Romantic literature and poetry – in the work of Heinrich Heine (1797–1856) and Joseph von Eichendorff, among others – but also in painting, the enigmatic term and its interpretation became an image of identification serving national self-confirmation and simultaneously an artistic reorientation.

However, even in the period around 1800, the idealisation of the forest as a pristine natural landscape already blatantly contradicted the facts surrounding the excessive agricultural exploitation of Central Europe's forests. The forest was also in an ecologically catastrophic state at that point. The majority

8. Katharina Eppert, *Rund um den Feldberg findet man viel Schnee zum Langlaufen*, 23.01.2021, https://www.rnz.de/ratgeber/reise_artikel-einsamer-hochschwarzwald-rund-um-den-feldberg-findet-man-viel-schnee-zum-langlaufen-_arid,613252.html, accessed 17.11.2021.

9. Joseph von Eichendorff, 'Der Umkehrende', in *Sämtliche Werke: Historisch-kritische Ausgabe*, vol. 1.1, 314.

10. Nils Büttner, 'Landschaften des Exils? Anmerkungen zu Gillis von Coninxloo und der Geschichte der flämischen Waldlandschaft', *Zeitschrift für Kunstgeschichte* 66 (2003), 546–580.

11. Susanne Rabenstein, 'Ludwig Tiecks Der blonde Eckbert: Eine individualpsychologisch-analytische Deutung des "Wahnsinnsmärchens"', in *Zeitschrift für freie psychoanalytische Forschung und Individualpsychologie* 3.2 (December 2016), 76–77.

Waldeinsamkeit

Ein in der Rhein-Neckar-Zeitung veröffentlichter Artikel über Skilanglauf im Schwarzwald aus dem Winter 2021 legt zumindest nahe, dass alle etwas mit dem Begriff anfangen können: „Und durch dieses märchenhaft dunkle Geäst, das durch den vielen Schnee gar nicht so düster erscheint, kann man sich gleiten und zum ‚Waldeinsamkeit spüren' verleiten lassen, ganz ohne Druck."[8] Im Wald einsam sein, niemand ist da, außer man selbst und ein Gefühl, das sich aus räumlicher Distanz zum Weltgeschehen und der Gewissheit bestimmt, genau in diesem Moment am richtigen Ort zu sein. „Wie liegt so weit die Welt von hier", heißt es bei Joseph von Eichendorff (1788–1857).[9] Der stille Wald, bei Eichendorff noch ein Ort göttlicher Natur, der sich mit der schönen Metapher vom Sternenkleid der Mutter Gottes verbindet, hat in der Literatur und der Bildenden Kunst eine lange Tradition. Das Motiv des dunklen, undurchdringlichen Waldes, in dem Wanderer, Ausflügler oder Reiter allein mit sich selbst sind, findet sich ab 1588 bereits in den üppigen Waldstücken des flämischen Malers Gillis van Coninxloo (1544–1607), doch bleiben seine Waldstücke einmalig und ohne Nachfolge.[10] War es der überwältigende Eindruck der großen pfälzischen Waldgebiete, der den Antwerpener Maler während seines Frankenthaler Exils zu diesen Gemälden anregte? Wir wissen es nicht. Die komponierten Waldstücke, unschwer als kunstvolle Interventionen zu erkennen, vermitteln die mythische Verklärung des Waldes, die sinnbildliche Bedeutung desselben. Erst zweihundert Jahre später lässt sich diese Einsamkeit im Wald durch den Neologismus *Waldeinsamkeit* auch sprachlich fassen. Der Berliner Frühromantiker Ludwig Tieck (1773–1853), gerade einmal 23 Jahre alt und in puncto Einsamkeit bereits leidvoll erfahren,[11] hatte 1797 in seinem Kunstmärchen *Der blonde Eckbert* einem Vogel das Lied von der *Waldeinsamkeit* in den Schnabel gelegt. Mit einem erstaunlichen Erfolg: Schnell wurde der Neologismus *Waldeinsamkeit* im Laufe des 19. Jahrhunderts zur bekanntesten Einsamkeitsmetapher der deutschen Romantik. Nicht nur in der romantischen Literatur und Lyrik, unter anderem bei Heinrich Heine (1797–1856) und Joseph von Eichendorff, sondern auch in der Malerei wurde der schillernde Begriff und seine Ausdeutung zum Identifikationsbild nationaler Selbstvergewisserung und zugleich künstlerischer Neubesinnung.

8. Katharina Eppert, *Einsamer Hochschwarzwald. Rund um den Feldberg findet man viel Schnee zum Langlaufen*, 23.01.2021, https://www.rnz.de/ratgeber/reise_artikel,-einsamer-hochschwarzwald-rund-um-den-feldberg-findet-man-viel-schnee-zum-langlaufen-_arid,613252.html, abgerufen am 17.11.2021.

9. Joseph von Eichendorff, „Der Umkehrende", in: *Sämtliche Werke. Historisch kritische Ausgabe*, Band 1.1, 314.

10. Nils Büttner, „Landschaften des Exils? Anmerkungen zu Gillis von Coninxloo und der Geschichte der flämischen Waldlandschaft", in: *Zeitschrift für Kunstgeschichte* 66 (2003), 546–580.

11. Susanne Rabenstein, „Ludwig Tiecks Der blonde Eckbert. Eine individualpsychologisch-analytische Deutung des ‚Wahnsinnsmärchens'", in: *Zeitschrift für freie psychoanalytische Forschung und Individualpsychologie* 3.2 (Dezember 2016), 76–77.

of the population saw it as a utilitarian space, and the 'forest feeling' of the Romantic 'Waldgefühl' and the idea of the forest as a site of longing developed solely among intellectual elites. It was only 'the spatial and spiritual distancing from the non-forms of nature', coupled with the flourishing of cities, that led to an awareness of the personal loss of the forest as an experienced space over the course of the 19th century.[12]

In keeping with this, the term *Waldeinsamkeit* describes a feeling that emerged out of the Romantics' ideas about beauty to spread through the broader populace in the late 19th century and still defines Germans' understanding of the forest – though not their psyche – with an astonishing degree of continuity today. The myth of the beauty of the German forest is paired with a generalised knowledge about forests that is scarcely based on any observation of nature: otherwise it would be almost impossible to explain how phenomena like the current dieback in the Harz region, which is one of Germany's largest national forests and even provided the inspiration for Tieck's neologism of *Waldeinsamkeit*, could go on with so little comment. Anyone can still enjoy *Waldeinsamkeit* in the German forest today by staying away from tourist centres and going a few hundred metres into the woods: this may still be true for many forests, but it is now hardly true for the Harz.

The extent to which we are now endangering the places we long for, be it the forest or the sea – this, at least, unites the British and the Germans, unites the forest and sea as longed-for places. In 2013 a British heavy metal band called itself *Waldeinsamkeit*. In keeping with their national origin, it is the sea and not the forest that they sing about in their song *Between Madness and the Tides*: 'Always waiting for something resembling a feeling / There is a part of me that will not be alone / I stumble into the sea / Sink like a stone so I can finally be free / Beneath the waves maybe there is a hope.'[13] It sounds like German Romantic poetry on the theme of *Waldeinsamkeit* and, nonetheless, it could be something more for us today if we would listen very closely to our feelings in the face of the forest or the sea and not shy away from the consequences.

And so the term *Waldeinsamkeit*, which John Smith has selected for his exhibition, seems to be a little more than just a hint to focus our attention – just like all of his films in the exhibition can never be separated from the political and social situation of the period in which they were created.

12. Norbert Elias, 'Über die Natur', *Merkur* 40 (1986), 469–481.

13. Waldeinsamkeit, *Between Madness and the Tides*, music by Tom Woolnough, lyrics by Nicholas Aldrich, released 29.09.2014, accessed 18.11.2021.

Waldeinsamkeit

Doch die Idealisierung des Waldes als eine unberührte Naturlandschaft stand bereits an der Wende vom 18. zum 19. Jahrhundert im krassen Widerspruch zu den Tatsachen landwirtschaftlich übernutzter Waldflächen in Mitteleuropa. Der Wald befand sich auch damals in einem ökologisch katastrophalen Zustand; für die Mehrzahl der Bewohner*innen war er ein Nutzraum, und das romantische Waldgefühl, die Idee des Waldes als Sehnsuchtsort, war allein in den intellektuellen Eliten entstanden. Erst „die räumliche und geistige Distanzierung von den Unbilden der Natur“[12] führte im Laufe des 19. Jahrhunderts mit dem Aufblühen der Städte zum Bewusstwerden des persönlichen Verlustes des Erfahrungsraumes Wald.

Passend dazu beschreibt der Begriff *Waldeinsamkeit* ein Gefühl, das sich, ausgehend von den Schönheitsvorstellungen der Romantiker*innen, im Laufe des späten 19. Jahrhunderts in der Bevölkerung ausbreitete und bis heute, wenn auch nicht die Psyche, so doch das Waldverständnis der Deutschen in erstaunlicher Kontinuität bestimmt. Der Mythos von der Schönheit des deutschen Waldes wird von einem pauschalen Waldwissen begleitet, das wohl kaum von der Naturbeobachtung herrührt. Denn sonst wäre es kaum zu erklären, dass Phänomene wie das aktuelle Waldsterben im Harz, einem der größten Waldnationalparks in Deutschland, in dem ausgerechnet Ludwig Tieck seine Inspiration für den Neologismus *Waldeinsamkeit* fand, so lautlos vonstattengeht. *Waldeinsamkeit* können alle noch heute im deutschen Wald genießen, wenn sie sich abseits der Touristenzentren wenige hundert Meter in den Wald begeben: Für viele Wälder mag dies noch zutreffen, für den Harz kaum mehr. Wie sehr gefährden wir heute unsere Sehnsuchtsorte, sei es der Wald oder das Meer – dies mindestens verbindet die Brit*innen und die Deutschen, verbindet den Sehnsuchtsort Wald mit dem Sehnsuchtsort Meer. Eine britische Heavy Metal Band hat sich 2013 den Bandnamen *Waldeinsamkeit* gegeben und besingt in ihrem Song *Between Madness and the Tides* (Zwischen Wahnsinn und Gezeiten), nicht etwa den Wald, sondern ihrer Herkunft entsprechend das Meer: „Immer auf etwas warten, das einem Gefühl ähnelt [...] Unter den Wellen gibt es vielleicht eine Hoffnung / Es gibt einen Teil von mir, der nicht allein sein wird / Ich stolpere ins Meer“.[13] Es klingt wie die Lyrik der deutschen Romantiker*innen zum Thema *Waldeinsamkeit* und könnte doch heute mehr für uns sein, wenn wir genau hinhörten, auf unsere Gefühle gegenüber dem Wald oder dem Meer, und die Konsequenzen nicht scheuen würden.

Und so scheint der Begriff *Waldeinsamkeit*, den sich John Smith für seine Ausstellung ausgesucht hat, ein klein wenig mehr als ein Fingerzeig zu sein, so wie alle seine Filme in der Ausstellung sich nie von der politischen und gesellschaftlichen Situation der Zeit lösen lassen, in der sie entstanden sind.

12. Norbert Elias, „Über die Natur“, in: *Merkur* 40 (1986), 469–481.

13. Waldeinsamkeit, *Between Madness and the Tides*, Musik von Tom Woolnough, Songtext von Nicholas Aldrich, veröffentlicht 29.09.2014, abgerufen am 18.11.2021.

The Chronicles of John Smith

Erika Balsom

I.

In the looped video installation *Horizon (Five Pounds a Belgian)* (2012) [see page 70], Smith trains his camera on the meeting of sea and sky. Staring out from the shore over a period of several months in Margate, on England's southeast coast, he constructs an atlas of light and colour, like J. M.W. Turner before him. One shot gives way to the next with metric regularity, introducing a new blue, a different grey, a greater turbulence, a change of air. The void of this ever-transforming environment is periodically interrupted by human activity. Against the resolute division of the pictorial field, an array of sublunary occurrences intercede, claiming the viewer's recalibrated attention: the tide recedes to reveal the sand, dogs pass by, a child's laughter echoes in the air. Now and then the rhythm of the cuts will slow, allowing a boat to travel from one side of the frame to the other undisturbed, before resuming metronomic consistency.

Smith's undertaking seems a little like a cinematic iteration of Édouard Manet's serial views, capturing as it does the formal complexities of environmental stasis and change, grasping hold of the impression of a singular moment. But something is awry on the soundtrack. The same audio of crashing waves plays repeatedly over the bulk of the installation's images, slipping across varying degrees of verisimilitude. There are moments of illusionistic synchronization during which one can sink into the impression that a tranche of lost time has been resurrected in front of one's eyes, but these never last long. The cut arrives and the sound loops again, this time playing over an image it clearly does not match. All at once a schism between seeing and hearing erupts, affirming the artifice of construction, expelling the viewer from absorption in an elsewhere and elsewhen, leaving her to confront the materiality of the constructed image in the here and now.

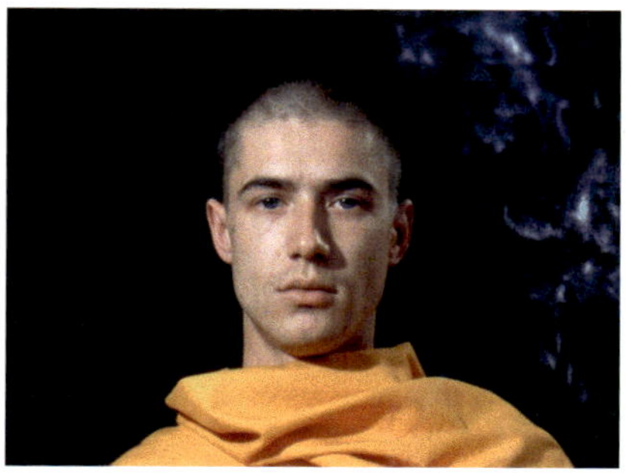

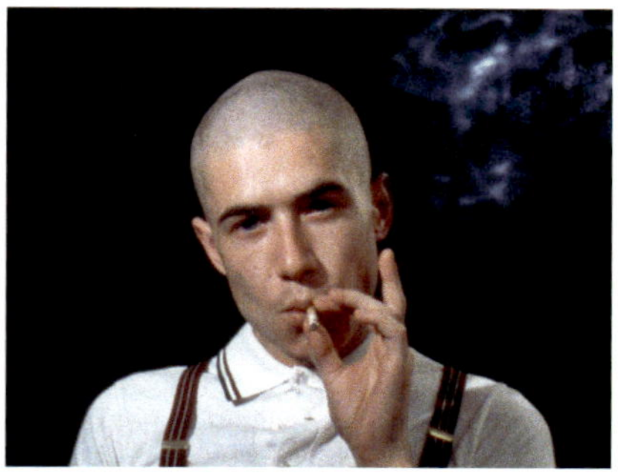

Om, 1986, 16mm, 4 minutes

Horizon extends key concerns that have animated Smith's practice for nearly fifty years. It combines a rapt attention to the small details of everyday life with a desire to disrupt the smooth operation of cinematic conventions and a fondness for self-imposed limitation. These qualities are central to the artist's most celebrated work, *The Girl Chewing Gum* (1976) [see page 44], a humorous critique of documentary naturalism achieved through a stark economy of means: twelve minutes, two shots, and two locations. By exploiting the habitual trust invested in voice-over narration, only to then reveal the speaker to be a patently unreliable demiurge, *The Girl Chewing Gum* tugs away at the precarious accord between sound and image, illuminating its central role in engendering meaning. Similarly, in the four-minute *Om* (1986), Smith plays with how the apprehension of a single humming sound and a limited number of visual signifiers – a saffron robe, wafting smoke, a young man with a shaven head – can invite radically different interpretations

Die Chroniken von John Smith

Erika Balsom

I.

In dem Videoloop *Horizon (Five Pounds a Belgian)* (2012) [siehe Seite 72] richtet John Smith seine Kamera auf das Zusammentreffen von Himmel und Meer. Über mehrere Monate starrt er vom Strand in Margate, an der Südostküste Englands, aufs Meer hinaus und konstruiert dabei einen Atlas aus Licht und Farbe, wie vor ihm William Turner. Mit metrischer Regelmäßigkeit folgt eine Aufnahme der anderen, um ein neues Blau, ein anderes Grau, eine stärkere Turbulenz, eine Veränderung in der Luft vorzustellen. Periodisch wird die Leere dieser sich stets verändernden Umwelt von menschlicher Aktivität durchbrochen. Dem streng aufgeteilten Bildfeld wirkt eine Reihe von sublunaren Ereignissen entgegen, die eine neu kalibrierte Aufmerksamkeit der Betrachter*in einfordert: Die Flut geht zurück und gibt den Blick auf den Sand frei, Hunde gehen vorüber, ein Kinderlachen hängt in der Luft. Gelegentlich verlangsamt sich der Schnittrhythmus und erlaubt einem Boot, ungestört von der einen Seite des Bildausschnitts zur anderen zu ziehen, bevor er seine metronomische Regelmäßigkeit wieder aufnimmt.

Smiths Unterfangen wirkt ein wenig wie eine filmische Iteration der seriellen Ansichten von Édouard Manet, insofern, als es die formale Komplexität von Stillstand und Wandel in der Umgebung einfängt und den Eindruck eines singulären Augenblicks festhält. Doch mit der Tonspur stimmt etwas nicht. Zu einem Großteil der Bilder dieser Installation wird immer wieder derselbe Ton von brechenden Wellen abgespielt, der dabei unterschiedliche Grade von Wirklichkeitsnähe durchläuft. Es entstehen Momente einer illusionistischen Synchronisation, bei denen man in der Anmutung versinken kann, eine Tranche verlorener Zeit sei vor den eigenen Augen gerade wieder zum Leben erweckt worden – doch sie dauern nie lange an. Es kommt der Schnitt und die Tonschleife spielt wieder von vorn, diesmal zu einem Bild, mit dem jede Übereinstimmung fehlt. Ein Spalt zwischen Sehen und Hören tut sich plötzlich auf, bestätigt das künstliche Wesen der Konstruktion, reißt die Betrachter*in aus der Vertiefung in ein Anderswo und Anderswann und überlässt sie bei der Konfrontation mit der Materialität des Hier und Jetzt sich selbst.

Horizon baut auf den zentralen Anliegen auf, die Smiths Praxis seit fast fünfzig Jahren motivieren. Das Werk vereint eine selbstvergessene Aufmerksamkeit für die Details des Alltags mit dem Willen, die glatten Abläufe filmischer Konventionen zu stören und eine Vorliebe für selbstauferlegte Beschränkungen. Von zentraler Bedeutung sind diese Qualitäten in dem berühmtesten Werk des Künstlers, *The Girl Chewing Gum* (1976) [siehe Seite 48], einer humorvollen Kritik am dokumentarischen Naturalismus, die in einer sparsamen Verwendung der Mittel zum Ausdruck kommt: zwölf Minuten, zwei Einstellungen, zwei Drehorte. Indem in *The Girl Chewing Gum* das gewohnte

(from a Buddhist monk to a skinhead) depending on slight shifts in their arrangement. In these reflexive works, the functioning of cinema itself is at stake. Ever a keen semiotician, Smith compels the viewer to confront how the apparatus casts its spell and how it conspires with our pre-existing expectations and biases. We are left to face the fragility and contingency of the suture that binds the vagaries of perception to what we think we know.

These enduring preoccupations tie Smith to the historical context from which he emerged: the circle of filmmakers associated with the Royal College of Art and the London Film-Makers' Cooperative in the mid-1970s, for whom the practice of avant-garde cinema was inseparable from an iconoclastic drive to puncture the spectacular plenitude of Hollywood. Narrative and illusionism alike were critical targets, coming under fire for their function as vehicles of ideological mystification. Any subjective expressivity on the part of the artist was rejected in favour of pared-down, rule-based approaches that asserted the hard edges of structure. The hope was to usher the spectator into a different form of perception, one that would give up on the seductions of representational space and instead contemplate the phenomenological reality of the encounter with the apparatus. In the words of filmmaker and theorist Malcolm Le Grice, this kind of cinema 'does not imitate or represent reality, nor create spurious illusions of times, places and lives which engage the spectator in a vicarious substitute for his own reality'; instead, filmmakers attend 'to the actuality of their materials and processes.'[1] Even if Smith's interest in storytelling, albeit intermittent and deconstructed, and his characteristic wit meant that his practice was never quite reconcilable with the prevailing 'structuralist-materialist' line of the day, his work nonetheless indelibly bears the mark of this influential moment and its focus on an anti-realist politics of form. As the artist put it in 1997, 'Although I did not embrace the movement wholeheartedly its propositions were fundamental in the formation of an approach to film-making that I have pursued consistently ever since.'[2]

With its compositional rigour, penchant for repetition, and emphasis on the spectator's own perceptual and cognitive processes, *Horizon* seems especially amenable to being considered in relation to this legacy. It seems to be a strong example of how steadfast Smith has been in his commitment to a particular mode of formal inquiry across the decades. And so it is. But there is perhaps more lurking within it than this. *Horizon* toys with cinematic codes and puts pressure on the allure of verisimilitude, certainly, but it does so while remaining ceaselessly oriented outwards, facing the expansiveness of the world, recording difference where some might see only sameness. It is worth recalling that, in addition to its function as a striking graphic device, the horizon line marks the limit of what may be perceived from the relative security of the shore,

1. Malcolm Le Grice, *Abstract Film and Beyond* (Cambridge: MIT Press, 1977), 152.
2. John Smith, *Real Fiction* (PhD dissertation, University of East London, 1997), 3–4.

Vertrauen in den Begleitkommentar ausgenutzt wird, nur um dann den Sprecher als einen offensichtlich unzuverlässigen Demiurgen zu entlarven, schwächt der Film allmählich die delikate Übereinstimmung von Ton und Bild und beleuchtet so ihre entscheidende Rolle bei der Bedeutungserzeugung. Ähnlich spielt Smith im vierminütigen *Om* (1986) damit, dass die Wahrnehmung eines einzelnen summenden Geräuschs und einer begrenzten Anzahl visueller Zeichen – ein safrangelbes Gewand, wabernder Rauch, ein junger Mann mit geschorenem Kopf – aufgrund von kleinen Verschiebungen in der Anordnung radikal unterschiedliche Interpretationen hervorzurufen vermag (vom buddhistischen Mönch zum Skinhead). In diesen selbstreferentiellen Arbeiten geht es um die Funktionsweise des Films selbst. Als engagierter Semiotiker zwingt Smith die Betrachter*in in die Konfrontation mit diesem Apparat, wie er uns verzaubert und sich mit unseren Erwartungen und Vorurteilen verschwört. Nun stehen wir der Fragilität und Bedingtheit des Fadens gegenüber, der die Unwägbarkeiten der Wahrnehmung mit dem verbindet, was wir zu wissen glauben.

Diese thematischen Konstanten verbinden Smith auch mit den historischen Zusammenhängen, aus denen er selbst hervorgegangen ist: der Kreis von Filmemachern, die Mitte der 70er Jahre aus dem Umfeld des Royal College of Art und der London Film-Makers' Cooperative kamen und für die der Avantgardefilm gleichbedeutend war mit einem bilderstürmerischen Verlangen, die spektakuläre Vollkommenheit von Hollywood zu entzaubern. Das Narrativ und der Illusionismus waren ebenso kritische Angriffsziele, die man ins Visier nahm, weil sie als Vehikel für ideologische Mystifizierung fungierten. Jegliche subjektive Ausdruckskraft aufseiten der Künstler*in wurde abgelehnt und ersetzt durch reduzierte, regelbasierte Ansätze, die harte strukturelle Kanten erzeugten. So sollten die Zuschauer*innen an eine andere Form der Wahrnehmung herangeführt werden, die die Versuchungen des Repräsentationsraums hinter sich ließ und stattdessen Überlegungen zur phänomenologischen Realität der Begegnung mit dem Apparat anstellte. Um den Filmemacher und Theoretiker Malcolm Le Grice zu zitieren, „imitiert oder repräsentiert [diese Art von Film] weder die Realität, noch schafft sie falsche Illusionen von Zeiten, Orten oder Leben, die den Betrachter in einen Ersatz für ihre eigene Realität verwickeln"; stattdessen befassen sich die Filmemacher*innen mit „der Tatsächlichkeit ihres Materials und ihrer Prozesse".[1] Wenn Smiths zugegebenermaßen periodisches und dekonstruiertes Interesse am Geschichtenerzählen sowie sein charakteristischer Witz zwar bedeuteten, dass seine Filmpraxis nie ganz mit der vorherrschenden „strukturalistisch-materialistischen" Linie seiner Zeit vereinbar war, so ist sein Œuvre dennoch mit bleibender Wirkung von diesem einflussreichen Moment und dem Fokus auf eine anti-realistische Politik der Form gekennzeichnet.

1. Malcolm Le Grice, *Abstract Film and Beyond* (Cambridge: MIT Press, 1977), 152.

tracing a frontier between the visible and invisible, the known and unknown, the near and the distant. The camera gazes out at a field of uncontrollable flux, radical otherness, and inhuman magnitude. As Herman Melville wrote in *Moby Dick*, the sea is 'masterless', for 'no mercy, no power but its own controls it.'[3] The closest we can come to glimpsing the vastness of the planet, it is an entreaty to humility.

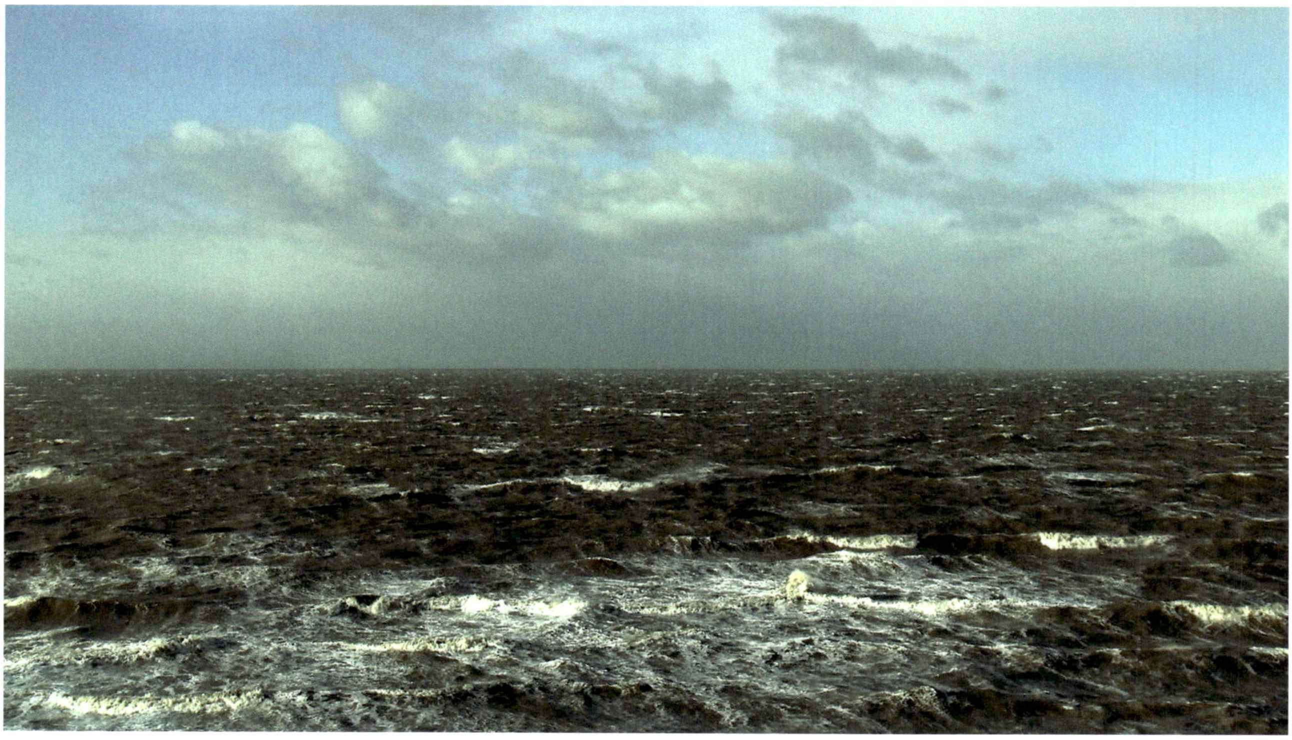

Horizon (Five Pounds a Belgian), 2012, HD video, seamless loop, 18 minutes cycle

Looking harder at *Horizon* – at how it subtly raises issues of mastery and masterlessness, how it emphasizes the filmmaker's positionality and routine, and foregrounds the smallness of any single person relative to the aquatic expanse – it becomes possible to discern the stirrings of a commitment very different than the politics of form with which Smith, like many other British avant-garde filmmakers of his generation, is so frequently associated. Critics often describe Smith's practice as exploring things like 'the power of language to direct and misdirect'[4] or 'the gulf between illusionism and formalism'[5] – and with ample reason. But in addition to these concerns, the artist has long been a chronicler of the world around him. This aspect of his work has become especially pronounced in the twenty-first century, when he has increasingly broached political questions in personal ways, casting new light on his earlier films and videos. For Smith, the fraught interval between the self and the world is a space of ethical responsibility, technological mediation, and eccentric humour. These concerns are articulated

3. Herman Melville, *Moby Dick: or The White Whale* (Boston: L.C. Page and Company, 1925), 262.
4. Martin Herbert, 'Mediate the Immediate: On John Smith', *John Smith*, ed. Tanya Leighton and Katrin Meyer (Mousse Publishing & Sternberg Press, 2013), 8.
5. Nick Bradshaw, 'Personal Space', *Sight and Sound* (September 2011), 15.

Wie der Künstler 1997 sagte: „Obwohl ich mich der Bewegung nicht voll und ganz verschrieben hatte, waren ihre Thesen grundlegend für die Entwicklung eines filmischen Ansatzes, den ich seitdem konsequent verfolge."[2]

Aufgrund der kompositorischen Strenge, dem Hang zur Wiederholung und der Betonung der perzeptiven und kognitiven Prozesse der Zuschauer*innen mag sich *Horizon* besonders gut dazu eignen, dass man es mit diesem Vermächtnis in Beziehung setzt. Es scheint ein gutes Beispiel für die Beharrlichkeit zu sein, mit der sich Smith seit Jahrzehnten einer bestimmten Art der formalen Befragung widmet, und das ist tatsächlich auch der Fall. Aber vielleicht schlummert hier noch etwas anderes im Verborgenen. Sicherlich, *Horizon* spielt mit filmischen Chiffren und setzt den Reiz der Realistik unter Druck, doch das Werk ist dabei stets nach außen gerichtet, stellt sich der Weite der Welt und registriert Unterschiede, wo andere vielleicht nur Gleichförmigkeit sehen würden. Es sei daran erinnert, dass die Horizontlinie, zusätzlich zu ihrer Funktion als markantes grafisches Mittel, auch das Ausmaß dessen markiert, was sich von der relativen Sicherheit des Ufers aus wahrnehmen lässt. Sie beschreibt eine Grenze zwischen dem Sichtbaren und dem Unsichtbaren, dem Bekannten und dem Unbekannten, dem Nahen und dem Fernen. Die Kamera blickt hinaus auf einen Bereich unkontrollierbarer Veränderung, radikaler Andersartigkeit und übermenschlicher Größe. Wie Herman Melville in *Moby Dick* schrieb, hat die See „keinen Meister", denn „außer ihrer eigenen, wird sie durch keine Gnade, keine Macht beherrscht."[3] Als unsere beste Vorstellung von der Größe des Planeten beschwört sie unsere Demut.

Betrachtet man *Horizon* näher – wie das Werk subtil Fragen von Herrschaft und Herrenlosigkeit aufwirft, wie es die Positionalität und die Routine des Filmemachers hervorhebt, wie es die Kleinheit jedes Menschen für sich im Vergleich zu den Weiten des Wassers in den Vordergrund stellt – dann kann man die Anzeichen eines Engagements erkennen, das sich deutlich unterscheidet von der Politik der Form, mit der Smith, wie viele andere britische Avantgarde-Filmemacher*innen seiner Generation, so gern in Verbindung gebracht wird. Von Kritiker*innen hört man oft, dass sich Smiths Praxis mit Dingen befasse, wie „der Macht der Sprache zu leiten und fehlzuleiten"[4] oder „der Kluft zwischen Illusionismus und Formalismus"[5], und damit haben sie recht. Doch neben diesen Interessen ist der Künstler schon seit langem ein Chronist der Welt, die ihn umgibt. Dieser Aspekt seines Schaffens ist im 21. Jahrhundert besonders deutlich geworden, wenn er politische Fragen zunehmend

2. John Smith, *Real Fiction* (PhD dissertation, University of East London, 1997), 3–4.
3. Herman Melville, *Moby Dick: or The White Whale* (Boston: L.C. Page and Company, 1925), 262.
4. Martin Herbert, „Mediate the Immediate: On John Smith", in: *John Smith*, hrsg. von Tanya Leighton und Katrin Meyer (Mousse Publishing & Sternberg Press, 2013), 8.
5. Nick Bradshaw, „Personal Space", in: *Sight and Sound* (September 2011), 15.

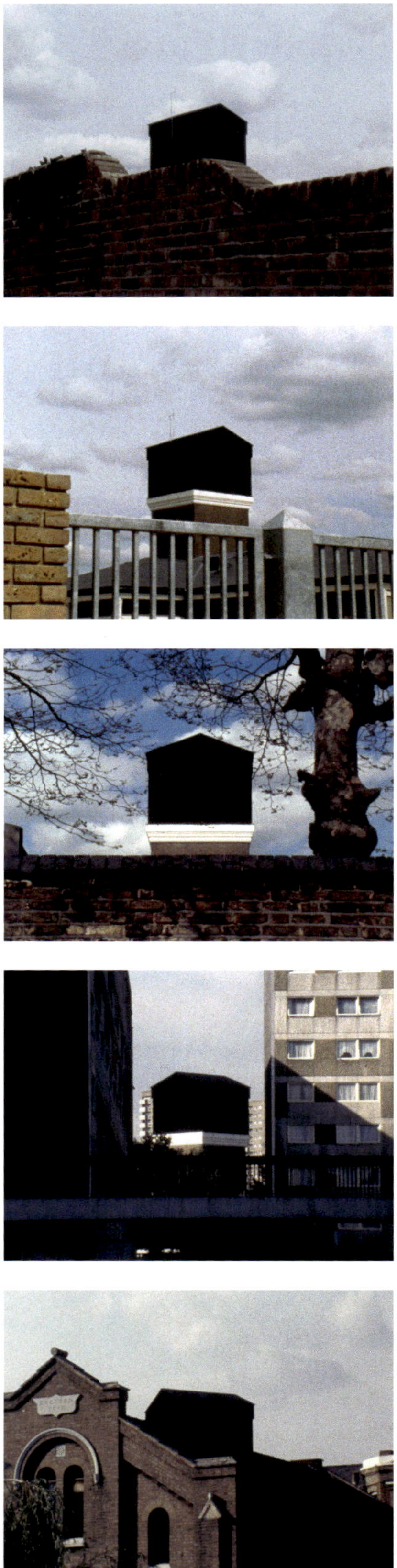

The Black Tower, 1985–87, 16mm, 24 minutes

more fully, more explicitly, in other recent works – but they are there, too, in *Horizon*, obliquely jostling with the rigour of form, as Smith stays rooted in place yet attuned to the vastness that lies beyond his grasp.

II.

Moving images are made to travel, which is perhaps part of why they have so often been employed as a means of describing the specificities of a given place. Those who will never visit Margate can encounter something of its atmospheric metamorphoses by standing in front of *Horizon*. Since the late nineteenth century, when the Lumière brothers sent their cameramen around the world to capture views of exotic locales, the cinema – particularly in its nonfiction iterations – has had a special affinity for collapsing distance by manufacturing unique vistas for mass circulation. For many filmmakers, this means making a journey to a faraway land. As Paula Rabinowitz has put it, 'One goes somewhere as a documentarian – Polynesia, Alabama, Poland, downtown; the documentarian is drawn elsewhere by an other.'[6] There are, of course, exceptions to this rule, and John Smith is one of them. He conceives of his practice differently: 'I'm very opposed to the kind of documentary tourism that takes place in the world an enormous amount, when people go somewhere to make a film about a subject they are not familiar with. The familiarity of place is important.'[7] Even if he cannot be considered a documentarian in the traditional sense of the word, his practice is marked by a pointed interest in actuality, one which ambivalently negotiates the inheritances of the documentary tradition and expands the latter's parameters through experimentation. Contrary to Rabinowitz's proposal, most of the time he does not to go anywhere to make his films and videos, or at least not very far. Rather than be 'drawn elsewhere by an other', he concentrates on what surrounds him, producing the bulk of his work using the locations and events that are nearby. From the start, his filmography is peppered with domestic interiors (e.g., *Leading Light* (1975), *Blue Bathroom* (1978–79)) and replete with the landscapes of East London, the historically working-class area where he has spent his life (e.g., *Hackney Marshes – November 4th 1977* (1977), *The Black Tower* (1985–87), *Blight* (1994–96)). While *The Girl Chewing Gum* contains no personal details, it was notably shot in Dalston, around the corner from where Smith lived at the time. Speaking of this film, the artist has compared himself to Sagar Mitchell and James Kenyan, Lancashire-based filmmakers who at the turn of the twentieth century produced hundreds of actualities of

6. Paula Rabinowitz, *They Must Be Represented: The Politics of Documentary* (London: Verso, 1994), 6.
7. Quoted in: Patrick Wright, 'Dalston, Then and Now: An Interview with John Smith', *In Focus: The Girl Chewing Gum 1976 by John Smith*, ed. Erika Balsom (Tate Research Publication, 2015), https://www.tate.org.uk/research/publications/in-focus/the-girl-chewing-gum-john-smith/dalston-then-and-now

auf eine persönliche Weise anschneidet und dabei neues Licht auf seine früheren Filme und Videos wirft. Für Smith ist das Spannungsfeld zwischen dem Selbst und der Welt ein Bereich der ethischen Verantwortung, der technologischen Vermittlung und des exzentrischen Humors. Diese Anliegen werden in neueren Werken ausführlicher und expliziter artikuliert – doch sie finden sich auch schon in *Horizon*, wo sie sich indirekt an der Strenge der Form stoßen, während Smith wie angewurzelt steht und dabei doch eingestimmt ist auf die Weite, die jenseits seines Fassungsvermögens liegt.

II.

Bewegte Bilder sind dafür gemacht, zu reisen, und das mag einer der Gründe sein, warum sie so oft als Mittel zur Beschreibung der Besonderheiten bestimmter Orte eingesetzt werden. Wer Margate nie besuchen wird, kann bei der Betrachtung von *Horizon* etwas über die atmosphärischen Metamorphosen des Ortes erfahren. Seit dem späten 19. Jahrhundert, als die Brüder Lumière ihre Kameraleute um die Welt schickten, um Ansichten exotischer Orte einzufangen, hat der Film – vor allem in seinen nicht-fiktionalen Varianten – eine besondere Affinität dazu, Entfernungen zu überwinden, indem er einzigartige Ansichten für die Massenverbreitung hervorbringt. Für viele Filmemacher*innen bedeutet das eine Reise in ein fernes Land. Wie Paula Rabinowitz schrieb: „Als Dokumentarist geht man irgendwohin – nach Polynesien, Alabama, Polen, in die Innenstadt; der Dokumentarist folgt der Anziehungskraft eines Anderen an einen anderen Ort.“[6]

Für diese Regel gibt es natürlich Ausnahmen, und John Smith ist eine davon. Er hat eine andere Vorstellung von seiner Praxis: „Ich bin vollkommen gegen diese Art von Dokumentartourismus, von dem es auf der Welt unheimlich viel gibt. Da gehen Menschen irgendwohin, um einen Film über ein Thema zu machen, mit dem sie sich nicht auskennen. Mit einem Ort vertraut zu sein, ist wichtig.“[7] Im traditionellen Sinne des Wortes kann man ihn zwar keinen Dokumentaristen nennen, seine Praxis zeichnet sich jedoch durch ein dezidiertes Interesse an der Wirklichkeit aus, ein Interesse, das das Erbe der dokumentarischen Tradition ambivalent verhandelt und deren Parameter durch das Experiment erweitert. Entgegen der These von Rabinowitz, muss er meist nirgendwo hingehen, um seine Filme und Videos zu drehen, oder zumindest nicht sehr weit weg. Anstatt der „Anziehungskraft eines Anderen zu folgen“, konzentriert er sich auf das, was ihn umgibt und produziert den Großteil seiner Arbeiten mit nahegelegenen Orten und Ereignissen. Von Anfang an ist seine Filmografie mit häuslichen Interieurs gespickt (z.B. *Leading Light* (1975), *Blue Bathroom* (1978–79)) und angefüllt

6. Paula Rabinowitz, *They Must Be Represented: The Politics of Documentary* (London: Verso, 1994), 6.

7. Zitiert nach: Patrick Wright, „Dalston, Then and Now: An Interview with John Smith“, in: *In Focus: The Girl Chewing Gum 1976 by John Smith*, hrsg. von Erika Balsom (Tate Research Publication, 2015), https://www.tate.org.uk/research/publications/in-focus/the-girl-chewing-gum-john-smith/dalston-then-and-now

everyday life in the United Kingdom.[8] The documentary aspect of *The Girl Chewing Gum* is sharply thrown into relief by Smith's 2011 'remake', *The Man Phoning Mum* [see page 46], which superimposes footage of the same street corner some thirty-five years later over the original film, graphically indexing the passage of time.

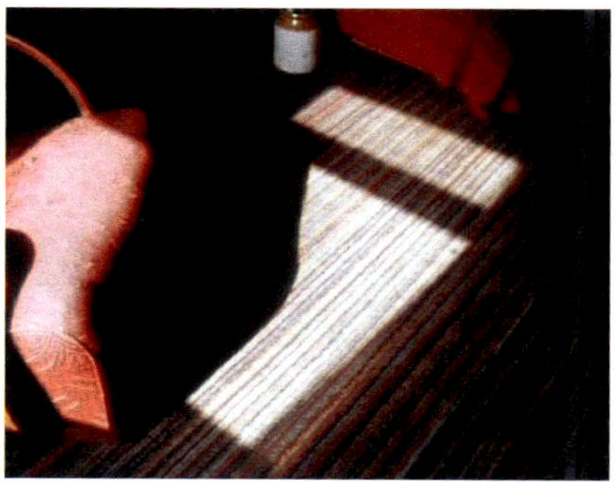
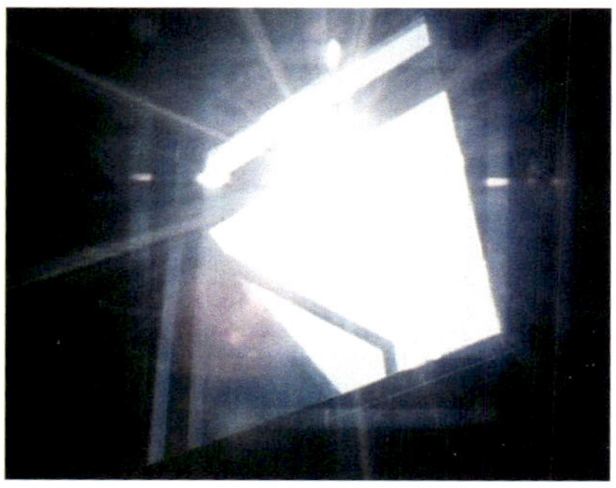

Leading Light, 1975, 16mm, 11 minutes

Alongside Smith's perspicacious interrogation of filmic language, then, there is a fascination with the medium's ability to capture traces of worldly reality, especially of that which exists closest to him and would likely never appear in the simulated perfection of advertisements or popular cinema. A realist conviction bubbles under the surface of his modernist inclination. Although realism and modernism are conventionally understood as opposed aesthetics, in Smith's hands they join together in a potent, two-pronged contestation of the form and content of the mass media, rubbing against each other in generative tension. Smith's modernist reflexivity claws away at the plenitude of illusion, reminding of the non-transparency of mediation, while his insistence on recording his surroundings in tremendous detail partakes of the spirit of democratization that has long animated realist aesthetics, which seeks to shift the frame of representation to encompass people and phenomena historically excluded from it. The desublimating granularity of these recordings also effects a semiotic intervention, as the image is pulled away from the readability of codes and towards what it always already was: a singular trace of the past. Put differently, this gesture underlines that every lens-based image is a hapax, irreducibly unique. Although cinema can and often does function somewhat like a language, governed as it is by the operation of recognizable conventions, it possesses no compositional unit precisely comparable to the stable iterability of the word. As Christian Metz puts it, 'The cinema can speak only in neologisms.'[9] Every shot will be different, even – or especially – those that seem to 'say' the same thing. By fastidiously documenting the specificity of place in a manner that attunes the viewer to this oft-forgotten uniqueness, Smith shatters the gelid formulas of the mass media, which seek to foster rapid and unambiguous communication, trimming away

8. Ibid.

9. See: Christian Metz, *Film Language: A Semiotics of the Cinema*, trans. Michael Taylor (Chicago: University of Chicago Press, 1991), 69.

mit den Stadtlandschaften von Ost-London, der traditionellen Arbeitergegend, wo er lebt (z.B. *Hackney Marshes – November 4th 1977* (1977), *The Black Tower* (1985–87), *Blight* (1994–96)). *The Girl Chewing Gum* enthält zwar keine persönlichen Details, ist aber wohlgemerkt um die Ecke von Smiths damaliger Wohnung in Dalston gedreht. Im Gespräch über diesen Film vergleicht sich der Künstler mit Sagar Mitchell und James Kenyan, zwei in Lancashire tätigen Filmemachern, die um die Wende zum 20. Jahrhundert hunderte von Gegebenheiten des täglichen Lebens in Großbritannien aufzeichneten.[8] Sehr deutlich tritt der dokumentarische Aspekt von *The Girl Chewing Gum* in Smiths „Remake" von 2011 hervor: In *The Man Phoning Mum* [siehe Seite 49] wird 35 Jahre später an derselben Straßenecke entstandenes Filmmaterial über den Originalfilm gelegt und verzeichnet das Verstreichen der Zeit anschaulich.

Neben seiner scharfsinnigen Befragung der Filmsprache befasst sich Smith also auch intensiv mit der Fähigkeit des Mediums, Spuren der materiellen Realität einzufangen, besonders derjenigen, die in seiner unmittelbaren Nähe besteht und wohl niemals in der simulierten Perfektion der Werbung oder des Unterhaltungskinos zu sehen sein wird. Unter der Oberfläche seiner modernistischen Einstellung brodelt die Überzeugung eines Realisten. Realismus und Modernismus werden zwar herkömmlich als gegensätzliche Ästhetiken verstanden, bei Smith jedoch vereinen sie sich zu einem wirksamen Zangenangriff auf die Form und den Inhalt der Massenmedien, reiben sie sich aneinander in einem fruchtbaren Spannungsverhältnis. Smiths modernistische Reflexivität kratzt an der Vollkommenheit der Illusion, erinnert daran, wie intransparent Vermittlung sein kann, während seine Beharrlichkeit, seine Umgebung in allen Einzelheiten aufzuzeichnen dem Geist der Demokratisierung entspricht, von dem die Ästhetik des Realismus schon seit langem erfüllt ist, welche den Repräsentationsrahmen dahingehend zu verschieben sucht, dass er Menschen und Phänomene einschließt, die historisch ausgeschlossen waren. Die desublimierende Granularität dieser Aufnahmen bewirkt zudem eine semiotische Intervention, da sie das Bild von der Lesbarkeit von Codes entfernt und dem näherbringt, was es immer schon war: eine singuläre Spur des Vergangenen. Anders gesagt unterstreicht diese Geste, dass jedes mit dem Objektiv erstellte Bild ein Hapax ist, irreduzibel einzigartig. Obwohl der Film annähernd wie eine Sprache zu funktionieren vermag, und es auch oft tut – schließlich wird er durch die Funktion erkennbarer Konventionen bestimmt – besitzt er doch keine kompositorische Einheit, die exakt vergleichbar wäre mit der stabilen Wiederholbarkeit des Wortes. Mit den Worten von Christian Metz: „Der Film kann nur in Neologismen sprechen."[9] Jede Einstellung ist anders, selbst

8. Ebd.

9. Siehe Christian Metz, *Film Language: A Semiotics of the Cinema*, übers. von Michael Taylor (Chicago: University of Chicago Press, 1991), 69.

anything extraneous. He beckons the viewer to descend from the loftiness of generality and hit the fascinating ground of endless particularity.

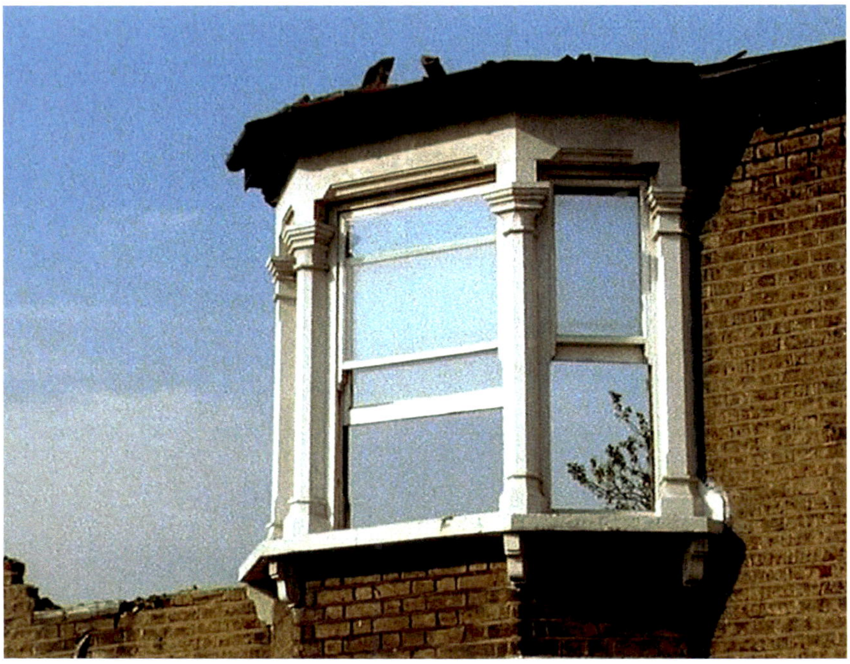

Blight, 1994–96, HD video from 16mm, 14 minutes

At the same time, this drive to accumulate audiovisual traces of a personal geography also speaks to a melancholic preoccupation with the moving image as a modern memento mori, able to embalm the small contingencies of the world for posterity in ways that at once deny and acknowledge the inevitability of finitude. André Bazin described this vocation as 'change mummified'; as Philip Rosen explains, this oxymoronic term registers how the cinema rests on a 'desire for *permanence* (of subjective existence, of identity), which can paradoxically open the spectating subject to the concrete, hence the flow of time and the fact of *change*.'[10] This tension between a desire for permanence and the inevitability of change is especially acute in a film such as *Blight*, which documents the demolition of houses to make way for the M11 Link Road in East London following a long, ultimately unsuccessful grassroots campaign by local residents to avert their displacement. To the rhythm of composer Jocelyn Pook's music, which incorporates snippets of residents' statements about their lives and homes, images of Victorian terraced houses in the midst of destruction – all alike and yet all distinct – succeed one another. By the film's end, construction on the road has begun. *Blight* evinces a tremendous formal precision while simultaneously foregrounding an urge to embalm time, as Smith acts as a witness to the difficulty of the present, creating an archive of a vanishing community. While the notion of 'change mummified' most immediately resonates in relation

10. André Bazin, 'The Ontology of the Photographic Image', *What is Cinema? Volume One*, ed. and trans. Hugh Grey (Berkeley: University of California Press, 1970), 15; Philip Rosen, *Change Mummified: Cinema, Historicity, Theory* (Minneapolis: University of Minnesota Press, 2001), 39.

oder besonders diejenigen, die dasselbe zu „sagen" scheinen. Indem Smith sorgfältig die Besonderheit des Ortes dokumentiert, auf eine Art, die die Betrachter*in auf diese oft vergessene Einzigartigkeit einstimmt, zerschlägt er die frostigen Formeln der Massenmedien, die eine schnelle und eindeutige Kommunikation anstreben und alles Unwichtige wegschneiden. Er lädt die Betrachter*in dazu ein, von den Höhen des Allgemeinen herabzusteigen und den faszinierenden Boden des endlos Partikularen zu betreten.

Gleichzeitig spricht dieser Drang, audiovisuelle Spuren einer persönlichen Geografie zu sammeln, auch für eine stark ausgeprägte, melancholische Beschäftigung mit dem bewegten Bild als einem modernen Memento mori, das es vermag, die kleinen Bedingtheiten des Lebens so für die Nachwelt einzubalsamieren, dass die Unabwendbarkeit der Endlichkeit gleichzeitig geleugnet und anerkannt wird. André Bazin beschrieb dies als „mumifizierte Veränderung"; und wie Philip Rosen erklärt, zeigt dieser oxymoronische Begriff an, dass der Film auf einem „Bedürfnis nach *Permanenz* (der subjektiven Existenz, der Identität) [beruht], welches das betrachtende Subjekt paradoxerweise für das Konkrete öffnen kann, daher also auch der Fluss der Zeit und die Tatsache der *Veränderung*."[10] Diese Spannung zwischen einem Bedürfnis nach Beständigkeit und der Unvermeidlichkeit der Veränderung wird besonders spürbar in einem Film wie *Blight*, der den Abriss von Häusern zugunsten der Verbindungsstraße M11 in Ost-London dokumentiert, nachdem eine ausdauernde basisdemokratische Initiative der Anwohner*innen gegen ihre Umsiedlung erfolglos ausgegangen war. Zum Rhythmus der Musik der Komponistin Jocelyn Pook – mit integrierten Ausschnitten einiger Aussagen von Anwohner*innen über ihr Leben und ihre Häuser – zeigt ein Bild nach dem anderen die in der Zerstörung begriffenen viktorianischen Reihenhäuser, die alle gleich und doch verschieden sind. Am Ende des Films hat der Bau der Straße begonnen. *Blight* bekundet eine enorme formale Genauigkeit und stellt dabei gleichzeitig das Bedürfnis die Zeit einzubalsamieren in den Vordergrund, denn Smith agiert hier als Zeuge der gegenwärtigen schwierigen Lage und erstellt ein Archiv der verschwindenden Gemeinde. Während der Gedanke der „mumifizierten Veränderung" am ehesten in der Auseinandersetzung des Individuums mit der Unausweichlichkeit des Todes seinen Widerhall findet, wird das emotionale Geflecht dieses Konzepts in *Blight* in einem kollektiven Kontext zur Geltung gebracht. Dem Protest der Anwohner*innen stellt Smith einen Protest gegen das Vergessen zur Seite. Die Häuser konnten nicht erhalten werden, doch wenigstens werden sie vor dem Vergessen bewahrt. Der Film bringt ein entscheidendes

10. André Bazin, „The Ontology of the Photographic Image", in: *What is Cinema? Volume One*, hrsg. und übers. von Hugh Grey (Berkeley: University of California Press, 1970), 15; Philip Rosen, *Change Mummified: Cinema, Historicity, Theory* (Minneapolis: University of Minnesota Press, 2001), 39.

to an individual coming to grips with the inevitability of death, in *Blight* the affective weave of this concept is brought to bear on a collective context. To the residents' protest, Smith adds a protest against forgetting. Even if the houses could not be saved, they will at least be spared from oblivion. The film draws out a crucial feature of the experimental atlas of East London that many of Smith's films together comprise: within the context of a country riven by class hatred and brutally dragged into neoliberalism by Margaret Thatcher, a prime minister who initiated a programme of social cleansing that continues into the present, the artist's devotion to the textures of ordinary life is a counter-hegemonic gesture of contestation.

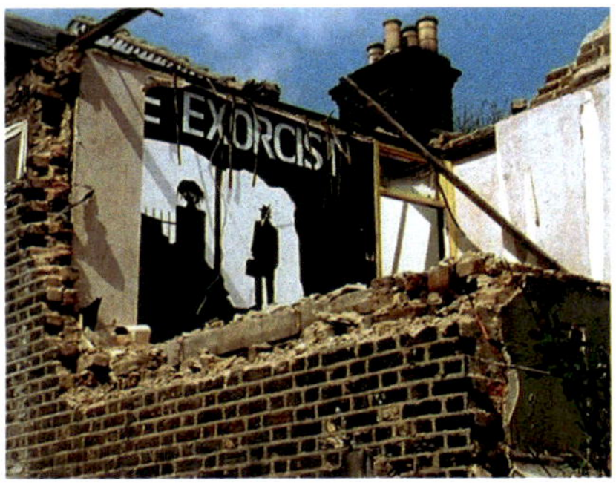

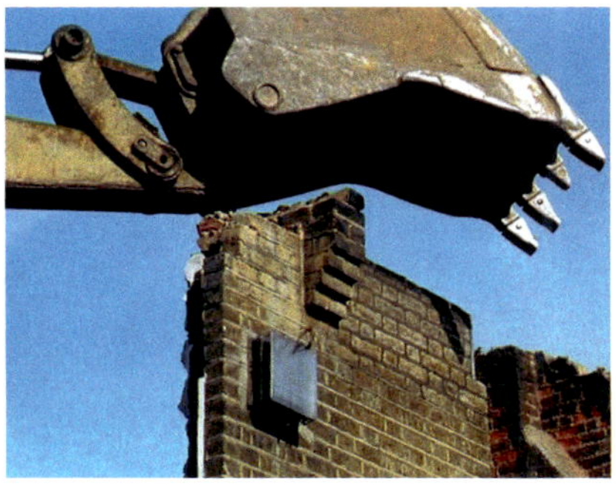

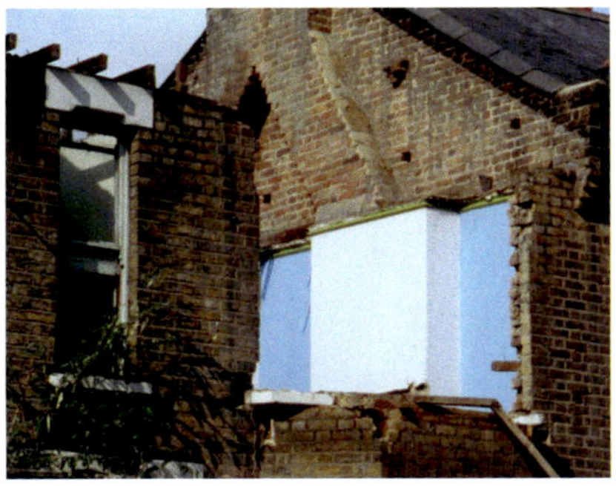

Blight, 1994–96, HD video from 16mm, 14 minutes

III.

From the mid-1990s on, Smith's emphasis on locality begins to be complemented by a strong autobiographical impulse, as he comes to occupy the role of protagonist in many of his works, appearing onscreen and/or as a voiceover narrator. In a stark departure from the aversion to subjective expressivity that is typical of structural-materialist filmmaking, he crafts a first-person cinema in which the idiosyncrasies of selfhood are coaxed out of the dim corners of private life and ushered into the light of public exposure, where they take on a form that will last. Coincidentally or not, this occurs around the same time as the artist shifts from 16mm film to video, the latter being a form of image-production that is more intimate and cheaper to use than its photochemical antecedent. From the beginning of his career, Smith had been, in his words, a 'cottage industry film-maker with a hands-on approach to all aspects of production', eschewing the capital-intensive modes of creation proper to most spheres of filmmaking.[11] Over the years, the once frugal domain of artists' moving image has moved steadily towards bigger budgets and higher production values, but Smith has stayed true to this artisanal conviction, buoyed by his transition to video, which enabled him to further explore how a moving image practice might take shape autonomously, as a habitual undertaking, wedded to quotidian rhythms.

For Smith, video becomes a diary form, true to itsetymological derivation from the Latin for 'I see', which

11. John Smith, 'John Smith', *Artists' Moving Image in Britain Since 1989*, ed. Erika Balsom, Sarah Perks, and Lucy Reynolds (London/New Haven: Paul Mellon Centre for Studies in British Art and Yale University Press, 2019), 478.

Merkmal des experimentellen Atlas von Ost-London hervor, den viele von Smiths Filmen zusammengenommen ergeben: Im Kontext eines Landes, das von Klassenhass zerrissen ist und brutal in den Neoliberalismus hineingezogen wurde, von Margaret Thatcher, einer Premierministerin, die ein Programm der sozialen Säuberung eingeleitet hat, das sich bis heute fortsetzt, ist die Hingabe des Künstlers an die Texturen des Alltags eine antihegemoniale Geste der Herausforderung, der Verweigerung.

III.

Seit Mitte der 1990er Jahre wird Smiths Betonung der Lokalität durch einen starken autobiografischen Impuls ergänzt, da er in vielen seiner Filme die Rolle des Protagonisten einnimmt, wobei er selbst im Film erscheint und/oder den Off-Kommentar spricht. In einer scharfen Distanzierung von der Aversion gegen den subjektiven Ausdruck, die das strukturalistisch-materialistische Filmemachen kennzeichnet, betreibt er nun ein Filmemachen aus der Ich-Perspektive, bei dem die Eigenarten des Selbstseins aus den dunklen Winkeln des Privatlebens hervorgelockt und in das Licht der Öffentlichkeit geführt werden, wo sie eine Form annehmen, die Bestand haben wird. Zufällig oder nicht, geschieht dies etwa zur gleichen Zeit, in der der Künstler vom 16-mm-Film zum Video wechselt, wobei Letzteres eine intimere und preisgünstigere Form der Bildproduktion darstellt als der fotochemische Vorläufer. Seit Beginn seiner Laufbahn ist Smith, wie er selbst sagt, immer ein „Filmemacher, der in Heimarbeit produziert und bei allen Aspekten der Produktion die Hände im Spiel hat“, und er meidet die kapitalintensiven Produktionsmethoden, die den meisten Bereichen des Filmemachens eigen sind.[11] Über die Jahre hat sich die einst genügsame Domäne des künstlerischen Bewegtbildes stetig auf größere Budgets und höhere Produktionswerte zubewegt, doch Smith bleibt seiner handwerklichen Überzeugung treu. Der Wechsel zum Video gibt ihm hier Auftrieb, denn so kann er noch weiter untersuchen, wie eine Praxis des bewegten Bildes sich unabhängig entwickeln könnte, als ein Unterfangen, das habituell ist, eingebunden in alltägliche Rhythmen.

Bei Smith wird das Video zu einer Tagebuchform und entspricht der etymologischen Herleitung aus der lateinischen Phrase für „Ich sehe“, die auf eine Ich-Beziehung zum Bild hinweist. In *Home Suite* (1993–94), dem ersten Werk des Künstlers in diesem Medium, ist seine eigene Ansicht nicht von der Kameraperspektive zu trennen, während er eine Bestandsaufnahme der baulichen Merkmale seines Hauses macht, inklusive abblätternder Farbe und undichter Toilette, kurz bevor er gezwungen wird, es zu räumen. In ungefähr 96 Minuten erläutert er diverse Elemente dieser Räumlichkeiten und berichtet im Off-Kommentar, woran sie ihn erinnern.

11. John Smith, „John Smith“, in: *Artists' Moving Image in Britain Since 1989*, hrsg. von Erika Balsom, Sarah Perks und Lucy Reynolds (London/New Haven: Paul Mellon Centre for Studies in British Art and Yale University Press, 2019), 478.

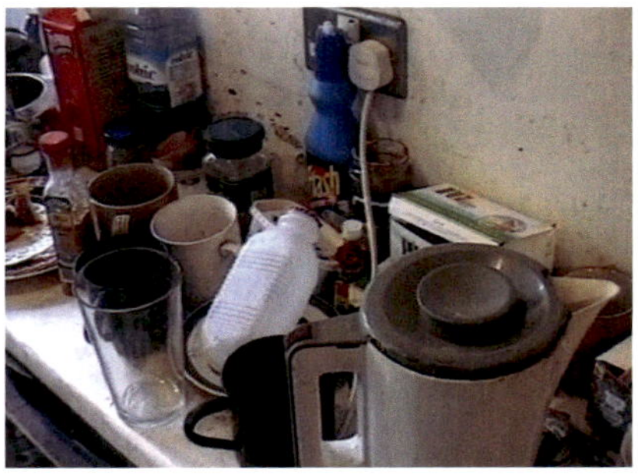

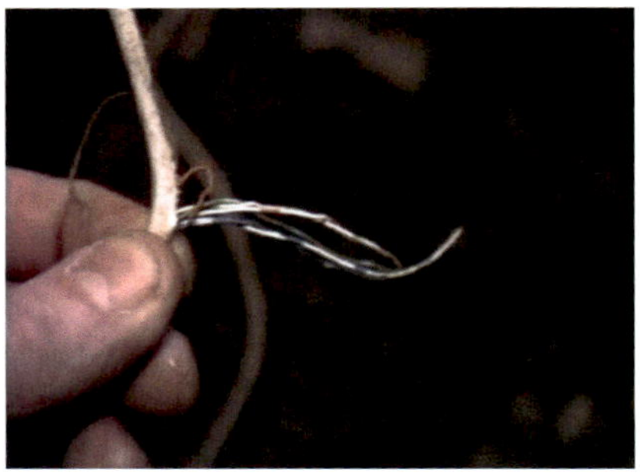

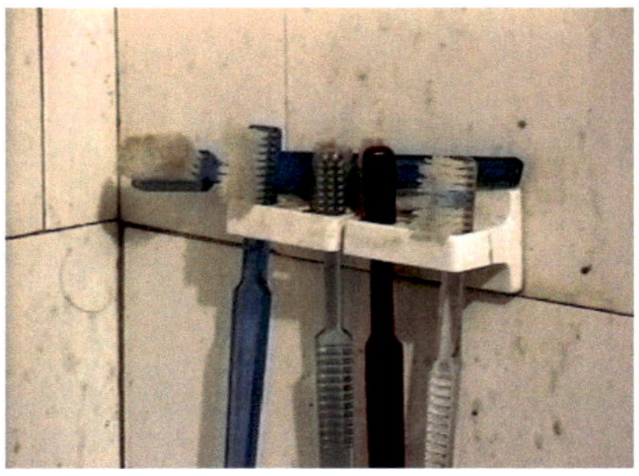

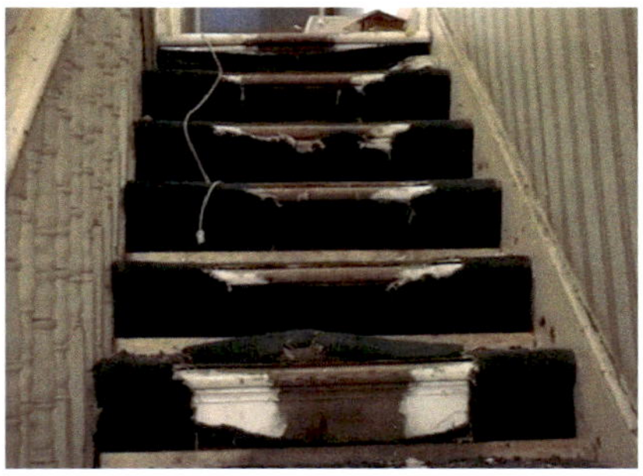

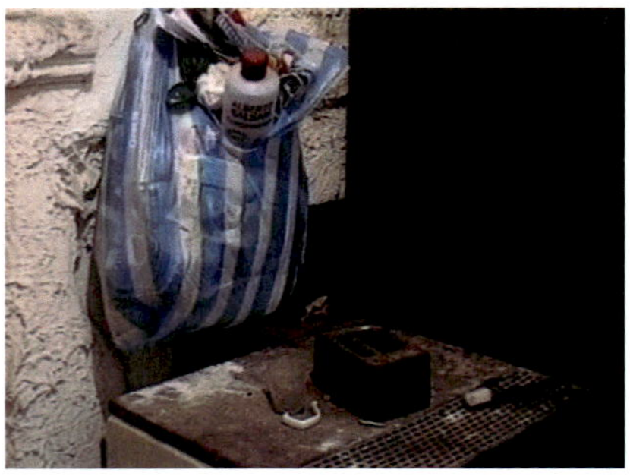

Home Suite, 1993–94, SD video, 96 minutes

suggests a first-person relation to the image. In *Home Suite* (1993–94), the artist's initial work in the medium, his own point of view is inseparable from that of the camera, as he takes stock of the architectural features of his house, flaking paint and leaky toilet included, just before he was to be evicted from it. Over some ninety-six minutes, he provides explanations of various elements of the space and recounts memories attached to them in voiceover. Whereas *The Girl Chewing Gum* ultimately reveals the incommensurability of sound and image, in *Home Suite* and later works such as the *Hotel Diaries* (2001–07) [see page 50], the whole endeavour rests on the copresence of the voice with the time and place of filming. However, instead of taking up the sort of commanding posture lampooned in the earlier film ('I want four boys to come from the left and I want one of them to look this way and flap his arms up and down'), in these later works Smith makes no effort to control the visual field through narration. Rather, he is a situated part of it, responding to its mundane complexity – sometimes humorously, sometimes hesitantly. In *Home Suite*, years of life lived are encrusted on the walls of the house, there for Smith to read like hieroglyphics decipherable to him alone.

Whereas a 16mm film of a length comparable to that of *Home Suite* would be relatively expensive to shoot and process, video allows the camera to roll and roll as Smith roams through the rooms he knows so well. The sharp articulations of filmic montage that he will pursue immediately after in the 16mm *Blight* are nowhere to be found. Why cut? There is no rush: the telephone can ring and he can go answer it, leaving the tape running. These electronic long takes allow time to pool generously, preserving spatio-temporal continuity and instilling a formal looseness within which details that would otherwise be lost to oblivion are mulled over with care and narrativized. While at first glance this might seem like a move away from the reflection on medium specificity that informs many of Smith's filmic works and towards a primacy of the signified, it would be more accurate to see it as a response to the specific affordances of his chosen technology. With its capacity for instant playback and extended recording, and its image made of ceaseless scanning, video is a medium of the present.

Despite the adoption of a very different form – taut rather than wandering, devoid of camera movement, with narration delivered in subtitles instead of in voiceover – a similar concern for how personal memory is embedded in the material world informs in the perversely punny *Dad's Stick* (2012) [see page 74]. Here, Smith seizes not on a place but an object, one that is seemingly banal yet loaded with significance and marked by unassuming beauty: the stick his father used for many years to stir housepaint. Over time, the stick accrued layer after layer of pigment, such that its sawed-off end served as an *aide mémoire* of all the lived-in rooms its owner had decorated. In a remarkably short duration, only five minutes, Smith constructs a moving elegy to his father, in which objects are shown to be

Während *The Girl Chewing Gum* letztlich die Unvereinbarkeit von Ton und Bild offenbart, hängt bei *Home Suite* oder auch bei späteren Werken, wie *Hotel Diaries* (2001–07) [siehe Seite 60] alles von der Kopräsenz der Stimme mit der Zeit und dem Ort des Filmens ab. Doch anstatt die in dem früheren Film verspottend präsentierte, befehlende Haltung einzunehmen („Ich will, dass vier Jungen von links kommen, und ich will, dass einer von ihnen in diese Richtung schaut und seine Arme auf und ab bewegt"), gibt sich Smith in diesen späteren Werken keine Mühe, das Blickfeld durch Kommentare zu kontrollieren. Stattdessen ist er als ein Bestandteil in selbigem vorhanden und reagiert auf dessen banale Komplexität – manchmal humorvoll, manchmal zögernd. In *Home Suite* sind die Zimmerwände dicht mit gelebtem Leben überkrustet, und Smith liest sie wie Hieroglyphen, die nur er zu entziffern vermag.

Wohingegen der Dreh und die Verarbeitung eines 16-mm-Films von der Länge von *Home Suite* relativ teuer wäre, kann Smith die Videokamera einfach laufen lassen, während er in den vertrauten Zimmern umherstreift. Die scharfe Artikulation der Filmmontage, die er unmittelbar im Anschluss in seinem 16-mm-Film *Blight* anwenden wird, ist hier nirgends zu finden. Warum schneiden? Es besteht keine Eile. Das Telefon klingelt und er kann drangehen und die Kamera laufen lassen. In diesen langen elektronischen Aufnahmen kann sich die Zeit weiträumig ausbreiten; die räumlich-zeitliche Kontinuität bleibt bewahrt, und es entsteht eine formale Lockerheit, in der Details, die ansonsten der Vergessenheit zum Opfer gefallen wären, ausführlich bedacht und in eine Erzählung überführt werden können. Auf den ersten Blick mag es scheinen, als würde sich Smith von der Reflexion über die Besonderheiten des Mediums, die viele seiner Filmwerke ausmacht, wegbewegen und sich dem Primat des Signifikats nähern, doch es wäre genauer, dies als eine Reaktion auf die spezifischen Möglichkeiten der von ihm gewählten Technologie zu sehen. Mit der Fähigkeit zur sofortigen Wiedergabe, einer verlängerten Aufnahmezeit und einem Bild, das durch ständiges Scannen entsteht, ist das Video ein Medium der Gegenwart.

Trotz der ganz anderen Form – straff anstatt schweifend, ohne Kamerabewegung, der Kommentar als Untertitel statt aus dem Off – ist das pervers wortspielerisch betitelte *Dad's Stick* (2012) [siehe Seite 78] ähnlich von der Frage geprägt, wie die persönliche Erinnerung in die materielle Welt eingeschrieben ist. Hier setzt Smith nicht an einem Ort an, sondern an einem Objekt, einem scheinbar banalen, dabei aber mit Bedeutung aufgeladenen Gegenstand, den eine schlichte Schönheit auszeichnet: der Stab, den sein Vater viele Jahre zum Umrühren von Wandfarbe benutzte. Mit der Zeit legte sich eine Pigmentschicht nach der anderen um den Stab, so dass sein abgesägtes Ende als Erinnerungsstütze für all die bewohnten Räume dienen konnte, die sein Besitzer gestrichen hatte. In bemerkenswert kurzer Zeit – in nur fünf Minuten – konstruiert Smith eine bewegende Elegie auf seinen Vater, in der man sieht, wie sich Objekte durch Gebrauch und Zeit verändern, wie sich

transformed by use and time, fond recollections mingle with intimations of patriarchal violence, and the border between abstraction and figuration is wilfully destabilized. The video is emblematic of Smith's devotion to remaking the possibilities of mediated memory outside of the hierarchies of significance that typically obtain.

When considering intimate works such as these, in which Smith occupies the role of subject and object at once, narrating various aspects of his life, it is tempting to borrow a term seldom applied to the moving image but which has of late enjoyed a tremendous vogue in literature: autofiction. Unlike autobiography, which is typically characterized by a predisposition for developmental, linear narratives that seek to make sense of the evolution of the self and which disavow any hint of fabulation, autofiction tends to dwell in the uncertain space between a life and its artistic representation. It frequently experiments with form in ways that make distinctions between documentary and fiction difficult, if not entirely futile, to legislate. There is, in other words, a reflexive dimension to the enterprise, albeit one that exists at some distance from the kinds of medium-specific experiments typical of avant-garde filmmaking in the 1970s. The site of inquiry is less the opaque materiality of technological mediation (although this may persist as an interest) than it is the question of how to draw upon the resources of artistic form to give shape to the scattered, contradictory, and sometimes eventful but often banal experience of living in the world.

Undoubtedly, there is a risk in holding up a mirror to one's own existence and making one's own processes of thought and creation the central subject of one's work. Autofiction can easily lapse into narcissism; it can perpetuate the myth of exceptional individuality, commodify the confessional self as a repository of authenticity, or stage a retreat from a world held in common. As such, it can seem perfectly consonant with neoliberal logics that champion independence and rely on the marketing of personality. For Smith, however, something rather different is at stake. With his droll, self-deprecating tone, he emphasizes the ordinary, not the exceptional. In the first-person, he finds a modality of expression capable of puncturing the replicable codes and templates of mass culture by making space for idiosyncrasy; it gives him, in other words, another way of staying close to the rumble of existence. As a storyteller, he is at ease with digression and averse to sensationalism. Whether he is recounting his relationship to particular objects or locations, as in *Home Suite* and *Dad's Stick*, or engaging in a session of self-googling and eBay auction browsing, as in *unusual Red cardigan* (2011) [see page 66], his narratives show that interiority and exteriority exist in dynamic dialogue, that the self is enmeshed within and produced by material and social contexts. Even when he seems to respond spontaneously to whatever sparks his curiosity at a given moment, there is no sense that he is spilling his guts to

liebevolle Erinnerungen mit Andeutungen patriarchaler Gewalt mischen, und die Grenze zwischen Abstraktion und Figuration mutwillig destabilisiert wird. Das Video steht sinnbildlich für Smiths Hingabe, die Möglichkeiten der medialen Erinnerung jenseits der üblichen Bedeutungshierarchien neu zu gestalten.

Bei der Betrachtung solch intimer Werke, in denen Smith gleichzeitig die Rolle des Subjekts und des Objekts einnimmt, wenn er von diversen Aspekten seines Lebens erzählt, ist man versucht, einen Begriff zu entlehnen, der selten auf das Bewegtbild angewendet wird, sich jedoch in letzter Zeit einer enormen Beliebtheit in der Literatur erfreut: Autofiktion. Im Gegensatz zur Autobiografie, die typischerweise zu linearen Entwicklungserzählungen tendiert, die die Entwicklung des Ichs nachvollziehen wollen und jeden Anflug von Fabulierkunst verleugnen, neigt die Autofiktion dazu, im ungewissen Bereich zwischen einem Leben und seiner künstlerischen Darstellung zu verweilen. Häufig experimentiert sie mit der Form, was die regelhafte Unterscheidung zwischen Dokumentation und Fiktion erschwert, wenn nicht gar sinnlos macht. Dem Unterfangen ist, mit anderen Worten, eine reflexive Dimension eigen, wenn sich diese auch recht stark unterscheidet von den mediumsspezifischen Experimenten, die für das Filmschaffen der Avantgarde in den 1970er Jahren typisch waren. Der Ort der Befragung ist nicht so sehr die undurchsichtige Materialität der technologischen Vermittlung (auch wenn dies als Interesse weiter bestehen kann), es geht vielmehr um die Frage, wie man die Ressourcen der künstlerischen Form nutzt, um die verstreute, widersprüchliche und manchmal ereignisreiche, oft aber banale Erfahrung des Lebens in der Welt in eine Form zu bringen.

Zweifelsohne geht man ein Risiko ein, wenn man der eigenen Existenz den Spiegel vorhält und die persönlichen Gedankens- und Schaffensprozesse zum zentralen Thema der eigenen Arbeit macht. Die Autofiktion kann leicht in Narzissmus verfallen; sie kann den Mythos der außergewöhnlichen Individualität verfestigen, das bekennende Selbst als Hort der Authentizität vermarkten oder den Rückzug aus einer gemeinsamen Welt inszenieren. So gesehen mag sie auch scheinbar perfekt mit neoliberalen Logiken übereinstimmen, die sich für Unabhängigkeit engagieren und auf die Vermarktung der Persönlichkeit setzen. Smith geht es aber um etwas ganz anderes. Mit seinem verschmitzten, selbstironischen Tonfall betont er das Gewöhnliche, nicht das Außergewöhnliche. In der Perspektive der ersten Person hat er eine Ausdrucksmodalität gefunden, mit der sich die replizierbaren Codes und Schablonen der Massenkultur durchbrechen lassen, weil er damit der Eigenheit Raum geben kann, will heißen: Sie eröffnet ihm eine weitere Möglichkeit, um dem Rumoren des Lebens nahe zu sein. Als Geschichtenerzähler ist ihm die Abschweifung angenehm und die Sensationslust zuwider. Ob er nun von seiner Beziehung zu bestimmten Objekten oder Orten erzählt, wie in *Home Suite* oder *Dad's Stick*, oder ob er sich selbst googelt und in eBay-Auktionen stöbert, wie in *unusual Red cardigan* (2011)

the viewer, pouring out deep inner truths. Rather, the accounts he offers are twinged with performative contrivance without ever leaving a sense of lived reality entirely behind. (He is, for instance, a great fan of the punchline.)

Smith's decision to take his own life as a subject of representation is consonant with his rejection of the role of the documentarian-tourist, and all its accompanying associations of imperial fantasy and the fetishization of otherness that such a position implies. His focus on the self is no withdrawal into the safety of an insular individualism. Rather, it bespeaks a desire to tamper with the asymmetries of power that have traditionally obtained in cinematic nonfiction between the one who wields the camera and those who are fixed in its crosshairs, a theme central already to *The Girl Chewing Gum*, however differently approached. Breaking with the aspiration to objectivity and allure of exoticism that have long been part of the documentary tradition, Smith charts another path, one that is modest and yet radical in how it affirms the inexhaustible interest of what is nearest to hand. Like facing the untameable ocean in *Horizon*, like staging the omnipotence of the narrator in *The Girl Chewing Gum* only to reveal him to be delusional, Smith's emphasis on his own life is an ethical wager, a way of staying clear of the arrogance of those who claim mastery over others via the camera's mechanical eye.

IV.

In an array of recent works, this aspect of Smith's practice takes on a geopolitical dimension. Consider *White Hole* (2014) [see page 80], in which the artist relays memories of traveling to Poland in 1980 and the former East Germany in 1998 in voiceover, economically crafting a parable that points to the limited trustworthiness of first impressions and the risk of romanticizing difference – in this case, state communism as compared to Thatcherism. When Smith first arrives in Poland, he is happy to be free of being surrounded by advertisements, to be in a country lacking in luxury and consumer choice. Before long, however, he realizes that he is idealizing the Polish context, just as some Poles idealize Thatcher's Britain. The video makes use of a binary construction, with a single voiceover first played backwards over a monochrome 'phantom ride' through a dark tunnel, then repeated forwards over the same image, but with the latter's black and white values inverted. The content of Smith's speech problematizes the stark divisions of the video's form, as he points to both the blind spots that inevitably exist as a product of one's own positionality and the incapacity of binary schemas to account for the complexities of worldly existence. Although the image of the tunnel relates most immediately to a 'new East German aphorism' that Smith hears about – amid rising unemployment and dashed hopes, 'people were saying that they could see a tunnel at the end of the light' – it also suggests a relation to epistemological limitation: like it or not, we all have tunnel vision to some degree.

[siehe Seite 68], seine Erzählungen zeigen, dass Inneres und Äußeres in einem dynamischen Dialog stehen, dass das Selbst in materielle und soziale Kontexte eingebettet ist und aus ihnen hervorgeht. Selbst wenn er scheinbar spontan auf irgendetwas reagiert, das seine Neugier weckt, hat man nie den Eindruck, dass er der Betrachter*in sein Herz ausschüttet und tiefe innere Wahrheiten hervorholt. Vielmehr sind seine Schilderungen von performativen Erfindungen durchzogen, ohne dass jemals der Sinn für gelebte Realität ganz verloren geht. (Er ist zum Beispiel ein großer Fan der Pointe.)

Smiths Entscheidung, sein eigenes Leben zum Gegenstand der Darstellung zu machen, stimmt mit seiner Ablehnung der Rolle des Dokumentartouristen und all den damit einhergehenden Assoziationen von imperialer Fantasie und einer Fetischisierung des Andersseins, die eine solche Position mit sich bringt, überein. Seine Konzentration auf das Selbst ist kein Rückzug in die Sicherheit eines insularen Individualismus. Stattdessen drückt sich darin das Verlangen aus, sich in die asymmetrischen Machtverhältnisse einzumischen, die im nicht-fiktionalen Film traditionell zwischen der- oder demjenigen bestehen, die die Kamera führt, und der- oder denjenigen, die im Fadenkreuz der Kamera stehen – ein Thema, das, wenn auch mit einem anderen Ansatz, schon in *The Girl Chewing Gum* zentral war. Indem er mit dem Anspruch auf Objektivität und der Verlockung des Exotischen bricht, die schon lange Teil der dokumentarischen Tradition sind, schlägt Smith einen anderen Weg ein, einen bescheidenen und zugleich radikalen, der das unerschöpfliche Interesse an dem bekräftigt, was uns am nächsten ist. Wie die Konfrontation mit dem unbezähmbaren Ozean in *Horizon*, wie die Inszenierung der Allmacht des Erzählers in *The Girl Chewing Gum*, die letzten Endes dazu dient, ihn als wahnhaft zu entlarven, ist auch Smiths Fokus auf sein eigenes Leben eine ethische Wette, eine Art und Weise, sich von der Arroganz derjenigen zu distanzieren, die mittels des mechanischen Kameraauges Herrschaft über andere beanspruchen.

IV.

In mehreren neueren Werken nimmt dieser Aspekt von Smiths Praxis eine geopolitische Dimension an. In *White Hole* (2014) [siehe Seite 84] zum Beispiel teilt der Künstler über einen Off-Kommentar seine Erinnerungen an eine Reise nach Polen im Jahr 1980 und nach Ostdeutschland im Jahr 1998. Dabei konstruiert er sehr effizient eine Parabel über die eingeschränkte Verlässlichkeit von ersten Eindrücken und das Risiko, Unterschiede zu romantisieren – in diesem Fall zwischen Kommunismus und Thatcherismus. Bei seiner Ankunft in Polen freut sich Smith darüber, dass er nicht mehr von Werbung umgeben ist, dass er sich in einem Land befindet, dem es an Luxus und Auswahlmöglichkeiten für die Konsument*innen mangelt. Doch schon bald merkt er, dass er die polnischen Zusammenhänge idealisiert, genau wie einige Pol*innen

If *White Hole* stages the failure of mutual understanding and the myopia of the distant gaze, the *Hotel Diaries* series – comprising seven videos,[12] all shot in hotel rooms, all but one of which are located in European cities – suggests a possible way out: attend to the particularity of one's own surroundings in rigorous detail, paying special attention to how distinctions between the 'here' and the 'elsewhere', the 'us' and the 'them' are leaky and unstable, all the more so in the era of the so-called War on Terror than they were during the Cold War. Although the very notion of a hotel would seem to evoke displacement and mobility, the *Hotel Diaries* are works of confinement; while abroad, Smith loses none of his reluctance to be a tourist, nor his attachment to generative limitation. His focus on the personal, proximate, and mundane endures even when he is not at home. He sticks to the restricted setting of his room, straying only as far as the elevator in one instance, shutting out the possibility of directly documenting the specificities of the countries he visits, often to attend film festivals: England, Germany, Ireland, Israel, the Netherlands, Palestine, and Switzerland. In place of the touristic vista, he allows the corporate blandness of the hotel and the monologue of its solitary guest to prevail.

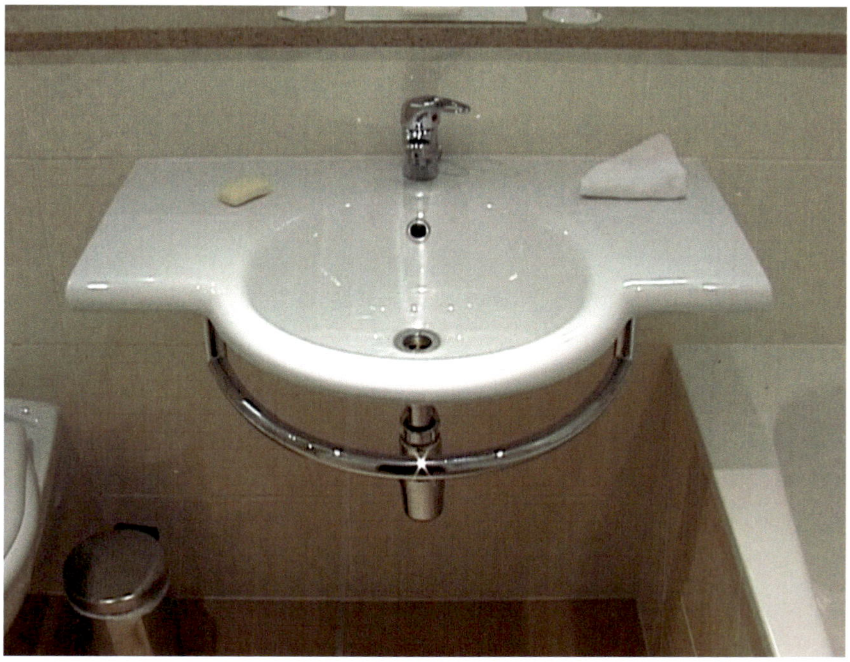

Hotel Diaries, 2001–07,
SD video in 7 parts, 82 minutes

At the start of *Six Years Later* (2007), the final instalment of the series, Smith evokes the fungible similarity of the various rooms that have appeared throughout it: 'I'm in a hotel in Antwerp or Brussels or Birmingham or Bremen or maybe Barcelona or Cork', he says, panning from one gleaming feature of the bathroom to the next in time with his alphabetical litany, before admitting that he is, in fact, in Ireland. In these works, the hotel room figures as an archetypal example of what

12. Or eight, depending on whether *Pyramids* (2006) and *Skunk* (2007), shot exactly one year apart in Rotterdam and always shown together as *Pyramids / Skunk* (2006–07), are to be considered one work or two.

Thatchers Großbritannien idealisieren. Das Video verwendet eine binäre Konstruktion, wobei ein und derselbe Off-Kommentar zuerst rückwärts zu einer monochromen „Phantomfahrt" durch einen dunklen Tunnel abgespielt und dann zum gleichen Bild vorwärts wiederholt wird, wobei die Schwarz-Weiß-Werte beim zweiten Mal umgekehrt werden. Der Inhalt von Smiths Sprache problematisiert die scharfen Trennungen in der Form des Videos, während er sowohl auf die blinden Flecken hinweist, die als Produkt der eigenen Positionalität unweigerlich bestehen, als auch auf die Unfähigkeit binärer Denkschemata, den Komplexitäten des Daseins Rechnung zu tragen. Obwohl das Bild vom Tunnel sich am direktesten auf einen „neuen ostdeutschen Aphorismus" bezieht, von dem Smith hört – inmitten steigender Arbeitslosigkeit und enttäuschter Hoffnungen „sagten die Menschen, sie sähen einen Tunnel am Ende des Lichts" – deutet es auch auf einen Zusammenhang mit erkenntnistheoretischen Einschränkungen hin: Ob es uns gefällt oder nicht, bis zu einem gewissen Grad haben wir alle einen Tunnelblick.

Wenn *White Hole* das Scheitern des gegenseitigen Verständnisses und die Kurzsichtigkeit des Blicks aus der Ferne inszeniert, so zeigt die Videoreihe *Hotel Diaries* – sieben Videos,[12] die in Hotelzimmern gedreht wurden, die sich alle, außer einem, in europäischen Städten befinden – einen möglichen Ausweg auf: Man achte genau auf die Besonderheit der eigenen Umgebung, besonders auch darauf, dass die Unterscheidungen zwischen dem „Hier" und dem „Anderswo", dem „Wir" und dem „Sie" instabil und nicht trennscharf sind, und zwar in der Ära des sogenannten Krieges gegen den Terror noch mehr als während des Kalten Krieges. Obwohl der Begriff Hotel an sich schon örtliche Verlagerung und Mobilität zu evozieren scheint, sind Smiths „Hoteltagebücher" Werke der Begrenzung; auch beim Reisen außer Landes verliert Smith nichts von seinem Widerwillen, ein Tourist zu sein, nichts von seiner Sympathie für die produktive Begrenzung. Sein Fokus auf das Persönliche, Naheliegende und Alltägliche bleibt bestehen, auch wenn er nicht zu Hause ist. Er bleibt in der begrenzten Umgebung seines Zimmers, nur in einem Fall geht er bis zum Aufzug und schließt so die Möglichkeit aus, die Besonderheiten der Länder, die er meistens besucht, um an Filmfestivals teilzunehmen, unmittelbar zu dokumentieren: England, Deutschland, Irland, Israel, die Niederlande, Palästina und die Schweiz. Anstelle des touristischen Blicks lässt er die kommerzielle Fadheit des Hotels und den Monolog des einsamen Gastes überwiegen.

Zu Beginn von *Six Years Later* (2007), der letzten Folge, erinnert Smith an die fungible Ähnlichkeit der diversen Zimmer, die in der Reihe zu sehen sind: „Ich bin in einem Hotel in Antwerpen oder Brüssel oder Birmingham oder Bremen oder vielleicht Barcelona oder Cork", sagt er und schwenkt im Takt seiner alphabetischen

12. Oder acht, je nachdem, ob man *Pyramids* (2006) und *Skunk* (2007) – im Abstand von genau einem Jahr in Rotterdam gedreht und als *Pyramids / Skunk* (2006–07) immer zusammen gezeigt – als ein oder zwei Werke betrachtet.

anthropologist Marc Augé calls the 'non-place': anonymous and generic, marked by none of the relation to history and memory that defines place, it is emblematic of 'a world… surrendered to solitary individuality, to the fleeting, the temporary and the ephemeral.'[13] It is, in other words, a perfect location for a first-person narrator who wishes to confront the strange dislocations of travel, globalization, and – crucially – the experience of distant war in the twenty-first century.

The *Hotel Diaries* mostly take place in the middle of the night. Smith shoots an unbroken take using a handheld camera while he speaks in voiceover, assessing the room and relaying details of his travel. He is alone, suspended in time and space, shorn of the comforts and routines of home, with his camera as his only companion. Each instalment of the series ends by giving the date of its production, underlining its status as a record of the specific moment when its maker decided to execute a videotaped performance. Given these parameters, one might assume the *Hotel Diaries* to be a work in which Smith is thrown back on himself in a cocoon of solipsism, deracinated and isolated, even more deeply immersed in a personal universe than he had been before. This would not be altogether wrong, but it is only part of the picture: thoughts about the minibar and the routines of the housekeeping staff are relayed alongside an anxious concern with conflicts occurring in the Middle East. The trivial and the serious mix in a way that seems like a category violation – until one realizes that such collisions are precisely what make up the fabric of twenty-first-century experience. This is even more true now, with the endless scroll of social media, than it was when Smith began the series. In the immediate aftermath of the events of September 11, 2001, the *Hotel Diaries* parse issues which have lost none of their relevance in the intervening years: everyday life in a time of endless war, pervasive disinformation, new velocities of image circulation, and atrocities broadcast in real time.

In each instalment, these realities somehow find in their way into Smith's nocturnal musings. The first episode, *Frozen War* (2001), was made on 8 October 2001, the day after the United States and United Kingdom began bombing Afghanistan. Smith turns on the television, 'dreading what the news tonight was going to be', only to find that the image has frozen at 1:41 a.m., with the headline 'STRIKE ON AFGHANISTAN' emblazoned on the screen. Has something gone wrong in London? When perpetual crisis is perpetually transmitted via television, a rupture in the image flow becomes an occasion to unfold ideas of fear, distance, and intervention. As it figures in Smith's video diary, the broadcasting error becomes more than mere contingency; it claims an allegorical force, encapsulating the artist's overarching desire to jam the gears of the media machine and find an alternate way to approach the tense present in

13. Marc Augé, *Non-Places: Introduction to an Anthropology of Supermodernity*, trans. John Howe (London: Verso, 1995), 78.

Litanei von einer glänzenden Badezimmereinrichtung zur nächsten, bevor er zugibt, dass er tatsächlich in Irland ist. In diesen Werken tritt das Hotelzimmer als archetypisches Beispiel davon auf, was der Anthropologe Marc Augé den „Nicht-Ort" nennt: Anonym und universell, durch keinerlei Bezug zu Geschichte und Erinnerung ausgezeichnet, der einen Ort ausmacht, ist er Sinnbild „einer Welt, die sich der einsamen Individualität, dem Flüchtigen, dem Vorläufigen und dem Kurzlebigen hingibt."[13] Mit anderen Worten ist es der perfekte Ort für einen Ich-Erzähler, der sich mit den seltsamen Verwerfungen des Reisens, der Globalisierung und – ganz entscheidend – der Erfahrung eines fernen Krieges im 21. Jahrhundert auseinandersetzen will.

Die *Hotel Diaries* spielen größtenteils mitten in der Nacht. Smith dreht mit der Handkamera jeweils eine lange Einstellung, während er im Off-Kommentar spricht, den Raum begutachtet und Einzelheiten von seiner Reise erzählt. Er ist allein, schwebt in Raum und Zeit, ohne die Annehmlichkeiten und Routinen seines Zuhauses, mit seiner Kamera als einziger Begleiterin. Jeder Teil der Reihe endet mit der Angabe des Datums, was seinen Status als eine Aufzeichnung des speziellen Moments unterstreicht, in dem sein Schöpfer beschloss, eine mit Video aufgenommene Performance durchzuführen. Aufgrund dieser Parameter könnte man annehmen, dass *Hotel Diaries* ein Werk sei, in dem Smith in einem solipsistischen Kokon entwurzelt und isoliert auf sich selbst zurückgeworfen wird, sich noch tiefer in ein persönliches Universum versenkt als vorher schon. Das wäre nicht ganz falsch, ist aber auch nur ein Teil der Wahrheit: Neben Gedanken über die Minibar und die Routinen des Raumpflegepersonals teilt er auch seine ängstliche Sorge um die Konflikte im Nahen Osten. Triviales und Ernstes wird derart gemischt, dass hier Kategorien scheinbar unzulässig durcheinandergeworfen werden – bis man erkennt, dass solche Kollisionen genau das sind, was die Erfahrungsstruktur des 21. Jahrhunderts ausmacht. Dies gilt heute, wo die Sozialen Medien unaufhörlich über den Bildschirm rollen, noch mehr als damals, als Smith seine Reihe begann. Unmittelbar nach den Ereignissen des 11. September 2001 gefilmt, behandeln die *Hotel Diaries* Themen, die seitdem nichts von ihrer Aktualität verloren haben: Der Alltag in einer Zeit nicht endender Kriege, die allgegenwärtige Desinformation, ein neues Tempo bei der Zirkulation von Bildern, in Echtzeit übertragene Gräueltaten.

In jeder Folge tauchen diese Realitäten irgendwie in Smiths nächtlichen Überlegungen auf. Die erste Episode *Frozen War* (2001), entstand am 8. Oktober 2001, einen Tag, nachdem die USA und Großbritannien mit ihren Bombenangriffen auf Afghanistan begonnen hatten. Smith schaltet „mit der größten Befürchtung, was heute Nacht wieder in den Nachrichten sein würde" den Fernseher ein, stellt aber fest, dass das Bild um 1:41

13. Marc Augé, *Non-Places: Introduction to an Anthropology of Supermodernity*, übers. von John Howe (London: Verso, 1995), 78.

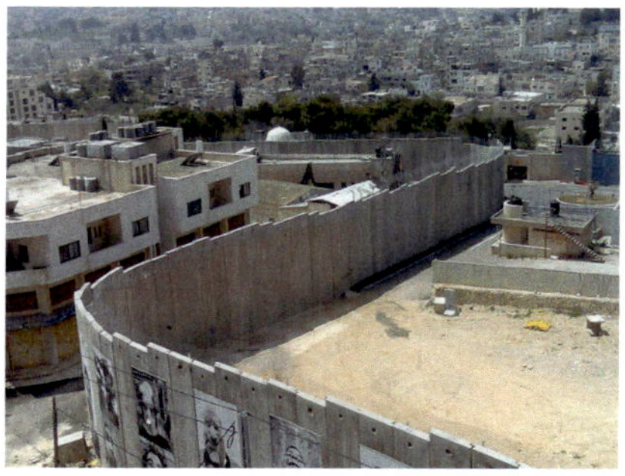

Hotel Diaries, 2001–07,
SD video in 7 parts, 82 minutes

the present tense. Against the sensationalism of planes crashing into buildings, the obscenity of photographs of torture, and the misleading bloviations of politicians and pundits, Smith is determined to provide a counterweight by dwelling in the realm of the unspectacular.

In *Dirty Pictures* (2007), the penultimate episode of the series, he diverges from the rules he had set for himself so as to dramatically throw the overall stakes of his project into relief. Recorded on 15 and 16 April, it is the only episode that takes place outside Europe and the only to feature two shots and two locations, the first in Bethlehem and the second in East Jerusalem. It is also the only time Smith offers a view of his surrounding city in daylight. After a prolonged observation of ceiling tiles moving in the wind, he pans to look out the window, where the Israeli West Bank Barrier – known in Arabic as the 'wall of apartheid' – is prominently visible. Political strife is now directly before his eyes. As he gazes at the divided landscape, Smith remains uncommonly silent, seemingly reluctant to impose his commentary on the image of humanitarian crisis and occupation he captures. After a cut, he explains that he has moved to a new hotel in East Jerusalem and reviewed the footage he shot the day before in Bethlehem. He was unhappy with the result, partly because of some dirt on the lens but also because he had said nothing about the image of the wall. Rather than speak about it retrospectively, he tells the story of passing through an Israeli checkpoint on foot – a story of his own privilege, the subjugation of Palestinians, and the pain of one woman in particular. The nights spent in Israel/Palestine are the only time in the whole of the *Hotel Diaries* that Smith witnesses first-hand the kind of conflict that consistently haunts the series from afar, and which is typically relayed to him via the news media. Here, too, however, a distance persists. While he shows, he cannot speak; while he speaks, he films the desk in his room or his shoes on the floor, allowing the narration to create a mental image for the viewer of a scene of state violence that remains absent.

In the subsequent, final episode, *Six Years Later*, Smith remarks, 'Seems like half the world's a swanky hotel and the other half's a bomb site.' He knows well where he stands and, unlike some, he is reluctant to cross to the other side with the intention of making an image. Even in *Flag Mountain* (2010) [see page 62] – a rare example of Smith shooting a landscape abroad – when he films a gigantic flag drawn on the side of a mountain in the Turkish Republic of Northern Cyprus from the other side of the island, it is from the single position of the balcony of an apartment where he had stayed two years previous. In the *Hotel Diaries*, Smith's decision to (almost) exclusively film the interiors of his various rooms must be understood not only as affirming the interest of those spaces but also as a refusal to make the genre of images most commonly associated with travel and Middle Eastern conflict. An iconoclastic impulse runs throughout the series, one directed against the regime of infotainment and a certain kind of documentary image produced

Uhr erstarrt ist – „ANGRIFF AUF AFGHANISTAN" steht groß auf dem Bildschirm. Ist in London etwas passiert? Wenn die andauernde Krise andauernd im Fernsehen übertragen wird, gibt eine Unterbrechung des Bilderflusses Anlass, sich Gedanken über Angst, Distanz und Intervention zu machen. Dadurch, dass er in Smiths Video vorkommt, ist der Sendefehler mehr als nur eine Bedingtheit; er behauptet eine allegorische Kraft, die das umfassende Bedürfnis des Künstlers einfängt, das Räderwerk des Medienapparats zu blockieren und eine alternative Möglichkeit zu finden, die angespannte Gegenwart in der Gegenwart zu behandeln. Zum Sensationalismus von Flugzeugen, die in Gebäude fliegen, der Obszönität von Folterfotos und dem irreführenden Gerede von Politikern und öffentlichen Experten will Smith ein Gegengewicht schaffen, indem er in der Sphäre des Unspektakulären verweilt.

In *Dirty Pictures* (2007), der vorletzten Folge der Reihe, weicht er von den Regeln ab, die er sich selbst gesetzt hat, um dramatisch hervorzuheben, was für ihn bei dem Projekt alles auf dem Spiel steht. Gefilmt am 15. und 16. April, ist dies die einzige Episode, die außerhalb von Europa angelegt ist und die einzige, für die Smith zwei Einstellungen an zwei Orten verwendet, die erste in Betlehem und die zweite in Ost-Jerusalem. Es ist auch das einzige Mal, dass Smith einen Blick auf die umliegende Stadt bei Tageslicht bietet. Nach einer längeren Beobachtung der Deckenplatten, die sich im Wind bewegen, schwenkt die Kamera für einen Blick ins Freie zum Fenster, von wo aus die israelischen Sperranlagen – im Arabischen als „Apartheidmauer" bekannt – deutlich zu sehen sind. Der politische Konflikt liegt nun direkt vor seinen Augen. Während er auf die geteilte Landschaft blickt, bleibt Smith ungewöhnlich schweigsam. Er scheint sich zu scheuen, das Bild der humanitären Krise und der Besetzung, das er einfängt, mit seinem Kommentar zu überlagern. Nach einem Schnitt erklärt er, dass er in ein anderes Hotel in Ost-Jerusalem umgezogen sei und begutachtet das Material, das er am Vortag in Betlehem gefilmt hat. Mit dem Ergebnis war er nicht zufrieden, teils, weil Schmutz auf der Linse gewesen war, aber auch, weil er nichts zu dem Bild von der Mauer gesagt hatte. Anstatt rückblickend darüber zu sprechen, erzählt er die Geschichte, wie er zu Fuß einen israelischen Grenzübergang passierte – es ist eine Geschichte von seinem eigenen Privileg, von der Unterwerfung der Palästinenser*innen im Allgemeinen und dem Schmerz einer Frau im Besonderen. Die Nächte, die er in Israel/Palästina verbringt, sind die einzigen in der gesamten Reihe, in denen Smith den Konflikt, der die *Hotel Diaries* beständig aus der Ferne heimsucht und ihm in der Regel über die Nachrichtenmedien übermittelt wird, aus erster Hand erlebt. Doch auch hier bleibt eine Distanz bestehen: Beim Zeigen kann er nicht sprechen; beim Sprechen filmt er den Schreibtisch in seinem Zimmer oder seine Schuhe auf dem Boden und ermöglicht der Erzählung dadurch, eine ausgeblendete Szene von Staatsgewalt vor dem geistigen Auge der Betrachter*in zu erzeugen.

by ostensibly progressive filmmakers who are 'drawn elsewhere by an other', especially to situations of emergency. Smith refuses the conventionally beautiful image and the image of suffering alike, seeing them as two sides of the same coin of spectacular seduction. The *Hotel Diaries* are charming and funny. Yet they also raise grave questions to which there are no easy answers. To what extent do we share a 'now'? How can one make an image of the present? How are we implicated in acts of imperial violence committed elsewhere, in our name, but against our convictions? When should the camera turn away?

V.

For many filmmakers, the coronavirus pandemic brought work to a halt. Unable to be in public or to travel, projects fell apart. For Smith, on the other hand, long accustomed to working alone and in confined spaces, it posed little professional difficulty. In May 2020, while the United Kingdom was in lockdown, he began an episodic series called *Covid Messages* (2020) [see page 106], made from repurposed footage of press conferences in which Prime Minister Boris Johnson briefs the public on the status of the pandemic. In some sense, the series is the inverted twin of the *Hotel Diaries*: it is based in a montage of appropriated images rather than the continuous recording of Smith himself, and it emerged from a protracted period spent at home instead of from the experience of travel, and yet both are rule-based serial works, bound to the unfolding present, tackling the role of isolation, politics, and media spectacle within it.

Through the six darkly funny instalments of *Covid Messages*, Smith plays with the press conference as a site of 'coded messages', assailing the vacancy of political speech and the grotesque manoeuvres of the Conservative government with his characteristic wit. In the first episode, *Twice*, he stands in front of a mirror, filming with an iPhone strapped to his head. As he washes his hands, he sings *Happy Birthday* twice through, set to the tune of Chopin's funeral march. The act seems absurd – but then a cut to Johnson reveals that the government has advised the public to do just this (minus the Chopin tune, of course). Otherwise, the UK prime minister says, 'for the vast majority of people in this country, we should be going about our business as usual.' Smith ends with a title card that twists the knife: 'Made in London during the sixth week of the lockdown, when Britain's Covid-19 related death toll reached 25,000.' With a tremendous economy of means, the artist marshals his dry humour in the service of outrage at the incompetence and cruelty of a Conservative government that has decimated the capacities of the NHS and other social services throughout a decade of austerity, now as ever ruling in the interests of the rich, the rest of the country – and particularly the most vulnerable – be damned.

In subsequent episodes, Smith's physical presence disappears, giving way to a more extensive use of text and a clever deployment of repetition and reverse motion. He frequently

In der darauffolgenden, letzten Episode von *Six Years Later* merkt Smith an: „Sieht so aus, als wäre die Hälfte der Welt ein Nobelhotel und die andere Hälfte ein Bombenabwurfplatz." Er weiß genau, wo er steht und im Gegensatz zu manch anderen zögert er, auf die andere Seite zu wechseln, nur mit der Intention, ein Bild zu machen. Selbst in *Flag Mountain* (2010) [siehe Seite 64] – ein seltenes Beispiel für eine Landschaftsaufnahme von Smith im Ausland – wenn er eine gigantische Flagge, die auf einer Bergseite in der Türkischen Republik Nordzypern abgebildet ist, vom anderen Teil der Insel filmt, findet dies ausschließlich von seiner Position auf dem Balkon einer Wohnung statt, die er zwei Jahre zuvor schon einmal gemietet hatte. In *Hotel Diaries* ist Smiths Entscheidung, (fast) ausschließlich in seinen diversen Zimmern zu filmen, nicht nur als eine Bestätigung der Interessantheit dieser Räume zu verstehen, sondern auch als eine Verweigerung, die Art von Bildern zu schaffen, die üblicherweise mit Reisen und den Konflikten im Nahen Osten in Verbindung gebracht werden. Durch die Reihe zieht sich ein bilderstürmerischer Impuls, der sich gegen das Regime des Infotainment und gegen eine bestimmte Art von dokumentarischem Bild richtet, das aus der Arbeit von ostentativ progressiven Filmemacher*innen hervorgeht, die sich „durch den Anderen woanders hingezogen fühlen", besonders zu Notsituationen. Smith lehnt das konventionell schöne Bild, wie auch das Bild vom Leiden ab, weil er sie als zwei Seiten derselben Medaille einer effektvollen Verführung versteht. Die *Hotel Diaries* sind charmant und witzig. Aber sie werfen auch ernste Fragen auf, auf die es keine einfachen Antworten gibt. Inwieweit teilen wir ein „Jetzt"? Wie lässt sich ein Bild von der Gegenwart erstellen? Inwiefern sind wir in Akte imperialer Gewalt verwickelt, die anderswo in unserem Namen, aber gegen unsere Überzeugung begangen werden? Wann sollte man die Kamera abwenden?

V.

Durch die Corona-Pandemie kam die Arbeit vieler Filmemacher*innen zum Stillstand. Ohne die Möglichkeit, in die Öffentlichkeit zu gehen oder zu reisen, mussten Projekte aufgegeben werden. Für Smith, der schon lange daran gewöhnt war allein und in begrenzten Räumlichkeiten zu arbeiten, ergaben sich jedoch daraus beruflich kaum Schwierigkeiten. Im Mai 2020, während Großbritannien im Lockdown war, begann er mit einer mehrteiligen Reihe mit dem Titel *Covid Messages* (2020) [siehe Seite 110], bestehend aus wiederverwendetem Filmmaterial von Pressekonferenzen, in denen Premierminister Boris Johnson die Öffentlichkeit über den Stand der Pandemie informierte. In gewisser Weise ist die Reihe der spiegelverkehrte Zwilling von *Hotel Diaries*: Sie basiert nicht auf kontinuierlichen Aufzeichnungen von Smith, sondern auf einer Montage von appropriierten Bildern, und sie ist während einer längeren Zeit entstanden, die Smith zu Hause verbrachte, anstatt aus der Erfahrung des Reisens. Und doch

fixates on small bodily gestures or fragments of speech, looping them in ways that are comedic and unsettling. A satirical narrative also takes shape: Smith transforms state rhetoric ('hands, face, space') and prime-ministerial performance into a story of failed sorcery. With scientific advice cast aside, surely some hocus-pocus will save us. The chief medical officer becomes the 'Chief Magical Officer'; Johnson tries out an array of incantations to ward off the virus, but to no avail. At the end of each brief episode – the six together amount to only twenty-two minutes – Smith punctures the delusion of bogus spells with the hard reality of facts, offering statistics concerning the effects of Covid-19 on the population of the United Kingdom, foremost among them a mounting death toll. *Covid Messages* is hilarious – or, rather, it would be if it weren't also a diary of catastrophe.

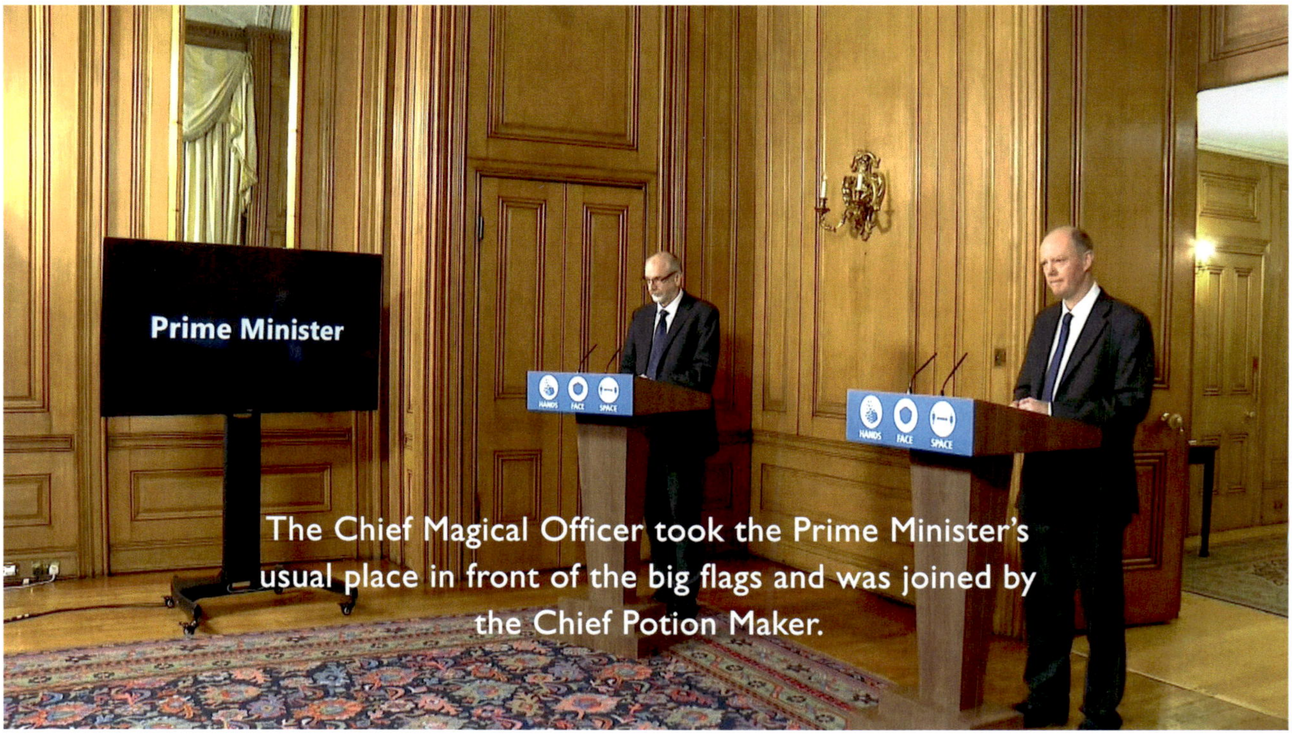

Covid Messages, 2020,
HD video, 22 minutes

Writing in 2021 about the post-2001 period in the United States – the same era documented in the *Hotel Diaries* and *Covid Messages*, one so profoundly marked by a creeping sense of unreality – the political theorist Bonnie Honig describes being 'enmeshed in a shock politics of disinformation that disorients and destabilizes democratic institutions, practices, and habits, aggravating inequalities of all sorts. Shock now is the impact on citizens of living in a world in which the real and the fake, the authentic and the corrupt, the public-minded and the self-serving can be hard to distinguish, and disorientation rules.'[14] She offers an excellent description of a long festering condition that has only been exacerbated by the Covid-19 pandemic. Honig notes the danger of succumbing to solipsism and paranoia under such circumstances, but also ventures a potential solution:

14. Bonnie Honig, *Shell-Shocked: Feminist Criticism After Trump* (New York: Fordham University Press, 2021), 8.

handelt es sich um regelbasierte, serielle Werke, die einer sich entfaltenden Gegenwart verpflichtet sind und sich mit der Rolle von Isolation, Politik und Medienspektakel in dieser Gegenwart auseinandersetzen.

In den sechs düster-komischen Folgen von *Covid Messages* spielt Smith mit der Pressekonferenz als einem Ort „verschlüsselter Botschaften". Mit seinem charakteristischen Scharfsinn greift er die Sinnleere der politischen Rede und die grotesken Manöver der konservativen Regierung an. In der ersten Folge, *Twice*, steht er vor einem Spiegel und filmt mit einem iPhone, das er sich an den Kopf gebunden hat. Während er sich die Hände wäscht, singt er zweimal *Happy Birthday* zur Melodie von Chopins Trauermarsch. Die Handlung wirkt absurd – aber der folgende Schnitt zu Johnson zeigt, dass die Regierung der Öffentlichkeit genau dazu geraten hat (natürlich abgesehen von der Chopin-Melodie). Ansonsten, so der britische Premierminister, „gilt für die überwiegende Mehrheit der Menschen in diesem Land, dass wir wie gewohnt weitermachen sollten." Smith endet mit einem Schlusstitel, der Salz in die Wunde streut: „Gedreht in London während der sechsten Woche des Lockdowns, als Großbritanniens Covid-19-bedingte Todesrate 25.000 erreichte." Mit einer enormen Sparsamkeit der Mittel stellt der Künstler seinen trockenen Humor in den Dienst der Empörung über die Inkompetenz und Grausamkeit einer konservativen Regierung, die während eines Jahrzehnts der Sparmaßnahmen die Kapazitäten des staatlichen Gesundheitssystems und anderer sozialer Dienste zusammengestrichen hat und heute wie eh und je im Interesse der Reichen regiert, völlig egal, was dies für den Rest des Landes – und insbesondere für die Schwächsten – bedeutet.

In den darauffolgenden Teilen nimmt die physische Präsenz von Smith ab. An ihre Stelle tritt zunehmend die umfangreiche Verwendung von Text sowie der geschickte Einsatz von Wiederholungen und Rückwärtsbewegungen. Häufig konzentriert er sich auf kleine körperliche Gesten oder Sprachfragmente, die sich komödiantisch und verstörend in Schleifen wiederholen. Zudem entfaltet sich hier eine satirische Erzählung: Smith verwandelt staatliche Rhetorik („Hände, Gesicht, Abstand") und die Leistungen des Premiers in eine Geschichte über gescheiterte Zauberei: Wo nun die Empfehlungen der Wissenschaft beiseitegeschoben wurden, wird uns sicher irgendein Hokuspokus retten. Der leitende Mediziner (Chief Medical Officer) wird zum „Chief Magical Officer"; Johnson probiert eine Reihe von Zaubersprüchen aus, um das Virus abzuwehren, aber ohne Erfolg. Am Ende jeder kurzen Folge – alle sechs zusammen ergeben lediglich 22 Minuten – durchbricht Smith den Wahn dieses faulen Zaubers mit der harten Realität der Fakten und bietet Statistiken über die Auswirkungen von Covid-19 auf Großbritanniens Bevölkerung, darunter vor allem die steigende Zahl der Todesopfer. *Covid Messages* ist urkomisch – beziehungsweise, es wäre urkomisch, wenn es sich nicht auch um ein Tagebuch der Katastrophe handelte.

through an attentiveness to stubborn particularity, we might resensitize our faculties, making it possible to grasp hold of sorely needed points of orientation. Close consideration of the small, unassuming detail has the power to refocus the gaze, unsettle received ideas, and loosen the grip of doxa. If this didn't already resonate with Smith's practice, it is worth mentioning that she assigns a special role to humour in this undertaking, recalling that 'Walter Benjamin noted nearly a century ago that laughter enables thinking by rendering the familiar strange' while also suggesting that the need today might be the inverse, 'to find in the strange something familiar by way of which to reorient ourselves and to relieve the exhaustion of the moment.'[15]

To look at the films and videos that John Smith has created over nearly fifty years is to find both methods at play: he renders the familiar strange and the strange, familiar. His medium and style may change over time, but this engagement with the politics of perception and the concreteness of the everyday is consistently there. He chronicles the present as it passes, piercing through the anaesthesia of shock with laugher, anger, and discernment.

Erika Balsom is Reader in Film Studies at King's College London. She is the author of four books including *TEN SKIES* (2021) and *After Uniqueness: A History of Film and Video Art in Circulation* (2017), and the co-editor of *Artists' Moving Image in Britain Since 1989* (2019) and *Documentary Across Disciplines* (2016). She regularly writes criticism for publications including *Artforum*, *4Columns*, and *Cinema Scope*.

15. Ibid., 9.

Die Chroniken von John Smith

In ihrer Beschreibung der Zeit nach 2001 in den USA – der gleichen Zeit, die in *Hotel Diaries* und *Covid Messages* dokumentiert ist und zutiefst von einem schleichenden Gefühl der Unwirklichkeit geprägt war – spricht die politische Theoretikerin Bonnie Honig 2021 von einer „Verstrickung in eine Schock-Politik der Desinformation, die demokratische Institutionen, Praktiken und Gewohnheiten verwirrt und destabilisiert und Ungleichheiten aller Art verschärft. Schock ist heute der Effekt, den das Leben auf die Bürger hat, weil sie in einer Welt leben, in der das Echte und das Gefälschte, das Authentische und das Korrupte, das Gemeinwohl und der Eigennutz schwer zu unterscheiden sind, und in der Desorientierung herrscht."[14] Honig liefert eine ausgezeichnete Beschreibung von einem schon seit langem schwelenden Zustand, der sich durch die Covid-19-Pandemie nur noch zugespitzt hat. Sie weist auf die Gefahr hin, unter solchen Umständen in Solipsismus und Paranoia zu verfallen, zeigt aber auch eine mögliche Lösung auf: Indem wir unsere Aufmerksamkeit auf eine hartnäckige Partikularität lenken, könnten wir unsere Fähigkeiten wieder wachrufen und so dringend benötigte Orientierungspunkte greifbar werden lassen. Die sorgfältige Erwägung kleiner, unscheinbarer Details hat die Macht, den Blick neu auszurichten, überkommene Vorstellungen aufzubrechen und den Griff der Doxa zu lockern. Wenn das nicht schon sehr nach der Praxis von Smith klingt, sei noch erwähnt, dass Honig bei diesem Unterfangen auch dem Humor eine besondere Rolle zuschreibt und daran erinnert, dass „Walter Benjamin vor fast einem Jahrhundert feststellte, dass Lachen das Denken fördert, indem es das Vertraute fremd erscheinen lässt", wobei sie ebenso zu bedenken gibt, dass das Bedürfnis heute umgekehrt sein könnte, dass wir „im Fremden etwas Vertrautes finden [wollen], um uns wieder zurechtzufinden und die Erschöpfung des Augenblicks zu lindern."[15] Bei der Betrachtung der Filme und Videos, die John Smith in fast fünfzig Jahren geschaffen hat fällt auf, dass beide Methoden im Spiel sind: Er lässt das Vertraute fremd erscheinen und das Fremde vertraut. Medium und Stil mögen sich über die Jahre geändert haben, doch seine Auseinandersetzung mit der Politik der Wahrnehmung und mit der Konkretheit des Alltäglichen bleibt konstant. Er zeichnet die vorüberziehende Gegenwart auf und durchbricht die Betäubung des Schocks mit Lachen, Zorn und einer trennscharfen Wahrnehmung.

Erika Balsom ist Dozentin für Filmwissenschaft am King's College London. Sie ist Autorin von vier Büchern, darunter *TEN SKIES* (2021) und *After Uniqueness: A History of Film and Video Art in Circulation* (2017), außerdem ist sie Mitherausgeberin von *Artists' Moving Image in Britain Since 1989* (2019) und *Documentary Across Disciplines* (2016). Sie schreibt regelmäßig Kritiken für Publikationen, darunter *Artforum*, *4Columns* und *Cinema Scope*.

14. Bonnie Honig, *Shell-Shocked: Feminist Criticism After Trump* (New York: Fordham University Press, 2021), 8.

15. Ebd., 9.

John Smith

The Girl Chewing Gum

1976, 16mm film transferred to HD video, 12 minutes

The Girl Chewing Gum was made in ideological opposition to the illusionism of mainstream cinema, at a time when many artists and filmmakers were creating films which sought to draw the viewer's attention to their material construction. Where most mainstream cinema attempts to make viewers identify with the actors in a story and forget that they are watching a film, myself and many others were making work which had the opposite ambition, to highlight cinema's inherent artifice. In a continuous shot showing everyday activity in a busy London street, *The Girl Chewing Gum* draws attention to the cinematic apparatus by denying its existence, treating representation as an absolute reality. The film achieves its ambition by using a voice-over to subvert the reading of the image, marking the beginnings of my ongoing love/hate relationship with the power of the word. Making *The Girl Chewing Gum* made me realise just how effectively the word can shape our perception of the world, a capacity that I've exploited in many of my subsequent films.

In 1976, as a 23-year-old art student, I never dreamt that my new film would still be watched by audiences in the 21st century. Although I have created more than 50 other films over the intervening years, *The Girl Chewing Gum* remains my best-known work. I have presented it personally on hundreds of occasions and it continues to be widely shown in museums, galleries, film festivals and independent cinemas, featuring in the syllabuses of universities, colleges and schools around the world. But over the 45 years since its debut it has gradually acquired an entirely new layer of meaning. When I devised the film I deliberately based it around the most ordinary present-day scenario, but 1976's mundane street scene has now become an almost exotic record of a distant time, where passers-by look like actors in period costumes, a difference made even more apparent by the ongoing gentrification of the film's East London location. To many young people the film looks like a relic from the early days of cinema, confirmed by school student blogs I have encountered which state that the black and white film, composed of only two shots, was made before colour film was invented, and before filmmakers learnt how to edit.

The Girl Chewing Gum

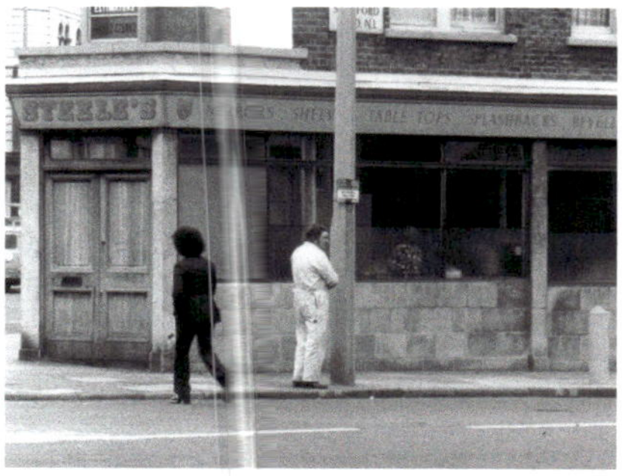

Let's have the man in the white boiler suit coming in from the right. Stop at the lamp-post and fold your arms... now look around you... walk back to the left again, and look left and right as you cross the road.

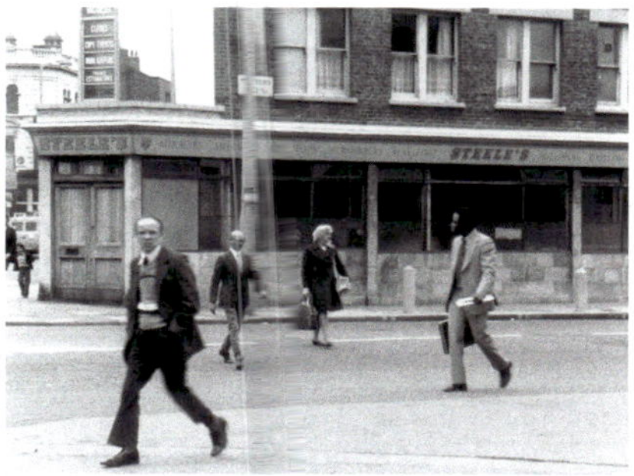

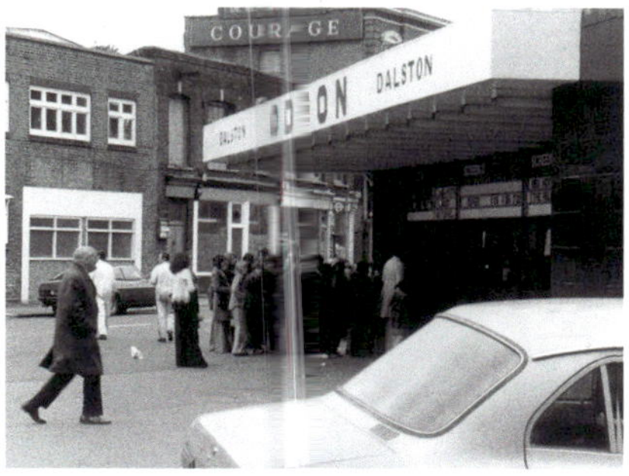

In the cinema queue I want to see a boy and his mother. The boy will be about eight years old and his mother about thirty-two. They will both have collar-length hair, his dark and hers fair. She will be wearing a suedette coat with a white imitation fur collar. They will be talking to each other and looking around them.

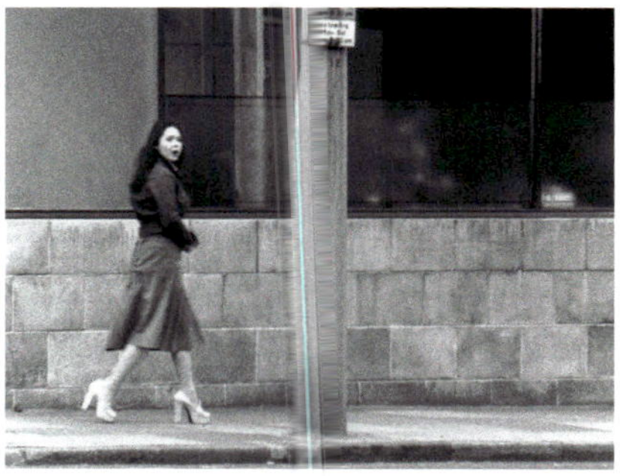

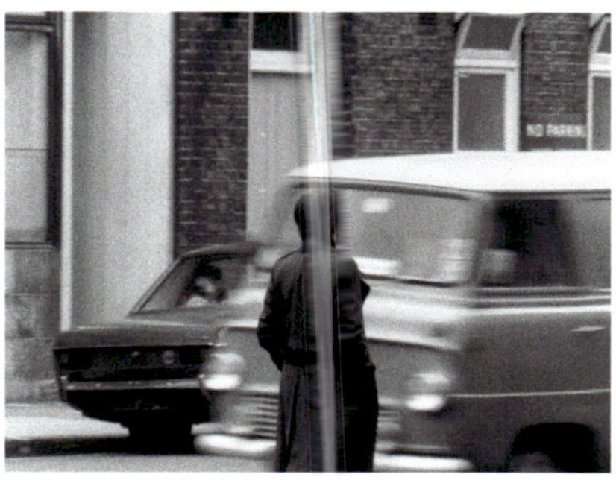

This young man has just robbed the local post office and is attempting to appear inconspicuous. He is trying to remain calm but his hand is sweating as he grips the butt of the revolver in his raincoat pocket even harder.

The Girl Chewing Gum

In 2011, acutely aware of the demographic and architectural changes that had taken place around the film's location in the area of London where I still live today, I decided to make a companion piece to *The Girl Chewing Gum*. I set my camera up in exactly the same spot that it had occupied in 1976 and attempted to duplicate the camera movements of the original footage. In post-production I superimposed this new high-definition colour video footage over the original black and white film, so that ghostly black and white passers-by from 1976 crossed paths with their colourful 2011 counterparts, oblivious to each other's existence. I had a fantasy that the eponymous Girl Chewing Gum, probably a grandmother by now, would bump into her former self in the street she had frequented for 35 years. Looking at the superimposed images I noticed that, presumably due to better nutrition, people were perceptibly taller in the recent footage than in the original film. I also realised that, at 59 years old, I was now more than half as old as cinema itself. Noting the ubiquitous presence of the smartphone, a device which was still science fiction in 1976, I titled the new work *The Man Phoning Mum*.

J.S.

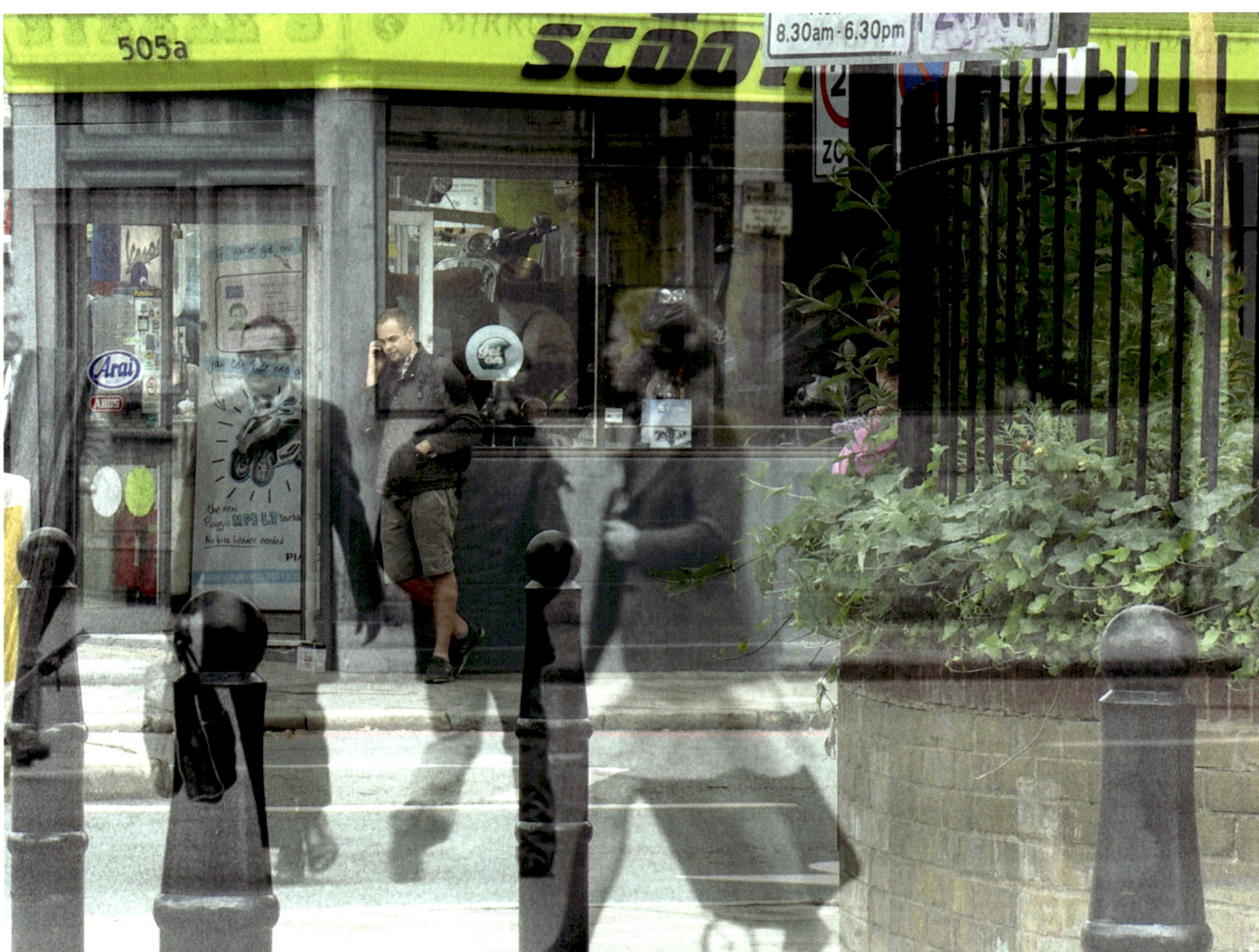

The Girl Chewing Gum — **The Man Phoning Mum**

Now I want the old man with white hair and glasses to cross the road. Come on, quickly… Look this way… Now walk off to the left.

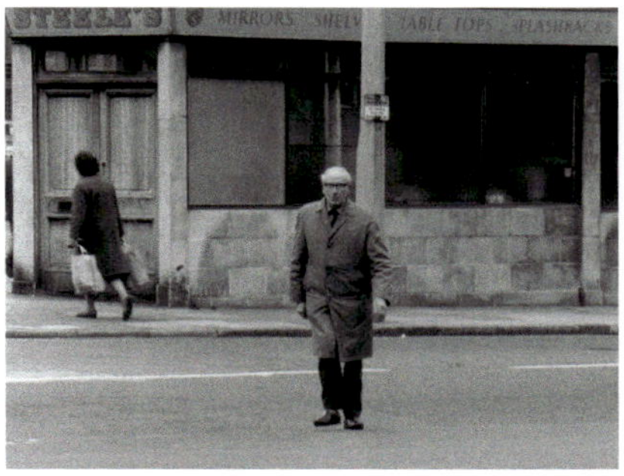

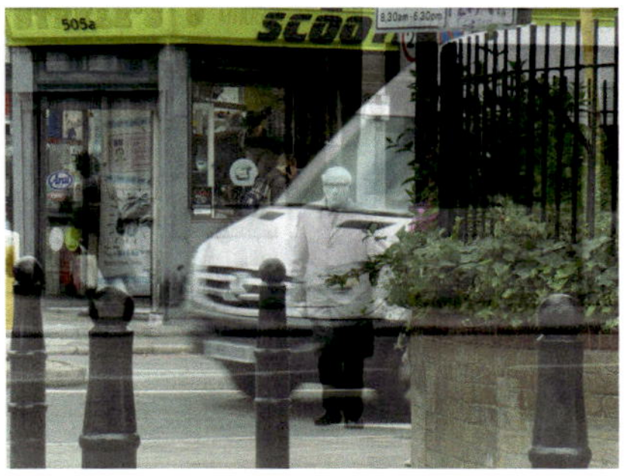

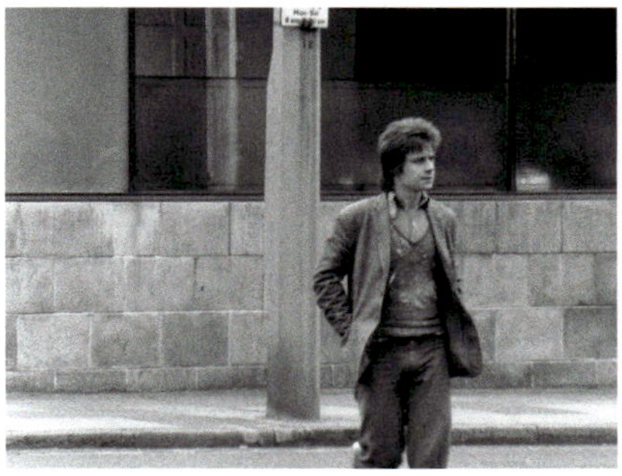

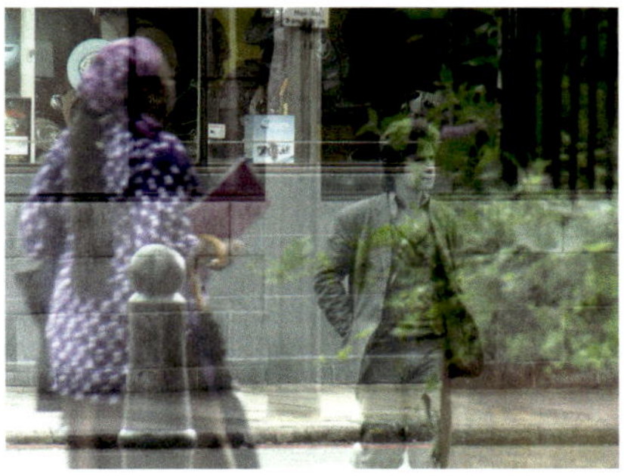

Now I want everything to sink slowly down as the five boys come by… hold it…

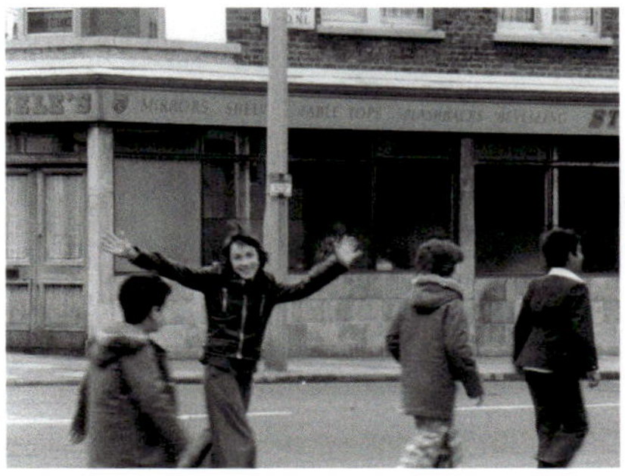

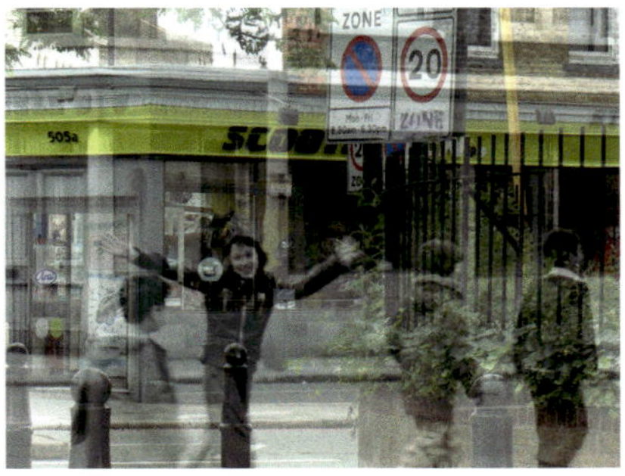

And I want the clock to move jerkily towards me… stop. Now I want the long hand to move at the rate of one revolution every hour, and the short hand to move at the rate of one revolution every twelve hours.

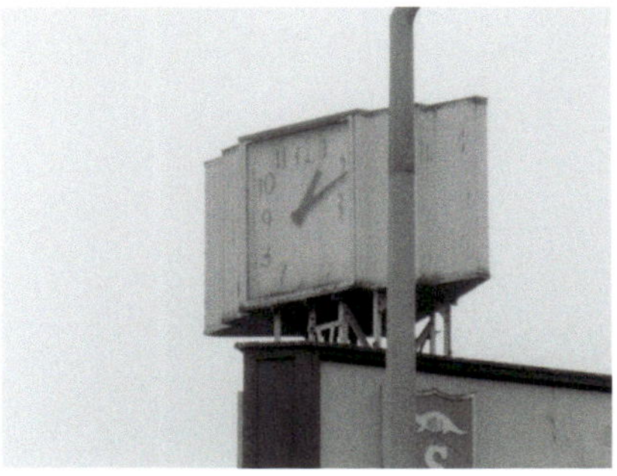

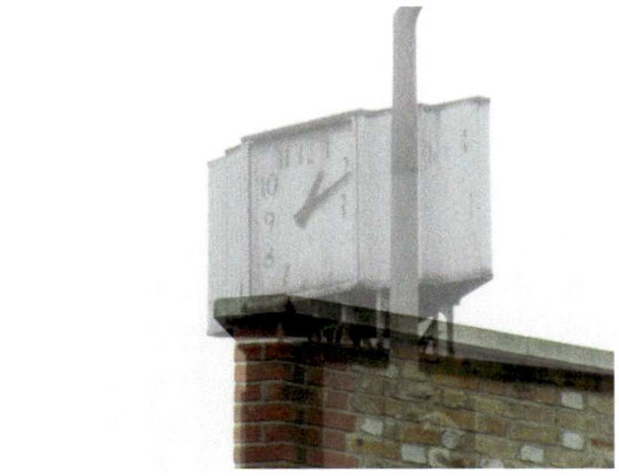

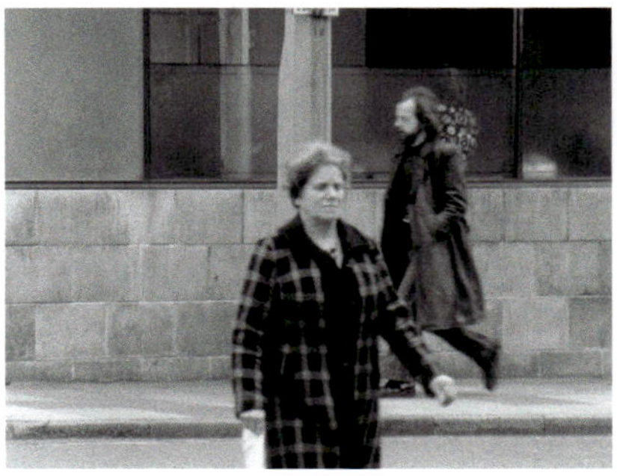

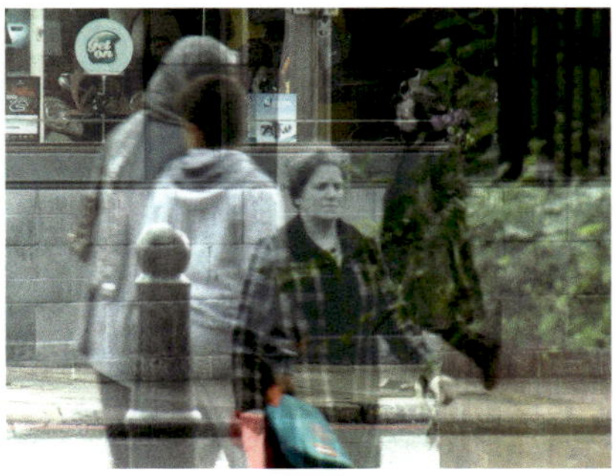

John Smith

The Girl Chewing Gum

1976, 16-mm-Film überspielt auf HD-Video, 12 Minuten

The Girl Chewing Gum wurde in ideologischer Opposition zum Illusionismus des Mainstream-Kinos zu einer Zeit gedreht, als viele Künstler*innen und Filmemacher*innen Filme schufen, die die Aufmerksamkeit der Zuschauer*in auf das Konstrukt des Films zu lenken versuchten. Während das Mainstream-Kino vorrangig versuchte, der Zuschauer*innen dazu zu bewegen, sich mit den Schauspieler*innen in einer Geschichte zu identifizieren und zu vergessen, dass sie einen Film anschauten, arbeiteten ich selbst und viele andere mit dem gegensätzlichen Bestreben, das dem Kino innewohnende Kunstwerk herauszustellen. In einer durchgehenden Einstellung, die das tägliche Leben in einer belebten Straße Londons zeigt, lenkt der Film *The Girl Chewing Gum* die Aufmerksamkeit auf den kinematischen Apparat, indem er seine Existenz leugnet, wobei Darstellung als eine absolute Realität behandelt wird. Der Film erreicht sein Ziel durch einen Voice-over, einen Off-Kommentar, um das Lesen des Bildes zu untergraben, was den Beginn meiner Hassliebe zur Macht des Wortes kennzeichnet. Durch die Produktion des Films *The Girl Chewing Gum* erkannte ich, welche starke Rolle das Wort in unserer Wahrnehmung der Welt spielt, eine Fähigkeit, die ich in vielen meiner späteren Filme ausgenutzt habe.

1976, als 23-jähriger Kunststudent, hätte ich mir nie träumen lassen, dass mein neuer Film im 21. Jahrhundert immer noch Zuschauer*innen haben würde. Obwohl ich in den folgenden Jahren mehr als 50 Filme produziert habe, bleibt *The Girl Chewing Gum* doch mein bekanntestes Werk. Ich habe es persönlich hunderte Male aufgeführt, es wird nach wie vor in Museen, Galerien, auf Filmfestivals und in unabhängigen Kinos gezeigt, es ist Teil des Lehrplans an Universitäten, Hochschulen und Schulen auf der ganzen Welt. In den 45 Jahren seit seiner Erstaufführung hat der Film jedoch schrittweise eine vollständig neue Bedeutungsschicht angenommen. Als ich den Film konzipierte, habe ich ihn absichtlich um eines der wohl normalsten Alltagsszenarien herum aufgebaut, aber diese alltägliche Straßenszene von 1976 ist nunmehr zu einem schon fast exotischen Beleg einer fernen Zeit geworden, in der Passant*innen wie Schauspieler*innen in zeitgenössischen Kostümen erscheinen, ein Unterschied, der durch die anhaltende Gentrifizierung an dem Drehort des Films, in East London, noch auffälliger wird. Auf viele junge Menschen wirkt der Film wie ein Relikt aus den Anfangszeiten des Kinos, was durch Blogs von Schüler*innen bestätigt wird, auf die ich gestoßen bin und in denen die Meinung geäußert wird, dass der Schwarz-Weiß-Film, der nur aus zwei Kameraeinstellungen besteht, produziert wurde, bevor der Farbfilm erfunden wurde und bevor die Filmemacher*innen gelernt hatten, wie ein Film bearbeitet wird.

2011, als ich mir der demografischen und architektonischen Veränderungen, die um den Drehort des Films in dem Stadtteil Londons, in dem ich noch heute lebe, sehr bewusst war, traf

ich die Entscheidung, ein Pendant zu *The Girl Chewing Gum* zu produzieren. Ich stellte meine Kamera an genau demselben Standort auf, an dem ich sie 1976 aufgestellt hatte, und versuchte, die Kamerabewegungen aus dem Schwarz-Weiß-Film nachzuvollziehen. Bei der Nachbearbeitung habe ich dieses neue, hochauflösende Farbfilmmaterial auf den originalen Schwarz-Weiß-Film überlagert, so dass geisterhaft erscheinende Schwarz-Weiß-Passant*innen von 1976 ihre Wege mit ihren farbigen Pendants von 2011 kreuzten, wobei sie sich ihrer jeweiligen Existenz nicht bewusst waren. Ich hatte die Eingebung, dass die Titelheldin – Girl Chewing Gum/das Kaugummi kauende Mädchen – die inzwischen wahrscheinlich Großmutter ist, mit ihrem früheren Selbst in der Straße, auf der sie vor 35 Jahren gelaufen war, zusammenstößt. Als ich mir die überlagerten Bilder ansah, bemerkte ich, dass die Menschen, wahrscheinlich wegen der besseren Ernährung, in dem neuen Filmmaterial wahrnehmbar größer waren als in dem alten Film. Ich stellte auch fest, dass ich, nunmehr im Alter von 59 Jahren, mehr als halb so alt war wie das Kino selbst. In Anbetracht der Allgegenwärtigkeit des Smartphones, eines Gerätes, das also 1976 noch Science-Fiction war, betitelte ich das neue Werk *The Man Phoning Mum*.

J.S.

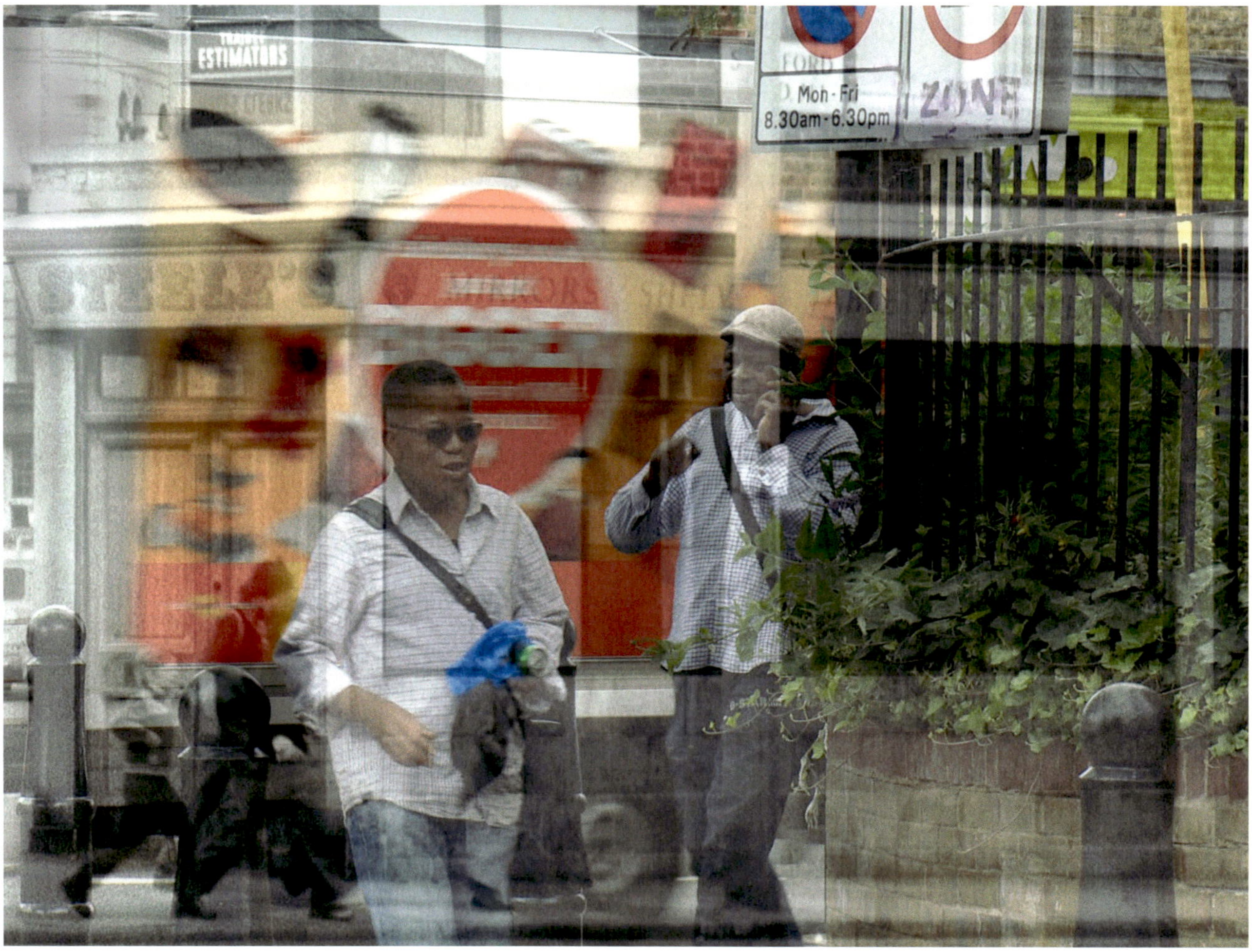

John Smith

Hotel Diaries

2001–07, series of 7 videos

On October 8th 2001, a few weeks after the September 11th attack on the World Trade Centre and two days after the USA and Britain started bombing Afghanistan, I was at the Cork Film Festival in Ireland. Returning to my hotel room very late at night I switched on the television, intending to catch up on the latest news. Expecting to see a moving image, I was surprised to discover that the close-up of a man's face that filled the screen was completely still, frozen in time. I watched the screen for several minutes but nothing changed, and the clock in the corner of the screen remained stopped at 1.41 a.m. What was happening? Why wasn't the image moving? Worried and confused, I picked up my video camera and attempted to talk about what was going on inside my head. I had no idea at the time that this spontaneous recording was the start of a project that would occupy me for the next six years.

Made over six years in the hotels of six different countries, *Hotel Diaries* charts the 'War on Terror' era of Bush and Blair through a series of video recordings that relate the ongoing conflicts in Afghanistan, Iraq and Israel/Palestine to my personal experiences while travelling. In these works, which play upon chance and coincidence, the hotel room is employed as a 'found' film set, where the architecture, furnishing and decoration become the means by which my own small adventures are linked to major world events.

J.S.

Because of film festivals in a variety of countries, John Smith has been accustomed to sleeping in hotels for a long time. We are all familiar with that moment when, under the impression of an unknown city, we move our things into a hotel room in the evening and are disappointed to find that these rooms are the same everywhere. We are thus also familiar with the gaze of Smith's camera, how it absent-mindedly drifts through the room's interior. The insignificant images are accompanied by the commentary of the filmmaker, who entertainingly evaluates and acknowledges his camera's discoveries. While his attentiveness seems slightly peculiar and exaggerated, his continuous observations metamorphose into open associations of ideas which provide the stimulus for the images that demonically force their way in, even though they point far beyond his camera's field of view. These officially disseminated images from news channels present sites of war and injustice that are known to us, are carried around within us and are a burden on our consciences. In the nocturnal confines of the hotel room, our own powerlessness becomes a nightmare. Tomorrow, the everyday political reality will already be spreading the same horrific images or others like them and will nonetheless still be maintaining its distance from solutions for them.

Hotel Diaries

While many of his other films are made up of montages that work with frequent cuts, Smith has deliberately reduced these to a minimum in this series. The films of the *Hotel Diaries* convey the impression that they began as improvisations, allowing us to follow along with every process and every thought in them: this is also suggested by the fact that the image and sound were recorded with a small hand-held camera, which is not concealed from the viewer. This makes us feel involved and present within the scenes as they unfold, regardless of where we actually are. These films are simultaneously a personal statement by the artist – his critique of shameless politics – and, seen collectively, a chilling chronicle.

U.G.

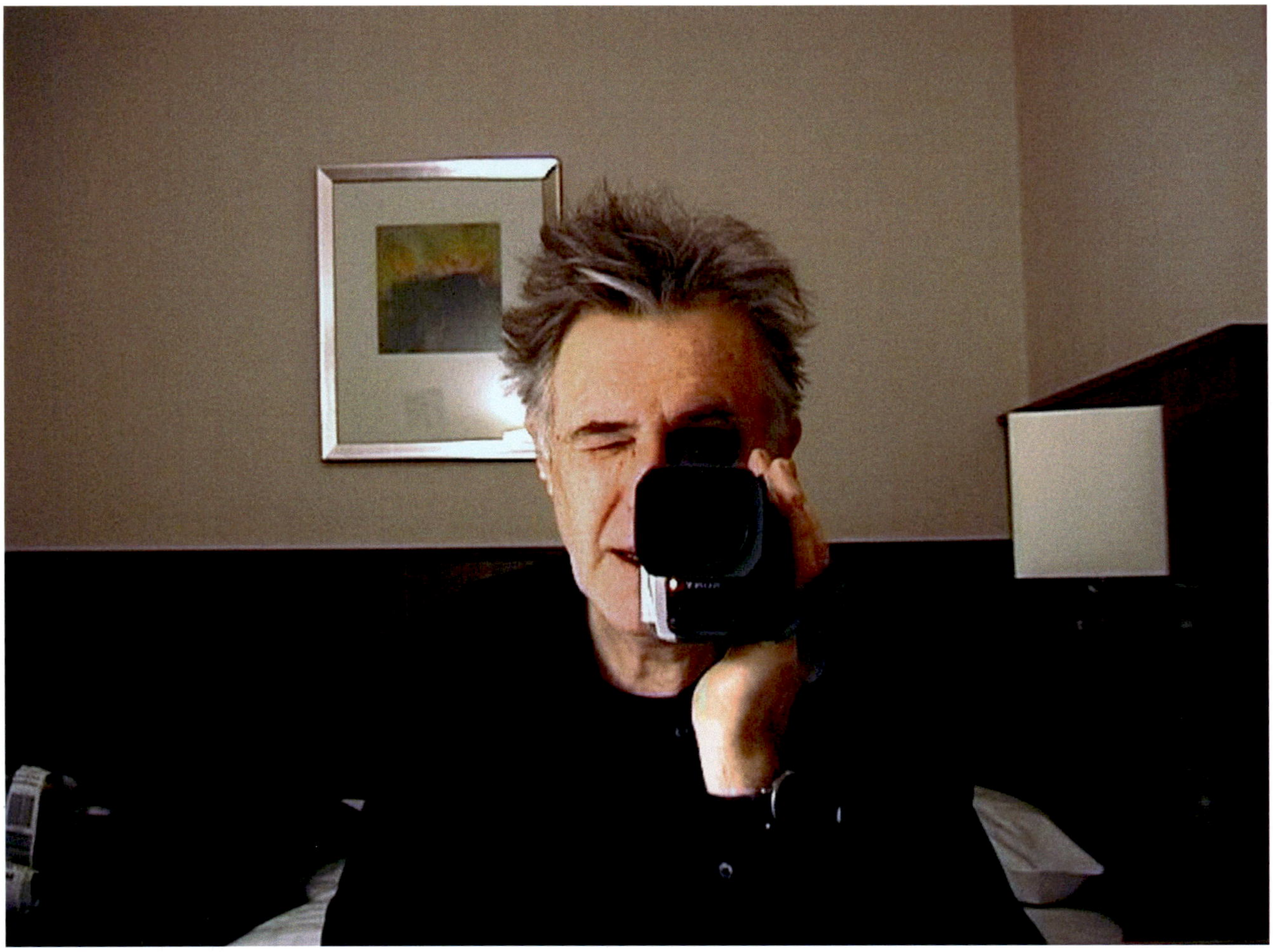

It's three-thirty in the morning, in early January 2006… no, it's late January 2006… and I'm in a hotel in Rotterdam. But, maybe before you start to lose interest in this, I should preface this video by letting you know that I'm actually one of the most famous experimental filmmakers in the world. I can prove this actually… I'll just show you if you'll bear with me.

Frozen War (Hotel Diaries 1)
Ireland, October 8th 2001
SD video, 11 minutes

A disorientating experience while attempting to watch the TV news in an Irish hotel room triggers a spontaneous response to the bombing of Afghanistan.

Frozen War (Hotel Diaries 1)
Irland, 8. Oktober 2001
SD-Video, 11 Minuten

Eine verwirrende Erfahrung bei dem Versuch, Nachrichten in einem irischen Hotelzimmer zu schauen, führt zu einer spontanen Reaktion zur Bombardierung Afghanistans.

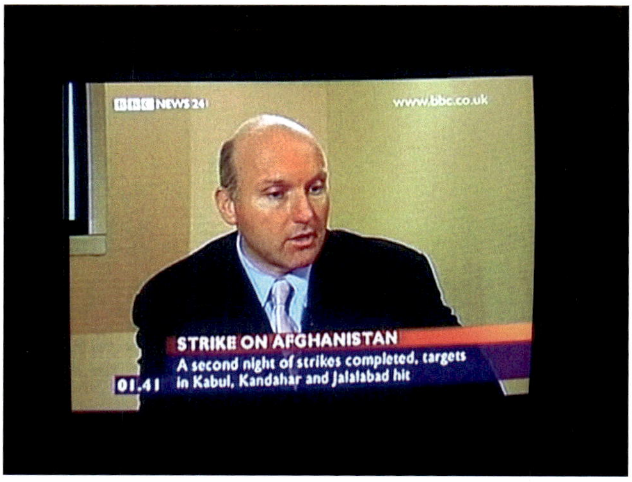

Outside in the street people are shouting. Their voices are raised, they're making a little bit of noise. In Afghanistan I'm sure that the voices are raised to an even higher pitch. Lives there have been cut short tonight as they were last night… Has something been cut short in London where this news was being transmitted, at one forty-one?

I'm looking at this image and this image is creating a fear in me, an insecurity about the place where I live, and that fear and insecurity is simply coming from the fact that the image on a TV screen is frozen. This man's face represents… I don't know… Shock?… Disbelief? Who is he? What was he talking about? Why is he still there on the screen? What has happened in London? Probably fuck-all, probably nothing has happened in fucking London.

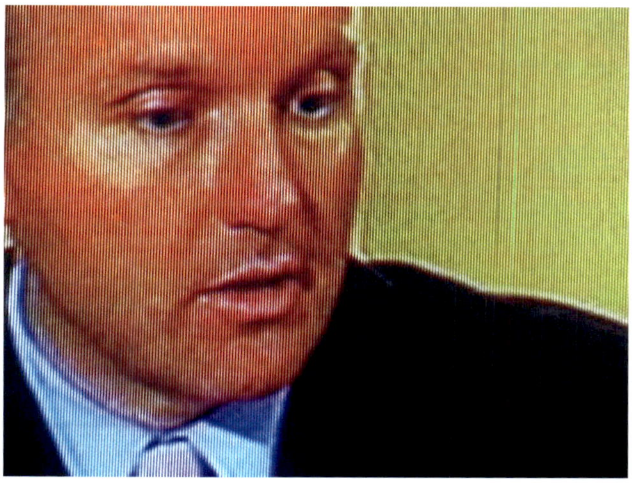

Museum Piece

Museum Piece (Hotel Diaries 2)
Germany, October 14th 2004
SD video, 12 minutes

While the Iraq war continues, a day's sightseeing and the features of a German hotel provoke a stream of thoughts about events large and small.

Museum Piece (Hotel Diaries 2)
Deutschland, 14. Oktober 2004
SD-Video, 12 Minuten

Während sich der Irakkrieg fortsetzt, provozieren eine eintägige Besichtigungstour und ein deutsches Hotel Gedankenströme zu größeren und kleineren Ereignissen.

But anyway, after I'd looked around outside I was going to go in and then… I couldn't… I just couldn't bring myself to go in. I know it's really stupid but somehow, with all the terrible things that the Israeli army are doing to the Palestinians at the moment, I just felt that I couldn't go in, that it would be expressing some kind of empathy with the Israeli government.

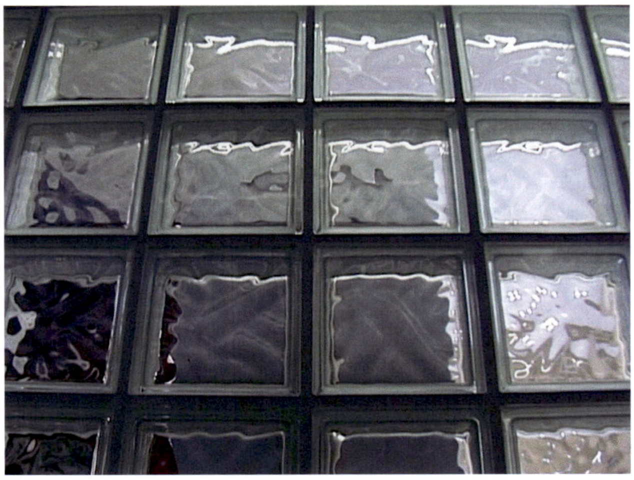

What else?… oh yeah, this here. The hotel used to be a Siemens factory, so it has got a lot of artefacts that have been placed in the corridors which are to do with machinery from the factory. I don't know what this is as I can't read the German sign which tells you what it is, but it's a bit of machinery from the Siemens factory. Which reminds me actually, somebody told me a terrible story today… it's really awful if it's true.

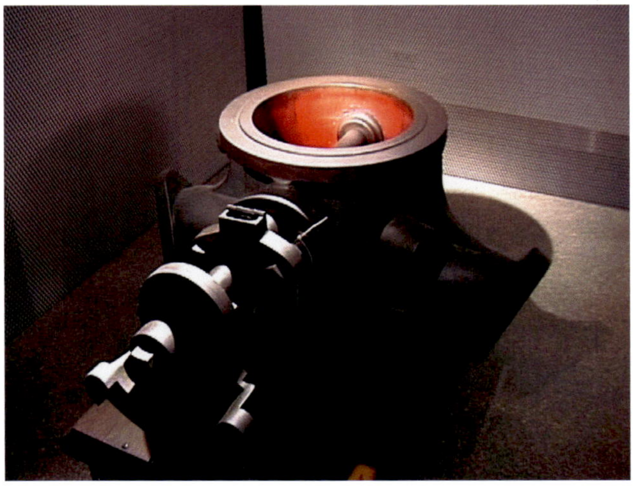

Throwing Stones

Throwing Stones (Hotel Diaries 3)
Switzerland, November 13th 2004
SD video, 11 minutes

As the camera looks out through a barred window and the clock strikes four in a Swiss city, the death of Yasser Arafat provides the starting point for a journey back in time.

Throwing Stones (Hotel Diaries 3)
Schweiz, 13. November 2004
SD-Video, 11 Minuten

Mit einer durch ein verriegeltes Fenster gerichteten Kamera und der Uhr, die in einer schweizerischen Stadt vier schlägt, ist der Tod von Yasser Arafat der Ausgangspunkt für eine Zeitreise zurück in die Vergangenheit.

So he was taken to a military hospital in Paris, where I believe he died yesterday, or maybe the day before. So over the last few days... I suppose one identifies with people... I've been thinking about what it must be like to be trapped in a place.

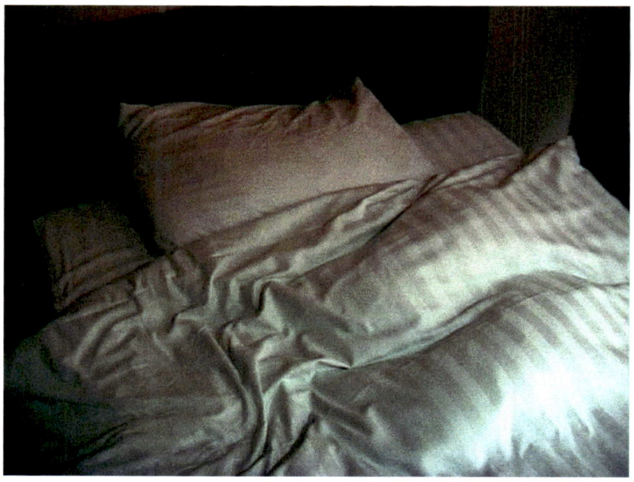

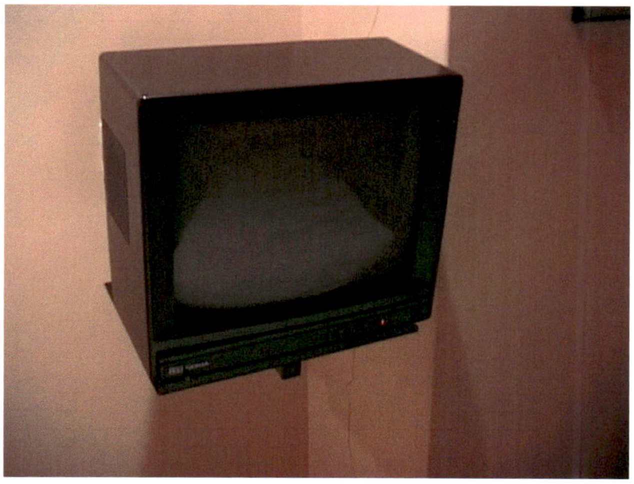

I remember when that happened that my first, my strongest reaction really was 'What are America going to do now?' And for three years of course we've been experiencing what they did do... But anyway, I was in New York until September the tenth, when I flew to Chicago. And on the morning of September the eleventh I woke up to see, on live TV, the World Trade Centre being attacked.

B & B (Hotel Diaries 4)
England, November 26th 2005
SD video, 6 minutes

The perception of an Anglo-American hotel room is coloured by new revelations about 'The War on Terror' and 'The Special Relationship' that exists between Britain and the USA.

B & B (Hotel Diaries 4)
England, 26. November 2005
SD-Video, 6 Minuten

Die Wahrnehmung eines anglo-amerikanischen Hotelzimmers ist gezeichnet von neuen Einsichten zu „The War on Terror" und „The Special Relationship" zwischen Großbritannien und den USA.

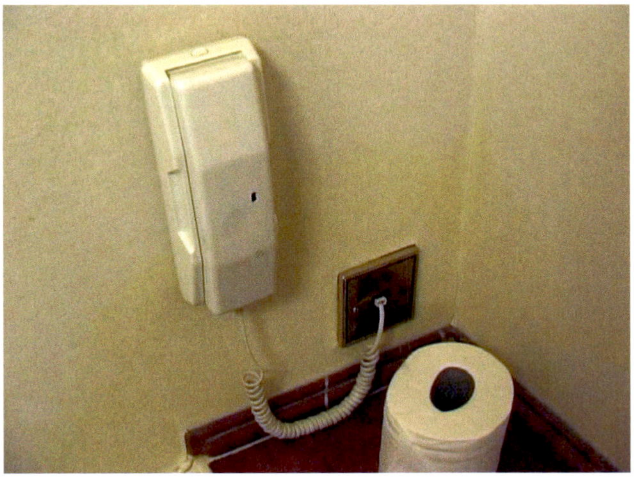

There was a leaked report about a telephone call that took place a while ago between Bush and Blair. Apparently, during this telephone call, Bush was suggesting to Blair that it might be quite a good idea to bomb the Al Jazeera TV station, because he felt that they were a little bit sympathetic to the enemy.

It's full of symbolism that I can't understand. It's quite cabalistic, it reminds me of Freemasonry. Or maybe, in this American British hotel, it represents something to do with the 'Special Relationship' that our two countries have. It gets weirder and weirder as you look across the picture… Here's a little scene from Abu Ghraib, or maybe Guantanamo.

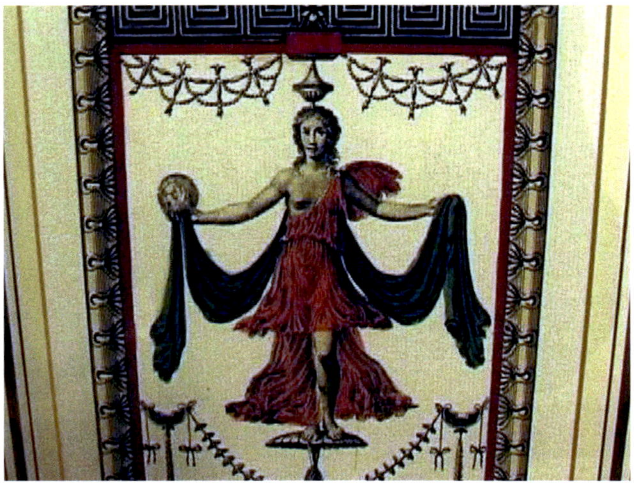

Pyramids / Skunk

Pyramids / Skunk (Hotel Diaries 5)
Netherlands, January 29th 2006 – January 29th 2007
SD video, 17 minutes

Hamas have just won the Palestinian elections and a chocolate bar in a Rotterdam hotel room eventually reminds the filmmaker that there are more important things going on in the world outside. Exactly one year later he returns to the same city and checks in at a very different hotel.

Pyramids | Skunk (Hotel Diaries 5)
Niederlande, 29. Januar 2006 / 29. Januar 2007
SD-Video, 17 Minuten

Die Hamas hat gerade die Wahlen in Palästina gewonnen, und ein Schokoladenriegel in einem Rotterdamer Hotelzimmer erinnert schließlich den Filmemacher daran, dass es wichtigere Dinge gibt, die sich draußen in der Welt abspielen. Genau ein Jahr später kehrt er in dieselbe Stadt zurück und checkt in ein völlig anderes Hotel ein.

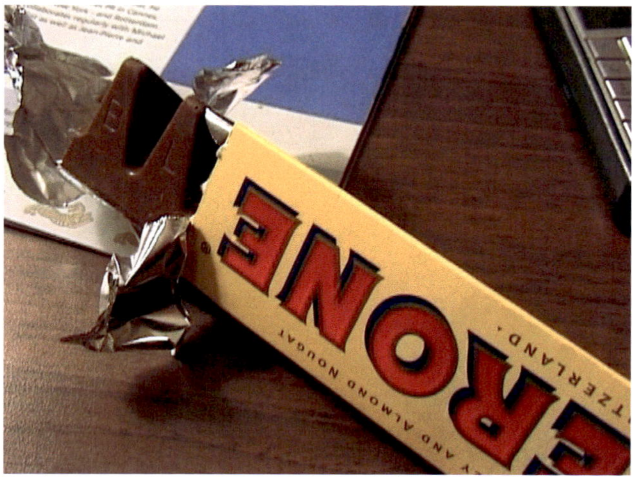

The only problem has been with the mini-bar… because the festival pays for the accommodation, but they don't pay for the mini-bar bill, and the cost of things from the mini-bar is unbelievable. This bar of chocolate here, this Toblerone… you can't tell how big it is but this is just a regular sized bar of Toblerone, and it was five euros fifty, for this eight inch long bar of Toblerone. It's ridiculous… five euros fifty… it's crazy.

Bambi, yeah, that was Tony Blair's nickname wasn't it, before he became a war criminal. Bambi… I never thought that it suited him myself but… anyway… it all seems like… it all seems like a really long time ago now.

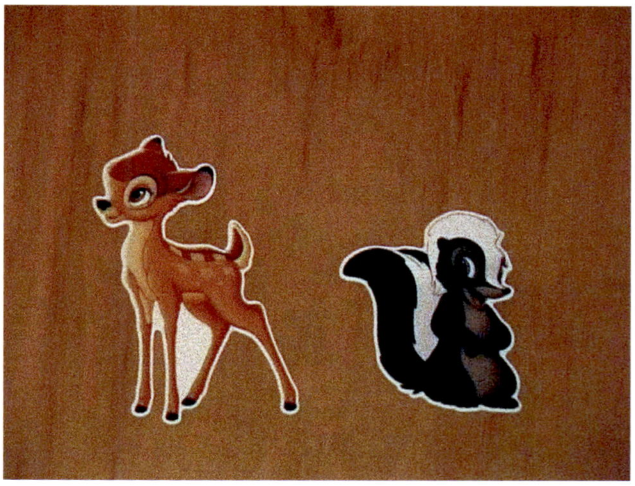

Dirty Pictures

Dirty Pictures (Hotel Diaries 6)
Palestine, April 15th–16th 2007
SD video, 14 minutes

Moving from one hotel in Bethlehem to another in East Jerusalem, the filmmaker encounters a series of problems involving a ceiling, a video camera and the Israeli occupation of Palestine.

Dirty Pictures (Hotel Diaries 6)
Palästina, 15./16. April 2007
SD-Video, 14 Minuten

Beim Umzug von einem Hotel in Bethlehem in ein anderes in Ostjerusalem wird der Filmemacher mit einer Reihe von Problemen konfrontiert, so im Zusammenhang mit einer Zimmerdecke, einer Videokamera und der israelischen Besetzung Palästinas.

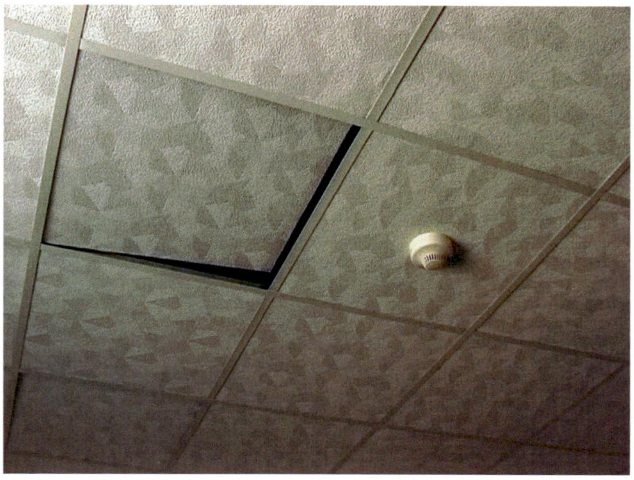

All these different tiles in the suspended ceiling started flying up and down. It was really nice to watch, so I've been hoping it would happen again when I got my camera out, but I haven't had a lot of luck so far. You get the odd little bit of flapping but nothing like I had last night. Anyway, I'm going to give up in a minute, but… oh… I can hear something happening… ah… here we go, something's happening now.

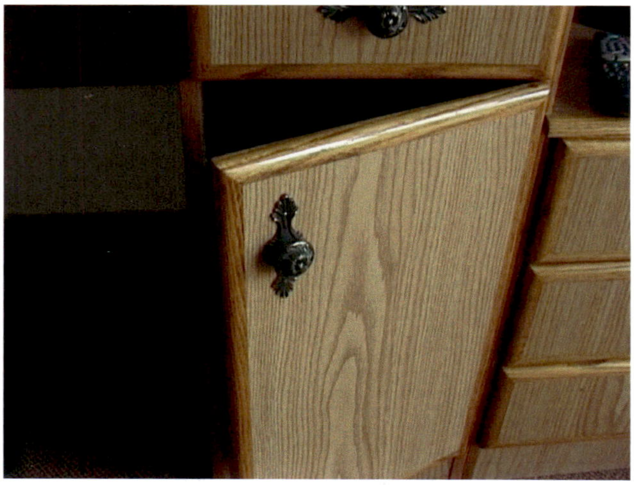

But anyway, she goes through the arch again, having taken the boot off, the boot goes through on the conveyer belt, she walks through the arch, and the thing still bleeps. So this disembodied voice is shouting these commands and saying 'Go. Go. Go'… I presume that's what it was saying… She's just standing there quaking and pleading to be let through, and… she doesn't have any luck. So, basically, after a while, she gives in and hobbles back, the way she came, back past us that are standing at the turnstile, and goes back into Bethlehem.

Six Years Later

Six Years Later (Hotel Diaries 7)
Ireland, October 20th 2007
SD video, 9 minutes

The filmmaker returns to the city where he made the first video in the series and looks back at the events of the past six years.

Six Years Later (Hotel Diaries 7)
Irland, 20. Oktober 2007
SD-Video, 9 Minuten

Der Filmemacher kehrt in die Stadt zurück, in der er das erste Video der Serie gedreht hat, und schaut auf die Ereignisse der vergangenen sechs Jahre.

I'm in a hotel in Antwerp... or Brussels... or Birmingham... or Bremen... or maybe... Barcelona... or Cork... Actually I am in Cork, in Ireland, six years after I made the first video in this series here. A lot has changed over that six years of course... to begin with, there certainly weren't any hotels like this in Cork in 2001. It could be any European city. Things are getting so homogenized now, but also so polarized... it seems like half the world's a swanky hotel and the other half's a bombsite.

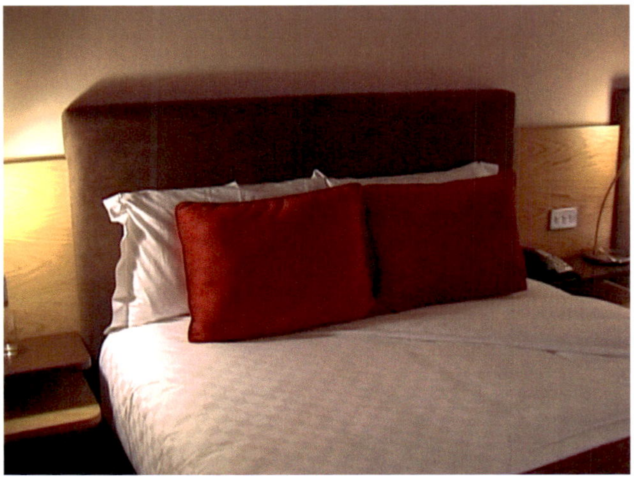

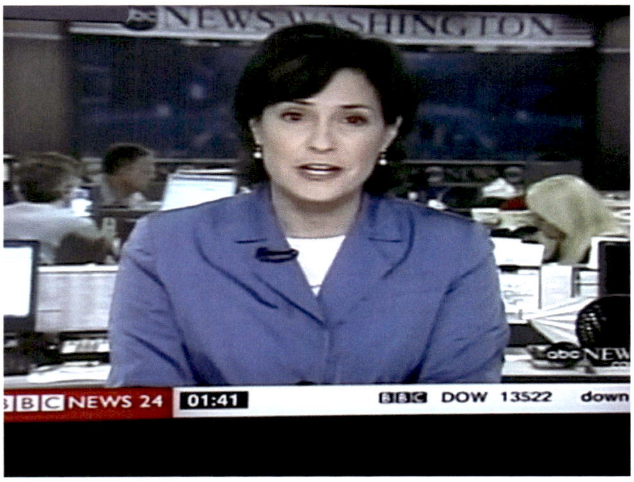

Anyway, we're just coming up to one forty-one, the time when the image was frozen on the TV screen in the last video I made here, so hopefully that's when we are going to arrive there... OK we're there... what's going on with the news?... Oh, here we go, here we go... the financial figures.

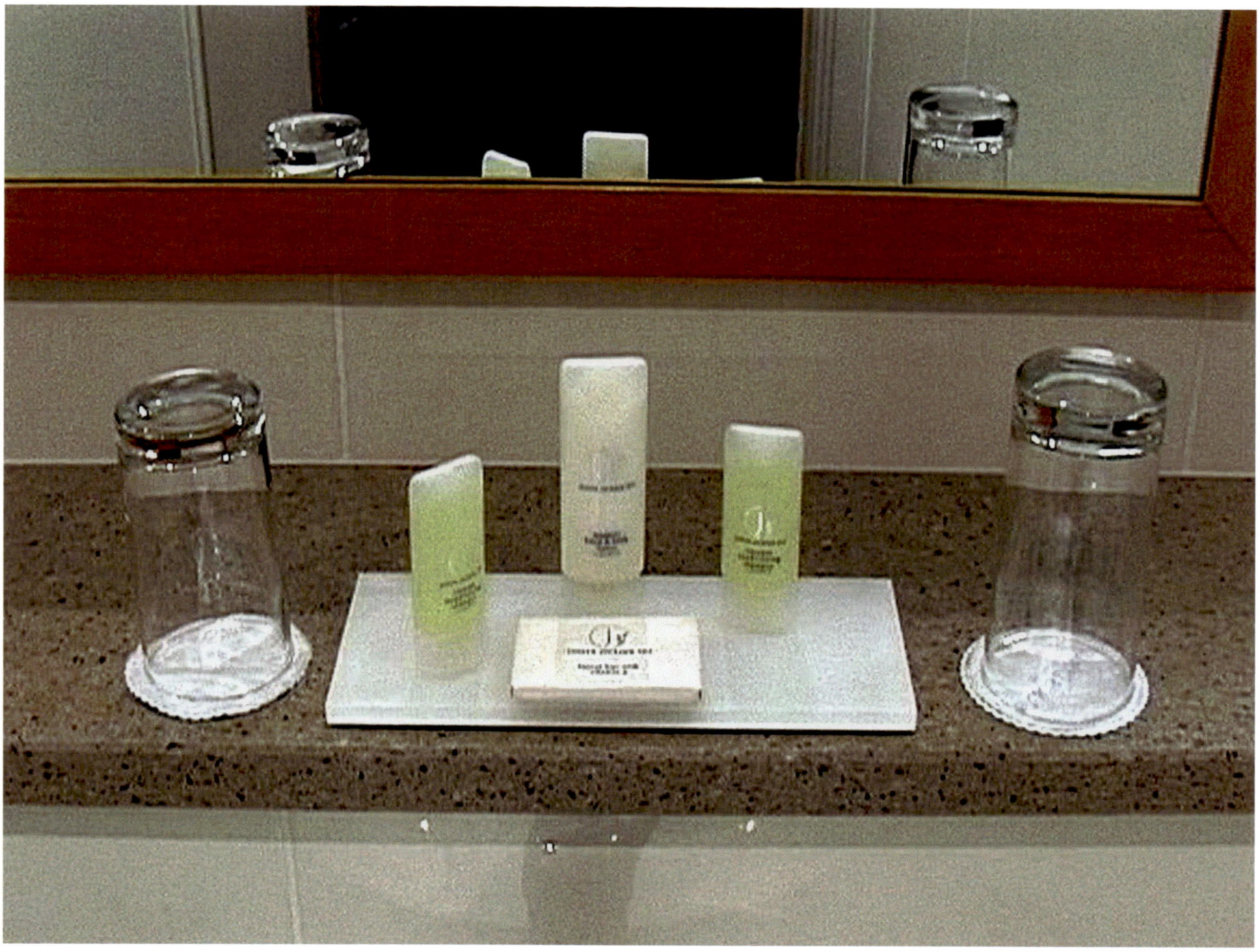

John Smith

Hotel Diaries

2001–07, 7-teilige Videoreihe

Am 8. Oktober 2001, einige Wochen nach dem Anschlag auf das World Trade Center am 11. September und zwei Tage nachdem die USA und Großbritannien mit der Bombardierung Afghanistans begonnen hatten, war ich auf dem Cork Film Festival in Irland. Als ich spätabends in mein Hotelzimmer zurückkehrte, schaltete ich den Fernseher ein, um mich über die neuesten Nachrichten zu informieren. Ich erwartete, ein bewegtes Bild zu sehen, stellte aber zu meiner Überraschung fest, dass die Nahaufnahme eines Männergesichts, das den Bildschirm ausfüllte, völlig unbeweglich war, in der Zeit erstarrt. Ich beobachtete den Bildschirm mehrere Minuten lang, aber nichts veränderte sich, und die Uhr in der Ecke des Bildschirms zeigte weiter 1:41 Uhr an. Was ging hier vor sich? Warum bewegte sich das Bild nicht? Besorgt und verwirrt nahm ich meine Videokamera in die Hand und versuchte zu erzählen, was in meinem Kopf vor sich ging. Damals ahnte ich noch nicht, dass diese spontane Aufnahme der Beginn eines Projekts war, das mich die nächsten sechs Jahre beschäftigen würde.

Hotel Diaries ist über einen Zeitraum von sechs Jahren in Hotels in sechs verschiedenen Ländern entstanden und zeichnet Bushs und Blairs Ära des „Kriegs gegen den Terror" anhand einer Reihe von Videoaufnahmen nach, die die anhaltenden Konflikte in Afghanistan, Irak und Israel/Palästina mit meinen persönlichen Erfahrungen beim Reisen verbinden. In diesen Arbeiten, die mit dem Zufall spielen, dient das Hotelzimmer als „gefundene" Filmkulisse, in der die Architektur, Einrichtung und Dekoration zum Mittel werden, um meine eigenen kleinen Abenteuer mit den großen Weltereignissen zu verbinden.

J.S.

Hotelübernachtungen sind John Smith von Filmfestivals in diversen Ländern seit langer Zeit eine Gewohnheit. Wir alle kennen den Moment, im Eindruck einer fremden Stadt abends das Hotelzimmer zu beziehen und die Enttäuschung, dass diese Zimmer sich überall gleichen. So kennen wir auch den Blick der Kamera von John Smith, wie er gedankenverloren die Zimmereinrichtung abwandert. Die belanglosen Bilder werden begleitet vom Kommentar des Filmemachers, der die Entdeckungen seiner Kamera unterhaltsam abwägt und würdigt. Wirkt diese Aufmerksamkeit leicht spleenig und übertrieben, so wandeln sich die laufenden Beobachtungen in Gedankenspiele, die zum Auslöser für Bilder werden, die sich dämonisch dazwischendrängen, obwohl sie weit über das Blickfeld seiner Kamera hinausweisen. Das sind offiziell verbreitete Bilder aus Nachrichtenkanälen, die Schauplätze des Krieges und des Unrechts aufzeigen, die wir kennen, in uns herumtragen und die unser Gewissen belasten. In der nächtlichen Enge des Hotelzimmers wird die eigene Ohnmacht zum Albtraum. Schon morgen wird der politische Alltag dieselben oder weitere

Schreckensbilder dieser Art verbreiten und dennoch deren Lösung weiter auf Distanz halten.

Während sich viele andere seiner Filme aus Montagen zusammensetzen, die mit häufigem Filmschnitt operieren, reduziert John Smith in dieser Serie den Schnitt bewusst auf ein Mindestmaß. Die Filme der *Hotel Diaries* rufen den Eindruck hervor, aus dem Stegreif begonnen zu sein, so dass wir alle Abläufe und Gedanken darin mitverfolgen können, wie es die kleine Handkamera bei der Aufnahme von Bild und Ton nahelegt, die den Betrachtenden nicht verborgen bleibt. Auf diese Weise fühlen wir uns in den laufenden Szenen anwesend und beteiligt, ganz gleich wo wir tatsächlich sind. Diese Filme sind zugleich das persönliche Statement des Künstlers, seine Kritik an einer schamlosen Politik und in ihrer Addition eine beklemmende Chronik.

U.G.

John Smith

Flag Mountain

2010, HD video, seamless loop, 8 minutes cycle

In 2007, on the way back to London from a study tour of Israel/Palestine led by the Israeli Committee Against House Demolitions, my partner and I visited Cyprus, where she had been engaged to teach a short filmmaking course. Glad to escape from a country scarred by the ongoing construction of the Separation Wall, I had forgotten that the capital Nicosia, where we were staying, was itself a divided city, bisected by the border between the Greek Cypriot south and the occupied Turkish Republic of Northern Cyprus. I was reminded of this fact in no uncertain terms when, on the night of our arrival, I looked across the city from the balcony of our apartment in the south. On the side of the Kyrenia mountains, overlooking the whole city, a gigantic flag of the Turkish Republic was illuminated in lights, provocatively flashing on and off in a choreographed sequence. I started to think about how this extreme display of nationalism, which dominated my perception of the scene, was probably all but invisible now to most of the city's inhabitants, who had witnessed it every night for many years. After returning to London I continued to think about this scenario, and two years later I rented the same apartment and returned to film the view from my balcony. Simultaneously horrified and amused by the directness of the nationalistic spectacle I decided to enhance it even further by filmic means, contrasting its drama against the everyday life of the city.

J.S.

The horizon marks the border of the visible. In *Flag Mountain*, it is formed by the Kyrenia Mountains. Another border is unrecognisable, but much more important: the border between the Turkish Republic of Northern Cyprus and the Republic of Cyprus, which contains the majority of the island.

John Smith has presented the nationalistically charged symbol of Northern Cyprus's flag in a way that could – without knowledge of its prior history and political controversy – be understood as an allusion to land art. It is joined by a nocturnal light spectacle that calls constellations to mind.

However, the link between the flag on the ground and that of Turkey already becomes apparent after a few shots, when Turkey's red and white flag is hoisted between two minarets, although this structure is a Gothic cathedral flanked by two towers like those typical of mosques.

In this film without words, the story is conveyed through sounds, some of which seem to resemble static. The calls to prayer for the Muslims and the tolling of the Greek-Orthodox church bells in Nicosia acoustically mark the work's beginning and end. Between them we hear the 'Independence March', Turkey's national anthem. However, the tones of everyday life also find their way in beneath this religious and patriotic

soundscape: hammering at a construction site, an aeroplane, cars. Shots from the film additionally point to this activity. Thus there are evidently different everyday worlds: a profane one, a staged one and a ritual one. For those without knowledge of this historical context, the film suggests the impression of a multicultural city.

U.F.

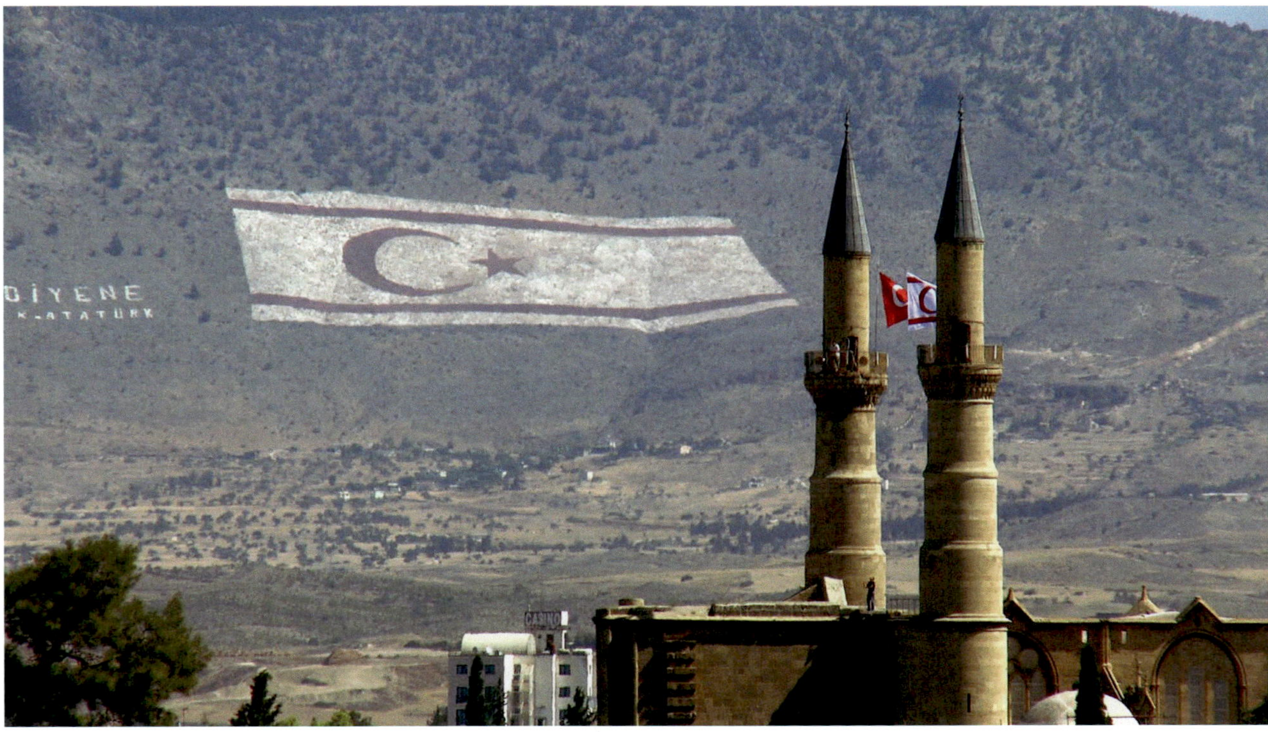

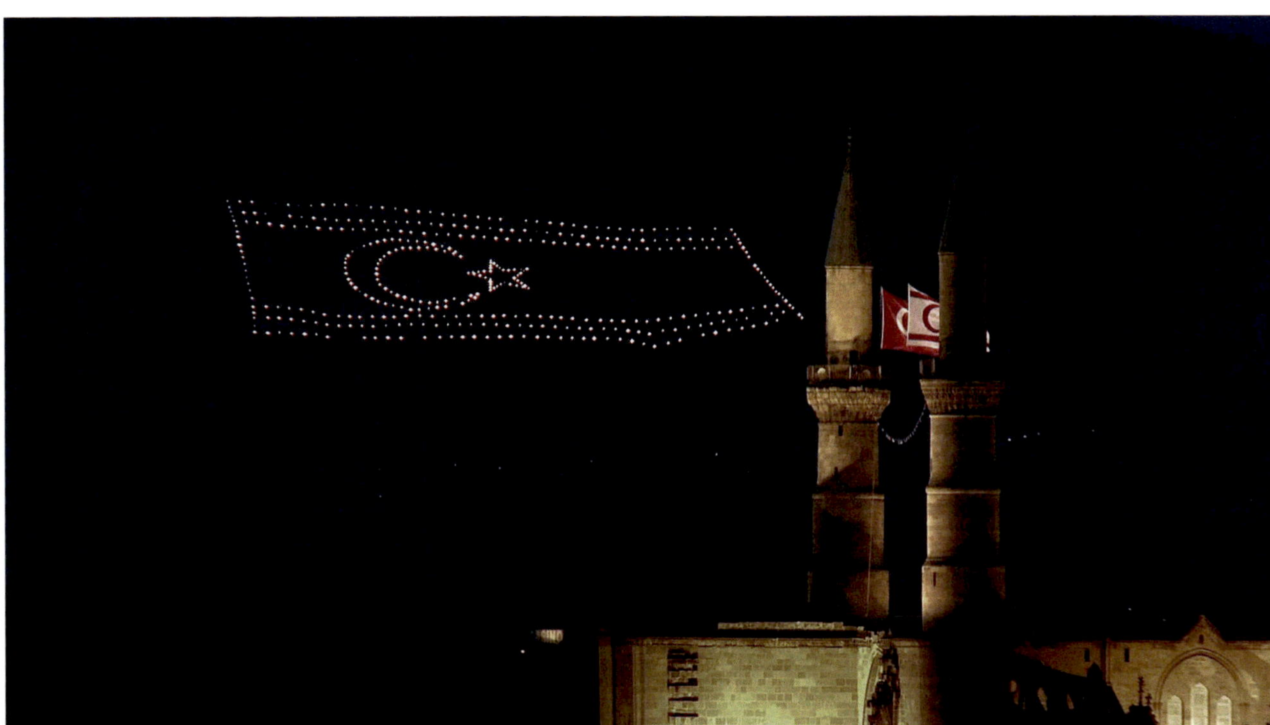

John Smith

Flag Mountain

2010, HD-Video, Endlosschleife, 8-minütiger Zyklus

Im Jahr 2007, auf dem Rückweg nach London von einer Studienreise in Israel/Palästina, die vom Israelischen Komitee gegen Häuserzerstörung organisiert war, besuchten meine Partnerin und ich Zypern, wo sie einen Kurzfilmkurs gegeben hat. Ich war so froh, einem Land zu entkommen, das vom Bau der israelischen Sperranlagen gezeichnet war, dass ich ganz vergessen hatte, dass die Hauptstadt Nikosia, wo wir untergebracht waren, selbst eine geteilte Stadt ist. Sie wird von der Grenze zwischen dem griechisch-zyprischen Süden und der besetzten Türkischen Republik Nordzypern zweigeteilt. Dieser Umstand wurde mir in der Nacht, in der wir ankamen, unmissverständlich in Erinnerung gerufen, als ich vom Balkon unserer Wohnung im Südteil über die Stadt blickte. An einem Berghang des Kyrenia-Gebirges, von wo aus man die gesamte Stadt überblickt, sah man eine gigantische Fahne der Türkischen Republik Nordzypern, beleuchtet mittels einer provokativ blinkenden, choreographierten Sequenz von Lichtern. Ich begann, darüber nachzudenken, dass diese extreme Zurschaustellung von Nationalismus, die meine Wahrnehmung dieser Ansicht beherrschte, für die meisten Bewohner der Stadt wohl fast schon unsichtbar geworden war, weil sie die Fahne seit Jahren jede Nacht gesehen hatten. Zurück in London dachte ich weiter über diese Umgebung nach, und zwei Jahre später mietete ich mir dieselbe Wohnung, um diesen Anblick vom Balkon aus zu filmen. Gleichzeitig entsetzt und amüsiert von der Unverfrorenheit des nationalistischen Spektakels, beschloss ich, es mit filmischen Mitteln noch zu verstärken und seine Dramatik in Kontrast zu setzen mit der Routine des Alltagslebens auf beiden Seiten der Stadt.

J.S.

Flag Mountain

Die Grenze des Sichtbaren ist der Horizont. Diesen bildet in *Flag Mountain* das Kyrenia-Gebirge. Eine andere Grenze ist jedoch nicht erkennbar, aber viel wichtiger, und zwar jene zwischen der Türkischen Republik Nordzypern und der Republik Zypern, die den größeren Teil der Insel umfasst.

John Smith setzt das nationalistisch aufgeladene Symbol der Flagge Nordzyperns auf eine Weise in Szene, die, ohne Wissen um die politische Brisanz und Vorgeschichte, auf eine Form von Land Art verweisen könnte, zu der sich nachts ein Lichterspiel addiert, das an Sternbilder erinnert.

Die Verbindung der Flagge auf dem Boden zu jener der Türkei wird aber schon nach wenigen Einstellungen deutlich, wenn zwischen zwei Minaretten die rot-weiße türkische Fahne gehisst wird, wobei es sich bei diesem Bauwerk ursprünglich um eine gotische Kathedrale handelt, die von zwei Türmen flankiert wird, wie sie für Moscheen typisch sind.

In diesem Film ohne Worte wird die Story von den Tönen getragen, die mitunter wie Störsignale erscheinen. Die Rufe zum Gebet für die Muslime und das Läuten der griechisch-orthodoxen Kirchen in Nikosia bilden eine akustische Klammer. Dazwischen erklingt der Unabhängigkeitsmarsch, die türkische Nationalhymne. Unter diese religiöse und patriotische Akustik mischen sich jedoch auch Töne des Alltags, das Hämmern auf einer Baustelle, ein Flugzeug, Autos. Einstellungen im Film verweisen zudem auf dieses Geschehen. Es gibt also offenbar unterschiedliche „Alltage": einen profanen, einen inszenierten und einen rituellen. Weiß man nichts vom historischen Hintergrund, entsteht der Eindruck einer multikulturellen Stadt.

U.F.

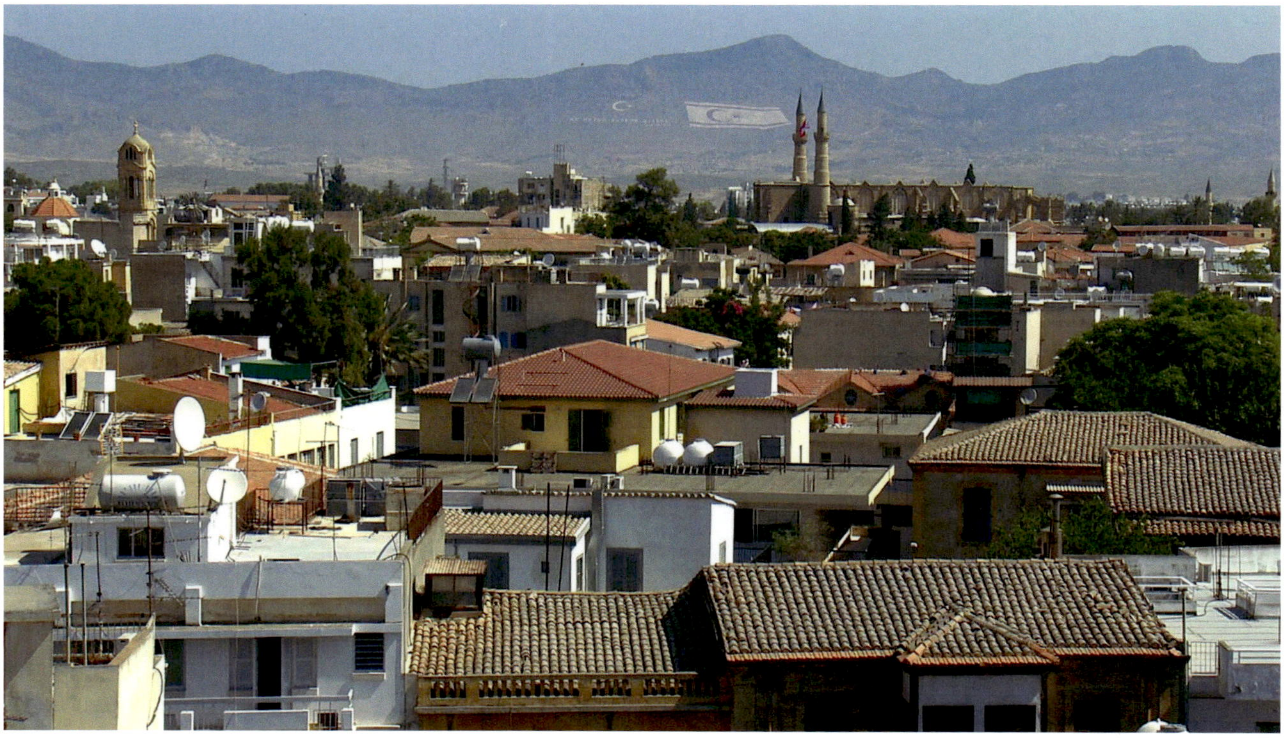

John Smith

unusual Red cardigan

2011, SD video, 12 minutes

In February 2010 I received a Google Alert informing me that a VHS compilation tape of my films was available for purchase on eBay. When I visited the eBay website I discovered that this second-hand tape, which had previously retailed for twenty pounds, was being offered for sale with a reserve price of five times that amount. Intrigued by the fact that anyone could attach a value of a hundred pounds to this technologically obsolete relic, I became curious about the seller's identity, which I soon decided to research. Studying the eBay page I found out that the seller, *serenporfor*, had 148 stars and 100% positive feedback. But who was *serenporfor*, and what else could I find out about him/her? Was there a clue in the name? Was it an anagram? If so, configurations like *Senor F Roper* and *Rose Pronfer* offered no illumination. The video *unusual Red cardigan* describes my journey of discovery, which led me to make some unplanned eBay purchases of my own.

J.S.

Thousands of eBay users do something similar every day: receive a package by post that contains the goods they have ordered. Sometimes it contains a personal greeting, but usually everyone remains a stranger to each other and places their trust in the anonymous routine of the system.

The internet platforms used by countless private sellers are primarily a market of things. John Smith ended up on eBay after finding out that someone had put one of his works up for sale there.

Later, as the camera turns to a package, we learn that he purchased a few of the items being offered. He initially thinks it might contain body parts, based on its form. Finally, we are there live for the opening of the package and, simultaneously, the virtual world's transformation into a three-dimensional one. We find out that the items are from a non-smoking household, which had no pets either. These details are also pieces of information that tell us something about the unknown person. This brief message brings her out of the realm of mere speculation and into that of facts. Thus the circulation of things is not exclusively an anonymous process: it is also a form of communication, although it is one that is carried out under difficult circumstances.

U.F.

unusual Red cardigan

I'm one of those people who spends too much of their time looking themselves up on the internet.

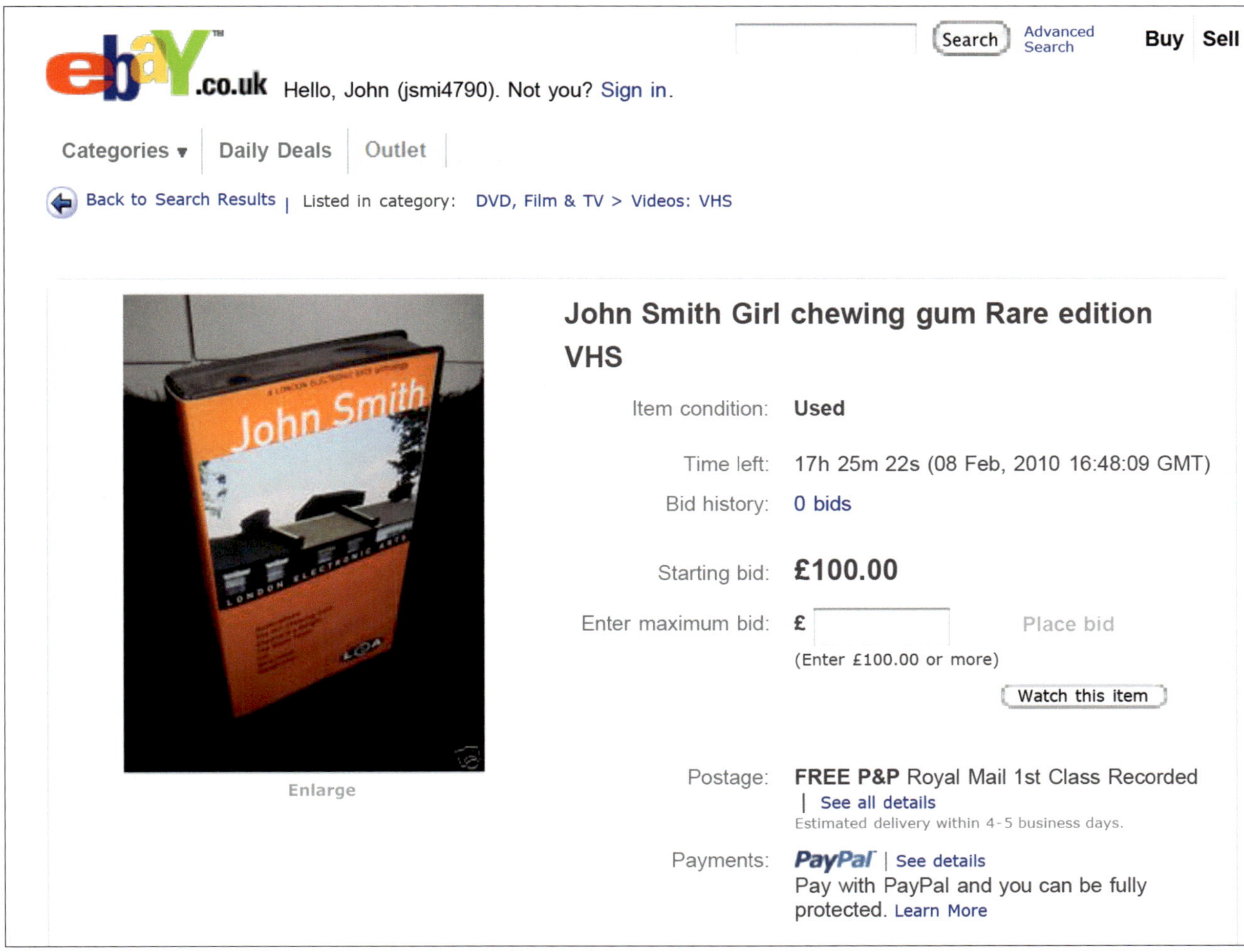

John Smith

unusual Red cardigan

2011, SD-Video, 12 Minuten

Im Februar 2010 erhielt ich eine Google-Benachrichtigung, die mich darüber informierte, dass auf eBay eine VHS-Kassette mit einer Zusammenstellung meiner Filme zum Kauf angeboten wurde. Als ich die entsprechende Seite auf eBay besuchte, sah ich, dass diese gebrauchte Kassette, die ursprünglich für zwanzig Pfund verkauft wurde, nun für einen Mindestpreis in der fünffachen Höhe angeboten wurde. Die Tatsache, dass irgendjemand dieses technologisch veraltete Relikt mit einem Wert von hundert Pfund versehen konnte, machte mich neugierig auf die Identität der Verkäufer*in, die ich bald zu recherchieren begann. Auf der eBay-Seite fand ich heraus, dass die Verkäufer*in mit Namen *serenporfor* 148 Sterne und 100% positive Bewertungen hatte. Aber wer war *serenporfor*, und was konnte ich sonst noch über ihn/sie herausfinden? Gab es einen Hinweis im Namen? War er ein Anagramm? Wenn ja, so waren Konfigurationen wie *Senor F Roper* oder *Rose Pronfer* doch wenig erhellend. Das Video *unusual Red cardigan* beschreibt meine Entdeckungsreise, die mich auch zu einigen ungeplanten eBay-Einkäufen führte.

J.S.

Tausende Nutzer*innen von eBay werden jeden Tag ähnliches tun – eine Postsendung mit bestellten Waren in Empfang nehmen. Manchmal liegt ein persönlicher Gruß dabei, aber zumeist bleibt man sich gegenseitig fremd und vertraut auf die routiniert gesteuerte Anonymität des Systems.

Die von unzähligen privaten Verkäufer*innen genutzten Plattformen im Internet sind in erster Linie ein Markt der Dinge. John Smith gerät durch den Hinweis, dass eine seiner Arbeiten dort von jemandem angeboten würde, zu eBay.

Später erfahren wir, dass er einige der angebotenen Sachen gekauft hat, als die Kamera zu einem Paket schwenkt. Zunächst denkt er, es könne Körperteile beinhalten, ausgehend von seiner Form. Schließlich erleben wir das Öffnen des Pakets live mit und zugleich, wie sich die virtuelle Welt in eine dreidimensionale verwandelt. Zu erfahren ist, dass die Dinge aus einem Nichtraucherhaushalt kommen, in dem es zudem keine Haustiere gibt. Diese Information ist zugleich eine Nachricht, die uns etwas über die unbekannte Person verrät. Sie wird durch diese kurze Mitteilung aus der bloßen Spekulation in das Feld der Tatsachen geholt. Die Zirkulation der Dinge ist somit nicht nur ein anonymer Prozess, sondern eine Form der Kommunikation, wenn auch unter erschwerten Bedingungen.

U.F.

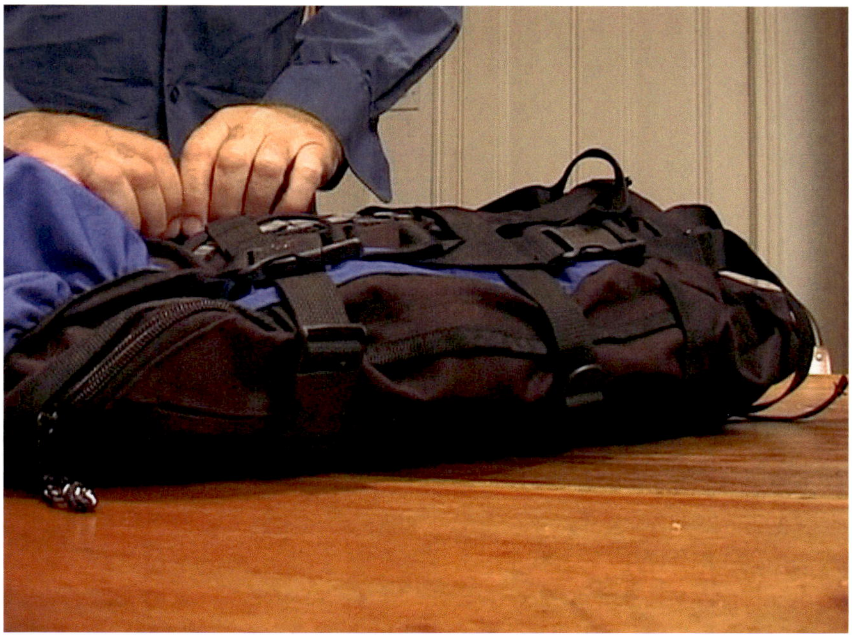

I'm hoping of course that this will contain some of the other items. It's nicely packed up… undo the drawstring… oh, what have we got here?

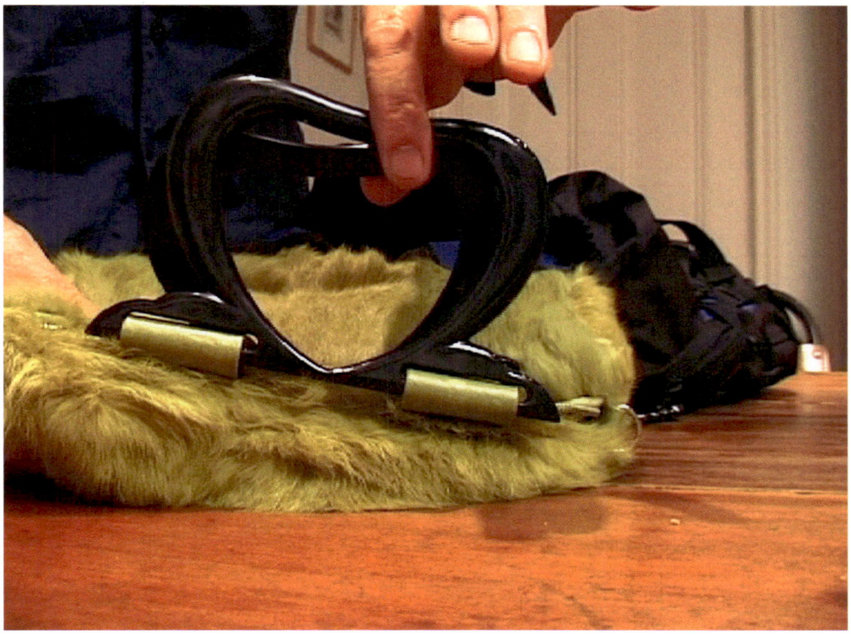

Ah, I think I remember what this is. Yes, it's the green rabbit fur handbag with heart-shaped handles. Very nice, good condition. Not quite sure what I'm going to do with it but it will definitely come in handy.

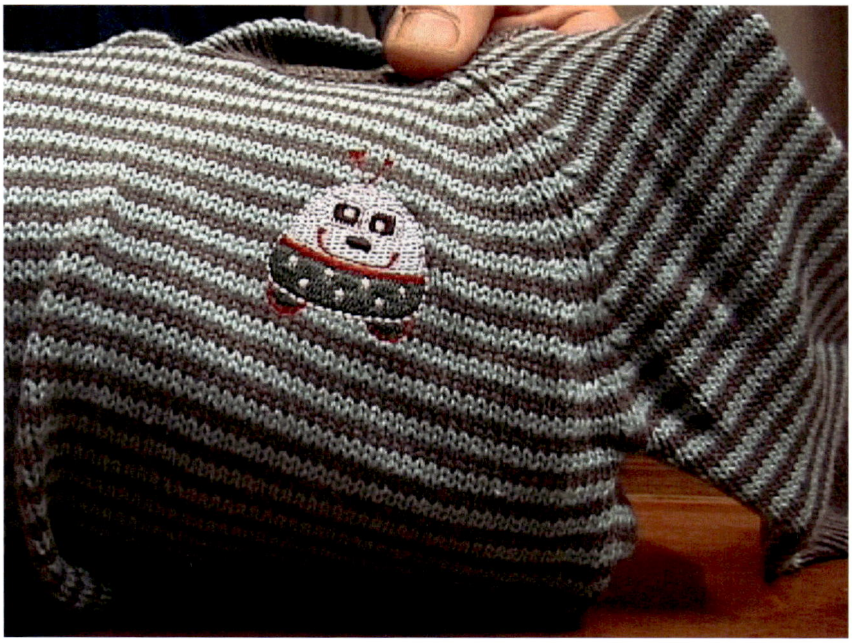

And also… what's this? Ah, the baby boy knitted cardigan, three to six months. It's still got the label, unused… yes, three to six months, Space-Dog… Space-Dog? Ah! Here we are… Space-Dog, on the front.

John Smith

Horizon (Five Pounds a Belgian)

2012, HD video, seamless loop, 18 minutes cycle

Towards the end of 2011 I received a commission to make a video installation for the Turner Contemporary gallery in Margate, which is situated next to the sea. At a meeting in the director's office, which looked directly out onto the water, I was immediately impressed by the panoramic view of the horizon, and by how much the appearance of the sea and the sky changed over short periods of time. I became interested in the possibility of recording the same view in dramatically different weather conditions and cutting between shots quite rapidly, to draw attention to just how spectacular these differences were. I got the director's permission to film from her office window at weekends, which I thought would allow me to set up my camera and observe and record the changes in weather in comfort (the proposed schedule meant that I would have to film during the depths of winter). Things didn't work out to plan. I rapidly discovered that in all but the calmest weather conditions the sea spray would lash against the gallery windows, making satisfactory filming impossible. I ended up filming ninety percent of my material from the seashore in midwinter, waiting around for hours for light and weather to change and for other events to take place in front of my camera, always frozen to the bone and frequently soaked to the skin. There's a story that the painter J. M.W. Turner once strapped himself to a ship's mast in a storm to observe its effects. I can imagine how he felt.

J.S.

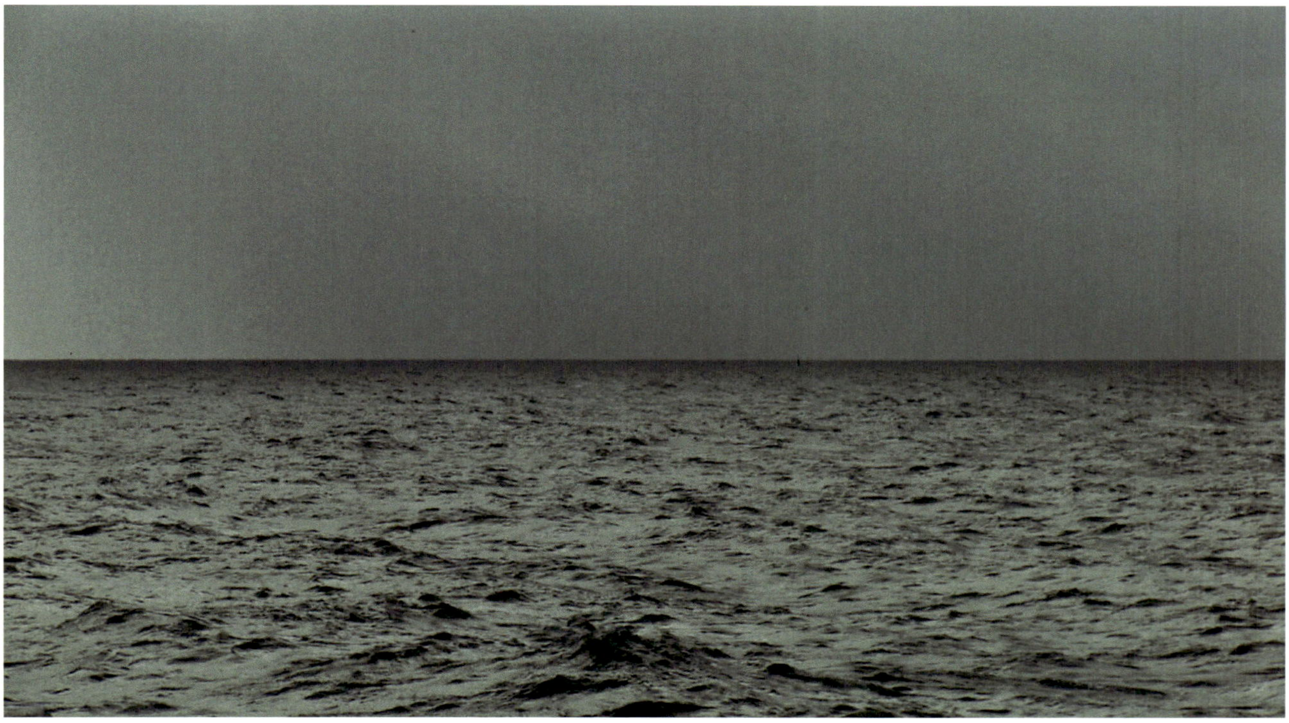

Horizon (Five Pounds a Belgian)

A greyish-blue sea, crashing waves: we immediately feel ourselves pulled into the midst of the scene. However, we quickly notice that something is not right, because the picture suddenly cuts to the image of a quite calm, blue expanse of water coupled with the full tone of the crashing sea.

Repeatedly changing, the sea is shown in various weather conditions. The loud crashing has nothing to do with these images. At times the crashing of the waves ceases completely or briefly corresponds to the actual filmed scene for a few seconds. Within the changing scenery, the horizon always remains on the same level and provides the only constant, forming a common thread running through the entire video work. The sound of the breaking waves is itself like a kind of 'prototype' – what we think of when we hear the term 'crashing' in connection with the sea. Ideal and reality collide in this collage of image and sound. At the same time, this soon raises the question of reality and fiction: is the inserted crashing of the sea a real recording at all or is it, for example, an artificially generated sound? In a world defined by media, we are able to unambiguously identify the real far less often than we would like. A reality based on our own experience is increasingly being replaced by a mediated reality – at the same time we are constantly consuming more and more media. Through the incongruity between the audio and the seemingly documentary footage of the sea, John Smith completely calls into question its actual authenticity. *Horizon* disrupts our sensory impressions, and its constantly changing images and sounds repeatedly and vividly demonstrate to us that we enjoy allowing ourselves to become ensnared in the trap of the reality or realities generated through media.

T.I.

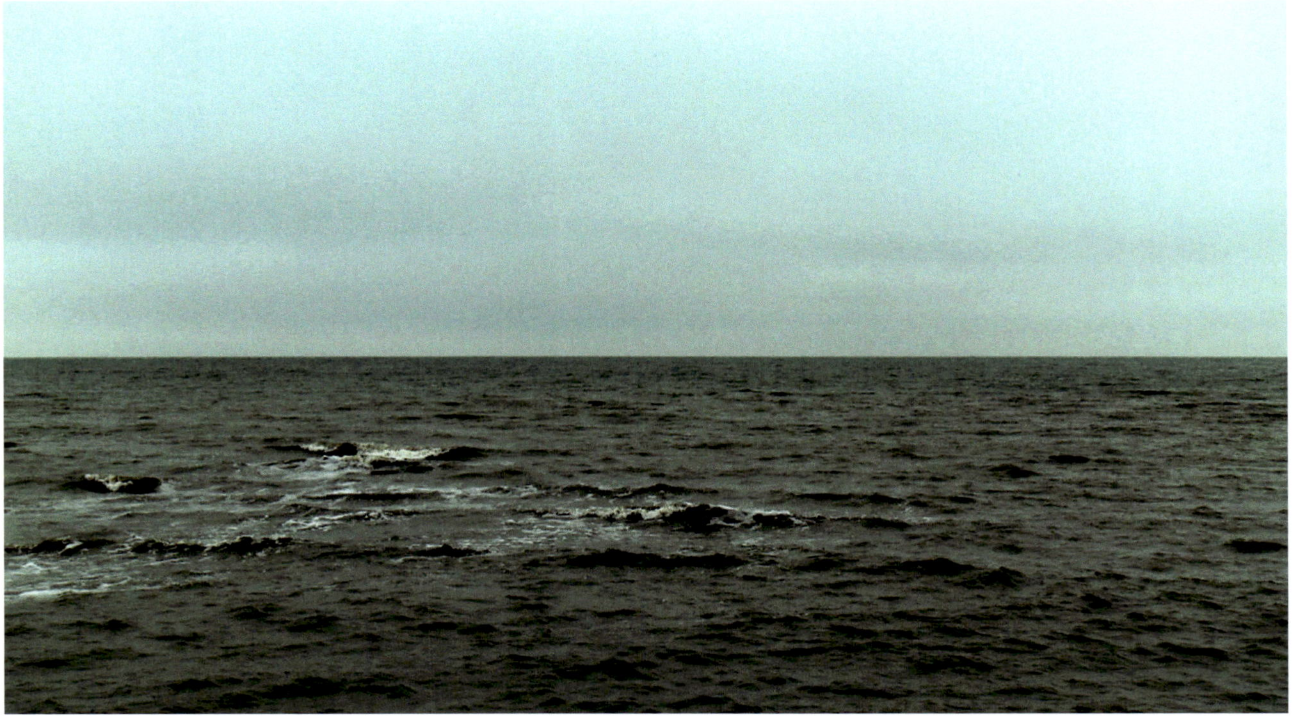

John Smith

Horizon (Five Pounds a Belgian)

2012, HD-Video, Endlosschleife, 18-minütiger Zyklus

Gegen Ende 2011 erhielt ich den Auftrag, eine Videoinstallation für die Galerie Turner Contemporary in Margate zu machen, die unmittelbar am Meer liegt. Bei einem Treffen im Büro der Direktorin, das direkt auf das Wasser hinausgeht, war ich sofort beeindruckt von dem Panoramablick auf den Horizont und davon, wie sehr sich das Aussehen des Meeres und des Himmels innerhalb kurzer Zeit veränderte. Mich interessierte die Möglichkeit, ein und dieselbe Ansicht bei dramatisch unterschiedlichen Wetterbedingungen zu filmen und recht schnell zwischen den Aufnahmen zu wechseln, um die Aufmerksamkeit auf die spektakulären Unterschiede zu lenken. Ich erhielt die Erlaubnis der Direktorin, an den Wochenenden von ihrem Bürofenster aus zu filmen, was mir die Möglichkeit geben sollte, meine Kamera aufzustellen und die Wetterveränderungen in aller Ruhe zu beobachten und aufzuzeichnen (der anvisierte Zeitplan bedeutete, dass ich mitten im tiefsten Winter filmen musste). Es lief nicht nach Plan. Ich stellte schnell fest, dass die Gischt, außer bei völlig ruhigem Wetter, ständig gegen die Fenster der Galerie peitschte und zufriedenstellende Filmaufnahmen unmöglich machte. Am Ende filmte ich neunzig Prozent meines Materials mitten im Winter vom Strand aus, wartete stundenlang auf Licht- und Wetterwechsel und auf andere Ereignisse, die sich vor meiner Kamera abspielen würden, immer bis auf die Knochen durchgefroren und oft bis auf die Haut durchnässt. Es gibt die Geschichte, dass der Maler William Turner sich einmal bei einem Unwetter mit Riemen an einem Schiffsmast festgezurrt hat, um die Auswirkungen des Sturms zu beobachten. Ich kann mir vorstellen, wie er sich gefühlt hat.

J.S.

Ein grau-blaues Meer, die Wellen rauschen, sofort fühlt man sich in die Szenerie hineinversetzt. Schnell merkt man jedoch, dass hier etwas nicht stimmt, denn mit dem vollen Ton des Meeresrauschens wird plötzlich das Bild einer recht ruhigen blauen Wasseroberfläche eingeblendet.

Immer wieder wechselnd wird das Meer in verschiedenen Wetterlagen gezeigt. Das laute Rauschen hat mit diesen Bildern nichts zu tun. Zwischenzeitlich setzt das Geräusch der Wellen gar ganz aus oder entspricht dann doch kurz für wenige Sekunden der tatsächlich gefilmten Situation. Innerhalb der sich verändernden Szenerie bleibt der Horizont stets auf gleicher Höhe und bietet die einzige Konstante, die sich wie ein roter Faden durch die videokünstlerische Arbeit zieht. Das Geräusch der brechenden Wellen selbst ist wie eine Art „Prototyp“ – das, woran man denkt, wenn man das Wort „Meeresrauschen“ hört. Ideal und Wirklichkeit stoßen in der Bild-Ton-Collage aufeinander. Wobei sich daraufhin schnell die Frage nach Realität und Fiktion stellt: Ist das eingeblendete Meeresrauschen überhaupt eine reale

Horizon (Five Pounds a Belgian)

Aufnahme oder etwa ein künstlich erzeugtes Geräusch? Die Identifizierung des Realen ist in einer medial geprägten Welt viel seltener eindeutig zu beantworten, als es uns lieb ist. Denn die auf eigener Erfahrung basierende Wirklichkeit wird zunehmend durch eine uns vermittelte Wirklichkeit während eines stetig steigenden Konsums von Medien ersetzt. Indem der Ton zu den vermeintlich dokumentarischen Aufnahmen des Meeres einfach nicht passt, stellt John Smith den tatsächlichen Wahrheitsgehalt komplett in Frage. *Horizon* irritiert die Sinneseindrücke und führt uns durch die stets wechselnden Bilder und Geräusche immer wieder vor Augen, dass wir gern dazu geneigt sind, in die Falle medial erzeugter Wirklichkeit(en) zu tappen.

T.I.

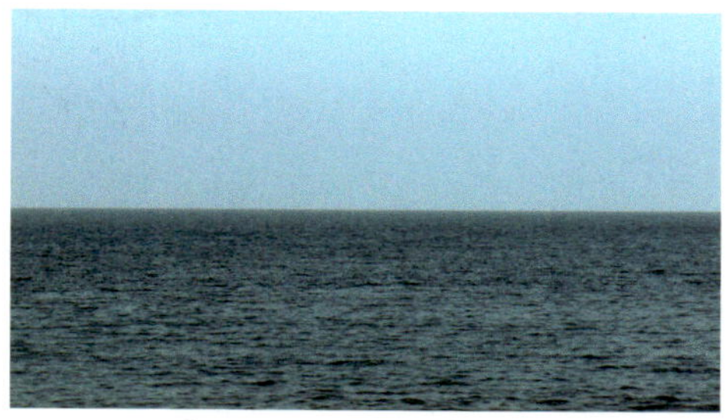

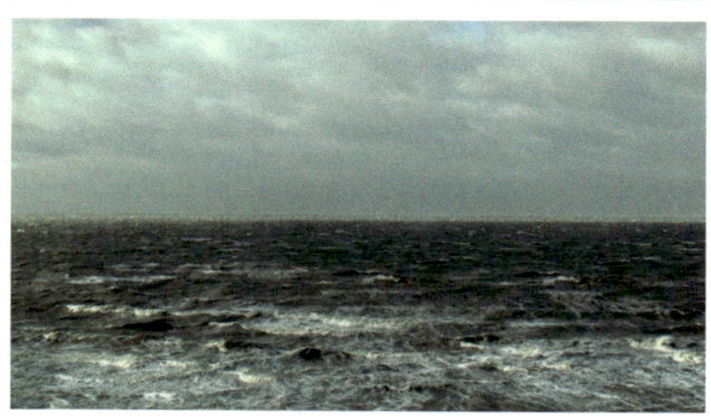

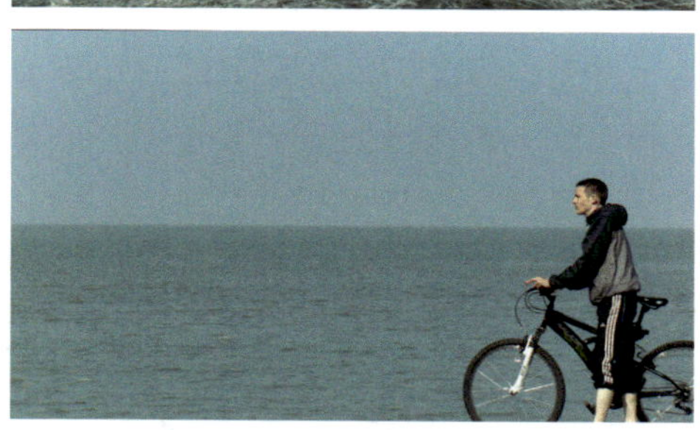

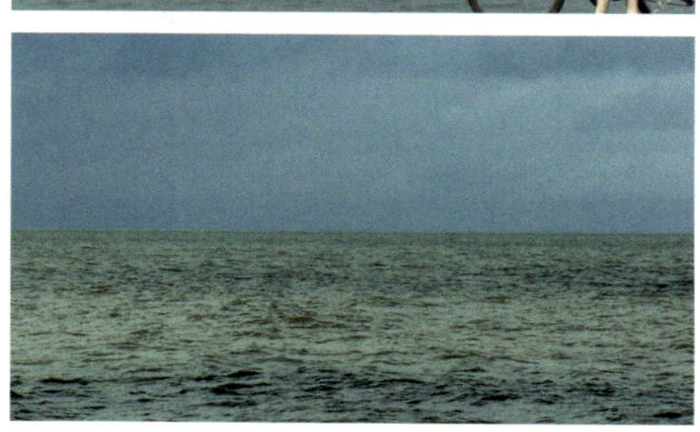

John Smith

Dad's Stick

2012, HD video, 5 minutes

My father always painted and decorated our family home. During one of my visits to his house not long before he died, he told me that he wanted to show me something. I followed him into his garage and he handed me a stick that he had used for stirring his house paint over the course of many years. He had cut off the end with a sharp saw, revealing layer upon layer of paint like the rings within a tree trunk, enabling him to look back at all the rooms he had painted over the decades. It was a poignant moment. Looking closely, I detected the bright orange of our hallway in the 1960s and the greyish green of our kitchen cupboards in the 1950s – more than 50 years of history encapsulated. I kept the stick after he died and five years later I made this film.

J.S.

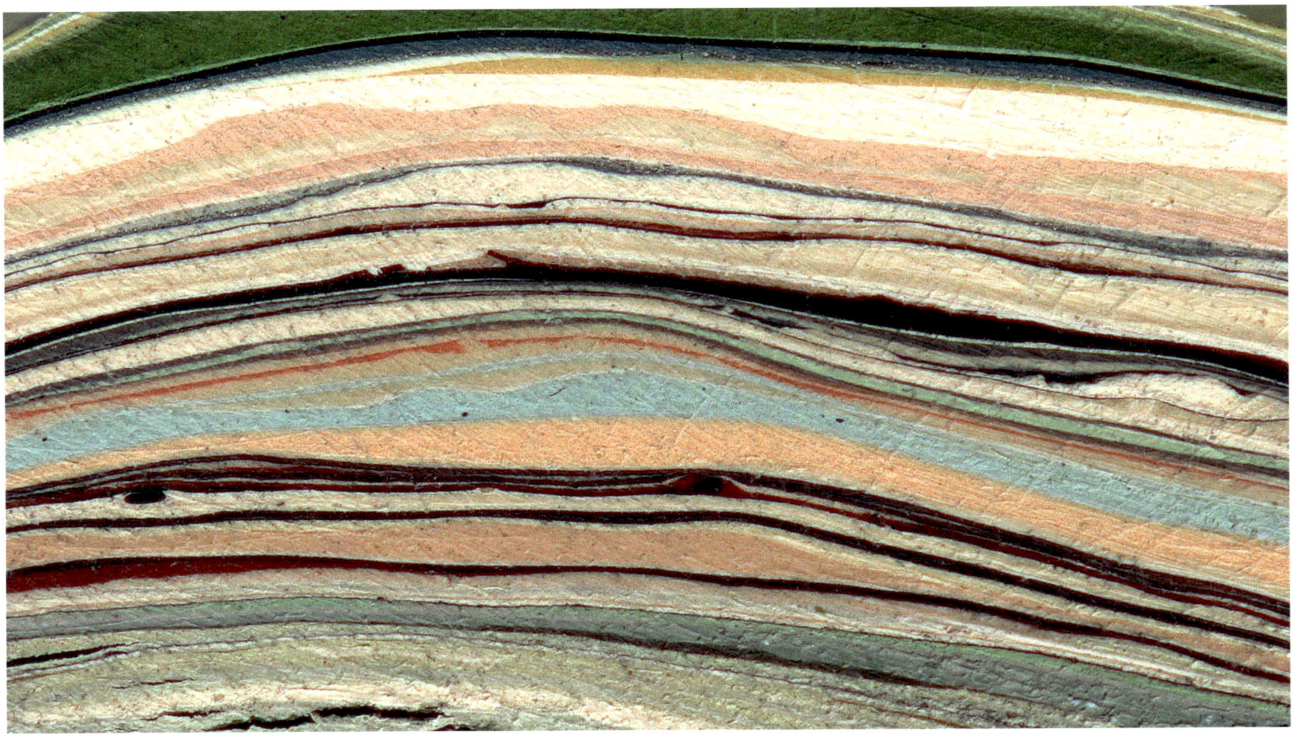

Dad's Stick

John Smith's work *Dad's Stick* sketches an unusually personal image of the artist by showing us a piece of wood covered with layers of paint and using the story behind it to provide us with a glimpse inside his relationship with his father. Nonetheless, as is the case in many of his films, the larger picture only gradually takes shape here. Smith deliberately chooses not to show any old footage of his home or his family – in the nostalgic aesthetic of a home video, for example. The short film begins with an abstract-looking image and, at first, it scarcely becomes more comprehensible for viewers as time passes. Only at the end do we learn what the object which provided the work's title is and what role it played. As is so often true of Smith's work, it is once again the power of language that first provides the images with a deeper meaning – as it applies to another, black wooden stick, which has lost its original function as a ruler.
In terms of the audio, the artist has selected just a handful of deliberately utilised elements to establish an auditory backdrop for his explanations of working processes or behaviours – or he also inserts new lines into the well-known melodies he sings to himself, just the way (as Smith tells us) his father used to like to do. Short sentences, superimposed on top of the visual material that changes every few seconds, continuously provide us with more and more information about what is being shown and with insights into the artist's relationship with his deceased father. The writing is sometimes also shown on monochromatic fields of colour which take up the tones from the stick and, with them, the walls of the house where the artist grew up.
The writing looks crude, almost as if the cheapest video software possible had been used to join it with the stills. Smith uses his approach to deconstruct the familiar clichés of the cinema and advertising, which rely again and again on an emotionalising musical accompaniment and the most simplistic optical stimulus-response mechanisms. As surprising as the intimate and moving effect which unfolds through his remembering his father in *Dad's Stick* is, the work nevertheless simultaneously retains Smith's customary reflective detachment, particularly in the visual elements utilised in the film.

D.B.

Dad's colour preferences changed over the years.

In the late 60s and 70s his palette was much more vivid.

As time passed by, his colours became more muted and his edges became softer.

In his later years he worked mainly in pastels and subtle shades of white.

Dad's Stick

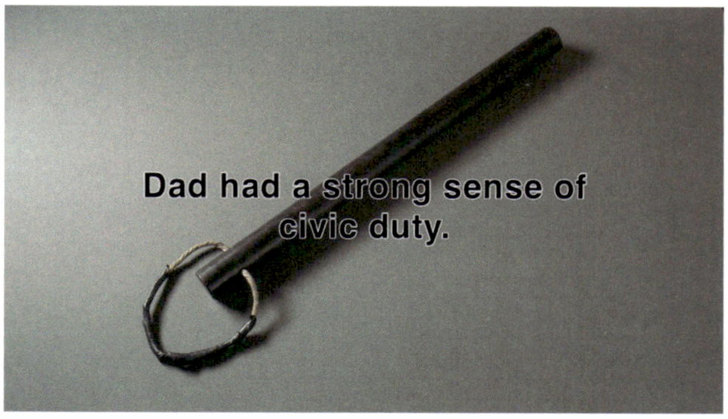
Dad had a strong sense of civic duty.

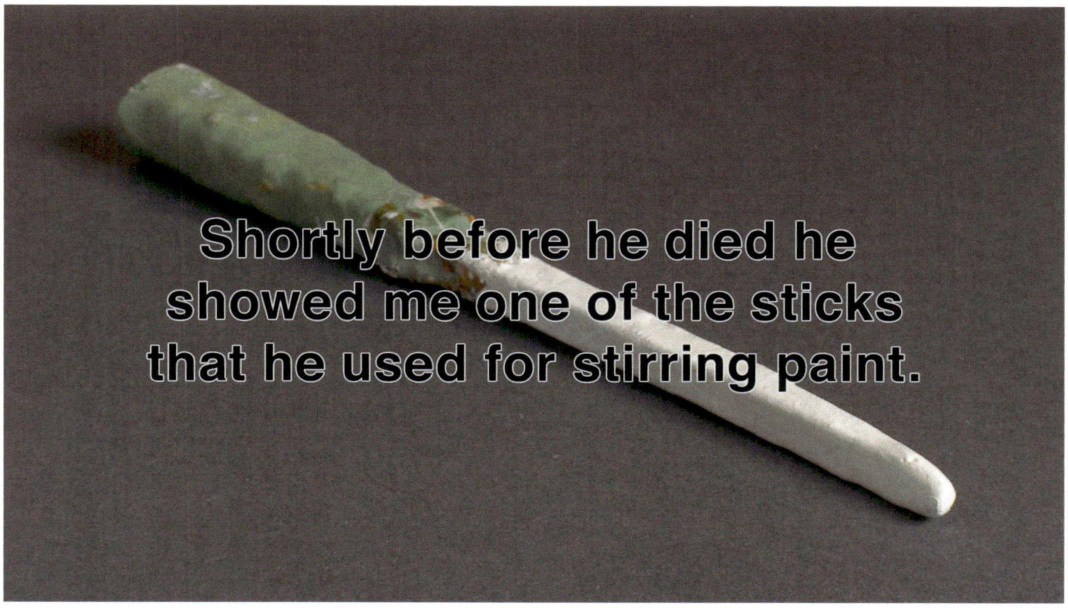
Shortly before he died he showed me one of the sticks that he used for stirring paint.

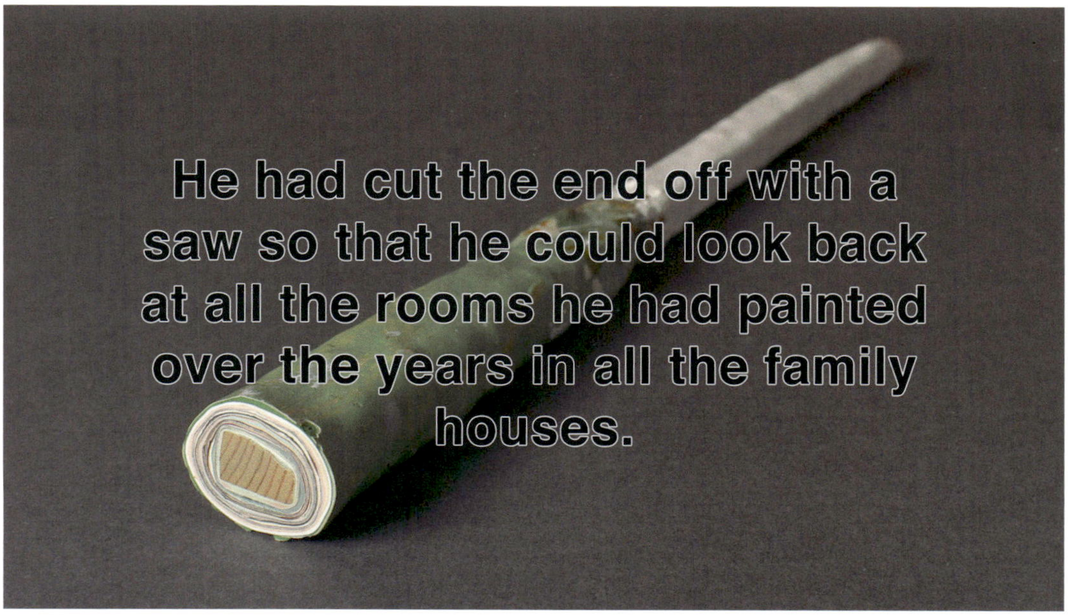
He had cut the end off with a saw so that he could look back at all the rooms he had painted over the years in all the family houses.

John Smith

Dad's Stick

2012, HD-Video, 5 Minuten

Mein Vater war stets derjenige, der unser Haus gestrichen und renoviert hat. Als ich ihn kurz vor seinem Tod wieder einmal besuchte, sagte er mir, dass er mir etwas zeigen wolle. Ich folgte ihm in die Garage, wo er mir einen Holzstab reichte, den er über viele Jahre zum Umrühren der Hausfarbe benutzt hatte. Das Ende hatte er mit einer scharfen Säge abgetrennt, so dass die vielen Farbschichten wie Ringe in einem Baumstamm sichtbar wurden und er auf all die Räume zurückblicken konnte, die er im Laufe der Jahrzehnte gestrichen hatte. Es war ein ergreifender Moment. Bei genauem Hinsehen entdeckte ich das leuchtende Orange unseres Flurs aus den 1960er Jahren und das Graugrün unserer Küchenschränke aus den 1950er Jahren – mehr als 50 Jahre Geschichte auf drei Zentimetern. Nach seinem Tod behielt ich den Stab, und fünf Jahre später habe ich diesen Film gedreht.

J.S.

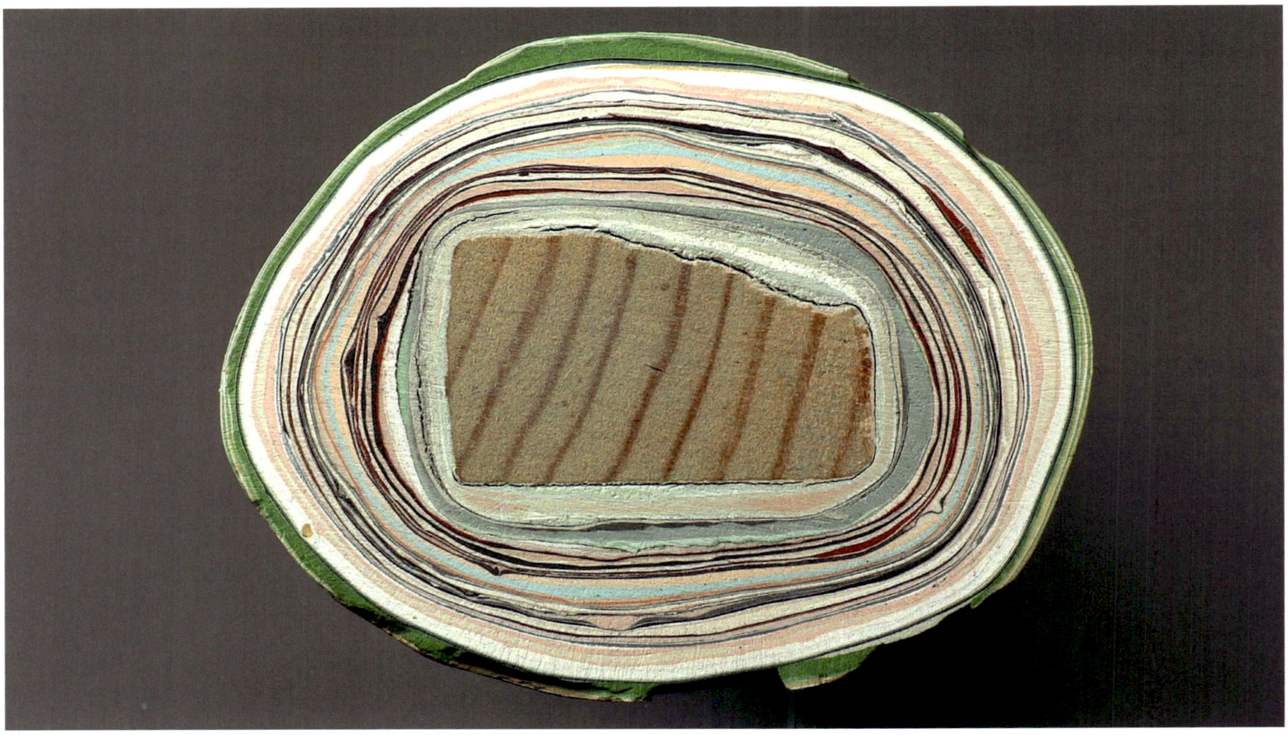

Dad's Stick

John Smiths Arbeit *Dad's Stick* zeichnet ein ungewöhnlich persönliches Bild des Künstlers, indem er einen mit Farbschichten überzogenen Stock zeigt und uns anhand dessen Geschichte einen Einblick in die Beziehung zu seinem Vater gewährt. Wie in vielen seiner Filme konstruiert sich das Gesamtbild doch auch hier erst mit der Zeit. Smith zeigt bewusst keine alten Aufnahmen seines Zuhauses oder seiner Familie, wie etwa in der nostalgischen Ästhetik eines Home-Videos.
Der Kurzfilm beginnt mit einem abstrakt anmutenden Bild, welches auch mit der Zeit für die Betrachtende*n zunächst kaum aufschlussreicher wird. Erst zum Ende hin erfahren wir, worum es sich bei dem titelgebenden Objekt handelt und welche Rolle es spielt. Wie so oft bei Smith ist es auch hier die Macht der Sprache, die den Abbildungen erst einen tieferen Sinn verleiht, so auch bei einem weiteren, schwarzen Holzstock, der seine ursprüngliche Funktion als Lineal verloren hat. Auditiv wählt der Künstler nur wenige, ganz gezielte Mittel, indem er erläuterte Arbeitsvorgänge oder Verhaltensweisen mit einer jeweils minimalistischen, aber signifikanten Geräuschkulisse untermalt. Oder indem er vor sich hinsingend altbekannten Melodien neu gedichtete Textzeilen verpasst, so, wie wir von Smith erfahren, es auch sein Vater gerne tat. Kurze Sätze, die über das alle paar Sekunden wechselnde Bildmaterial geblendet werden, geben uns stetig mehr Informationen zu dem Gezeigten und einen Einblick in das Verhältnis des Künstlers zu seinem verstorbenen Vater. Zuweilen wird die Schrift auch auf monochromen Farbfeldern gezeigt, die die Farben des Stocks und somit auch der Wände des Hauses, in dem der Künstler aufwuchs, aufgreifen.
Die Schrift wirkt simpel und fast so, als hätte sie in der möglichst billigsten Videosoftware ihre Einheit mit den Standbildern gefunden. John Smith dekonstruiert mit seiner Vorgehensweise die gewohnten Klischees des Kinos und der Werbung, in denen immer und immer wieder auf emotionalisierende Musikuntermalung und einfältigste optische Schlüsselreize gesetzt wird. So überraschend sich die intime und anrührende Wirkung seiner Erinnerung an den Vater in *Dad's Stick* entfaltet, so bleibt sie, vor allem mit den im Film gewählten visuellen Mitteln, doch zur gleichen Zeit für Smith gewohnt reflektiert distanziert.

D.B.

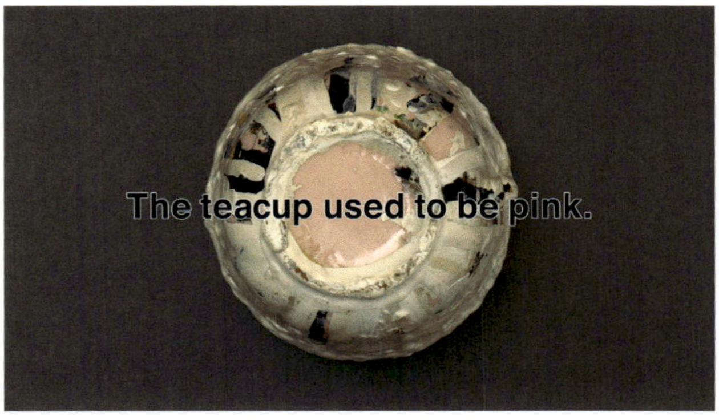

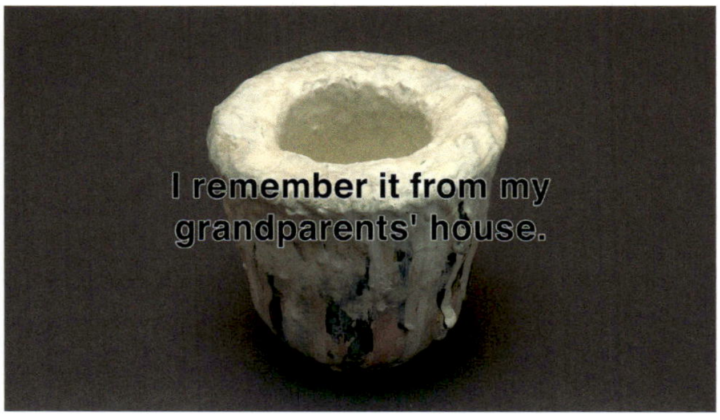

John Smith

White Hole

2014, HD video, seamless loop, 7 minutes cycle

In 2014 I was invited to create a work on paper for the Royal Academy Summer Exhibition by the artist Cornelia Parker, who was curating a room based around the theme of 'Black and White'. I soon started thinking about negative and positive images and remembered something I had been told when I visited a film festival in Leipzig in 1997. Eight years after the fall of the Berlin Wall, some people in the east were starting to say that they could see 'a tunnel at the end of the light'. I decided to make a negative print from a black and white photograph looking out of a railway tunnel, a black hole looming in its opening.

Having produced the print I felt that the idea had considerably more potential and went on to make a video work using the same image, based upon my own experience of visiting communist Poland in 1980. *White Hole* metaphorically alternates negative and positive imagery and backwards and forwards speech, questioning the idealisation of life in other places and political systems, remembering a time when we could at least imagine that the grass might be greener on the other side.

J.S.

White Hole

This film revolves around questions of memory and history. The two are interwoven and their content is extremely malleable, because they exist under the influence of the present. As a result, their essence often takes on a reductive form. Dramaturgically, John Smith deals with this by inviting us to take a journey in both directions along the path of time: to do this, he makes use of an old-fashioned black-and-white technique which simultaneously recurs back to history and is formally polarising.

The fact that his few encounters with the East – once before and once after the end of socialism, in Warsaw and Leipzig – can scarcely provide a basis for a deeper understanding is absolutely clear to Smith. However, fleeting episodes can also permit the past to resurface in an exemplary manner and describe valid generalities in retrospect. The video work conveys this semantic transformation.

A photo provides the shot that serves as the basis of the film's minimalist animation. Black and white, light and dark, and positive and negative image change places in it. As a loop successively played forwards and backwards, the film finds itself in a dichotomous continuity. The extreme visual symbolism is transparent, but extraordinarily suggestive. The text, which continues along above it, does not have to concern itself with the visual sequences. It develops its significance through the sound of the speech and the content of the narrative, together with the emotions and hopes contained in them. Image and text form a collage whose components are divided by their cut edges. This detachment is treacherous and causes semantic gaps to emerge; there are phases where any understanding regarding the past remains in the dark or incomprehensible.

U.G.

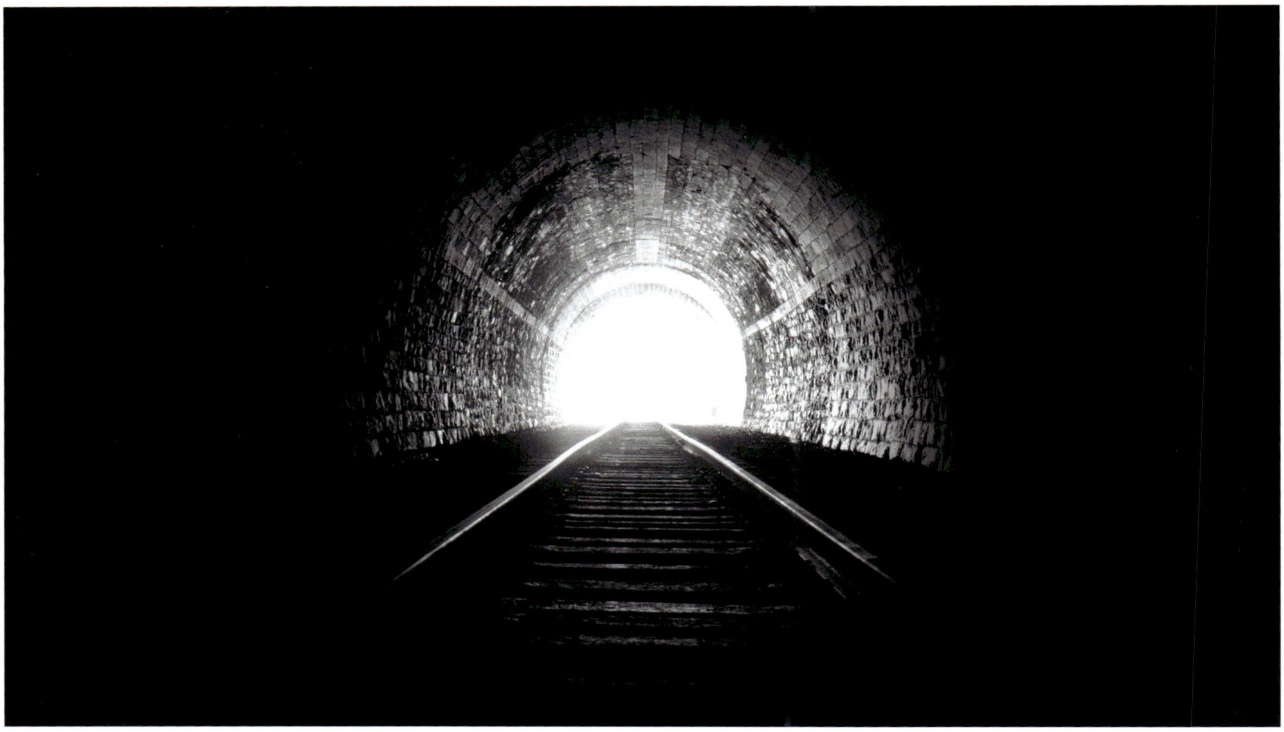

So entering shops, first through their closed doors and then through the thick winter curtains hanging inside, was always an adventure – when looking for a grocery store or a tobacconist I could just as easily find myself in a hairdresser's or a hardware shop. This was something that I really appreciated – I loved the absence of the hard-sell that pervaded everyday life in capitalist Britain. I loved the fact that the shops contained no decadent luxuries and that there was so little choice.

White Hole

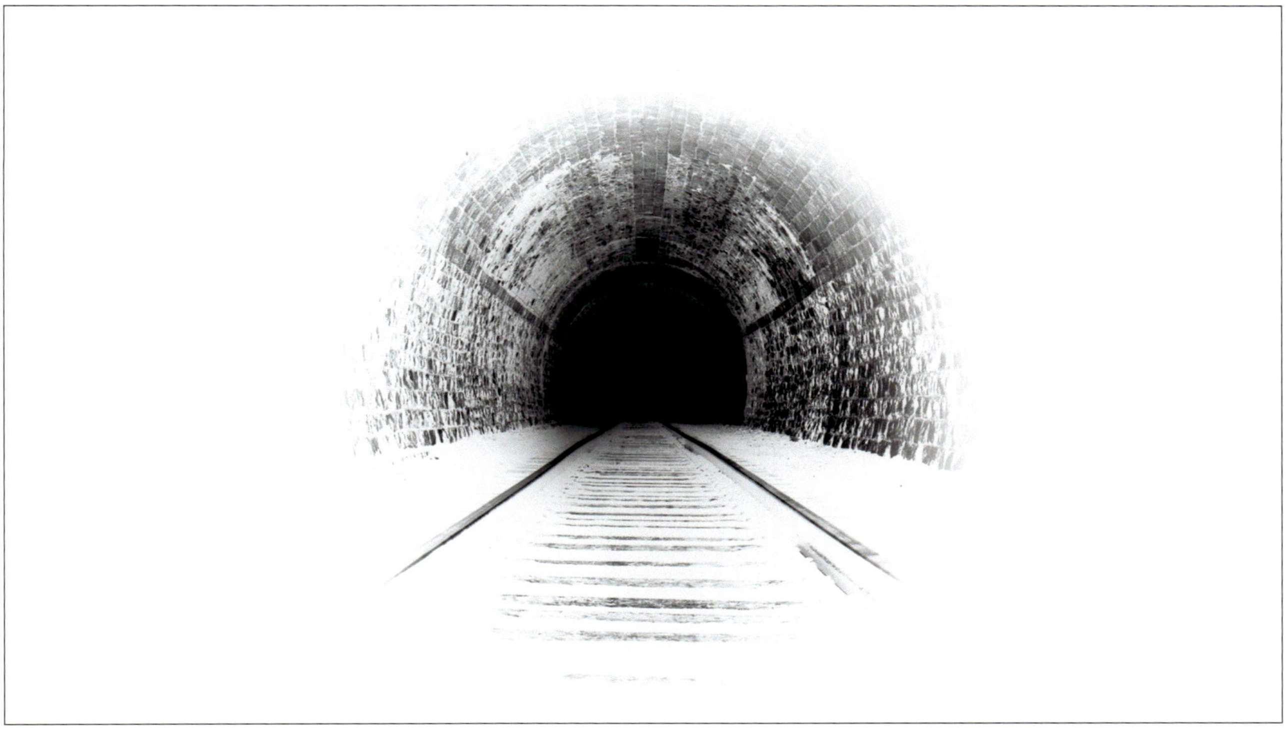

Most Poles that I spoke to did not agree. While I extolled the virtues of limited style options in the shoe shops, they seemed to be obsessed by Western democracy. I could of course understand their support for the fledgling Solidarity movement, but why did they sing the praises of Margaret Thatcher? I had several conversations where my own idealisation of communist Poland was matched by a Polish idealisation of the capitalist west.

John Smith

White Hole

2014, HD-Video, Endlosschleife, 7-minütiger Zyklus

Für die Royal Academy Summer Exhibition sollte ich 2014 eine Arbeit auf Papier schaffen. Cornelia Parker, die einen Raum zum Thema „schwarz und weiß“ kuratierte, hatte mich dazu eingeladen. Ich machte mir Gedanken über Negativ- oder Positivbilder und erinnerte mich an etwas, das man mir 1997 in Leipzig gesagt hatte, als ich dort ein Filmfestival besuchte: Acht Jahre nach dem Mauerfall begannen einige Menschen im Osten zu sagen, dass sie „einen Tunnel am Ende des Lichts“ sehen konnten. Ich entschloss mich, von einer Fotografie, die den Blick aus einem Eisenbahntunnel zeigt, einen Negativabzug zu machen – ein schwarzes Loch, das in der Öffnung erscheint.

Nach Fertigstellung des Abzugs hatte ich das Gefühl, dass der Gedanke noch einiges an Potenzial hatte und machte mich daran, eine Videoarbeit mit dem gleichen Bild zu produzieren, basierend auf eigenen Erfahrungen von einem Besuch im kommunistischen Polen im Jahr 1980. *White Hole* wechselt zwischen einer negativen und positiven Metaphorik hin und her sowie zwischen rückwärts und vorwärts abgespielter Sprache. So stellt das Werk die Idealisierung des Lebens an anderen Orten und in anderen politischen Systemen infrage und erinnert an eine Zeit, in der wir uns wenigstens noch vorstellen konnten, dass das Gras auf der anderen Seite vielleicht grüner ist.

J.S.

Der Film umkreist Fragen von Erinnerung und Geschichte. Beide, miteinander verwoben, enthalten äußerst formbare Inhalte, da sie unter dem Einfluss der Gegenwart stehen. Das bringt mit sich, dass ihre Essenz oft plakativ ausfällt. John Smith geht dramaturgisch darauf ein, indem er uns auf eine Reise in beide Richtungen entlang des Zeitstrahls einlädt und dafür auf altmodische Schwarzweißtechnik zurückgreift, welche zugleich auf die Geschichte rekurriert und formal polarisiert.

Dass seine wenigen Begegnungen mit dem Osten, einmal vor und einmal nach dem Ende des Sozialismus, in Warschau und in Leipzig, kaum die Basis für ein tieferes Verständnis liefern konnten, ist John Smith absolut klar. Aber auch flüchtige Episoden können exemplarisch die Vergangenheit aufscheinen lassen und im Nachhinein Allgemeingültiges zeichnen. Diesen Bedeutungswandel trägt die Videoarbeit.

Ein Foto liefert die Grundeinstellung für die filmisch minimalistische Bildanimation. Darin tauschen Weiß und Schwarz, Licht und Dunkelheit, Positiv- und Negativbild den Standort. Als Loop aufeinanderfolgend vorwärts und rückwärts abgespult befindet sich der Film in dichotomer Kontinuität. Die extreme Bildsymbolik ist durchschaubar, aber außerordentlich suggestiv. Der darüber hinweglaufende Text muss sich nicht um die Bildabläufe kümmern. Er entwickelt seine Bedeutung aus dem

White Hole

Klang der Sprache und dem Inhalt der Erzählung mit den darin enthaltenen Emotionen und Hoffnungen. Bild und Text sind eine Collage, deren Bestandteile ihre Schnittkanten trennen. Dieser Abstand ist tückisch und lässt semantische Pausen entstehen, phasenweise bleibt jede Verständigung über die Vergangenheit im Dunkeln oder unverständlich.

U.G.

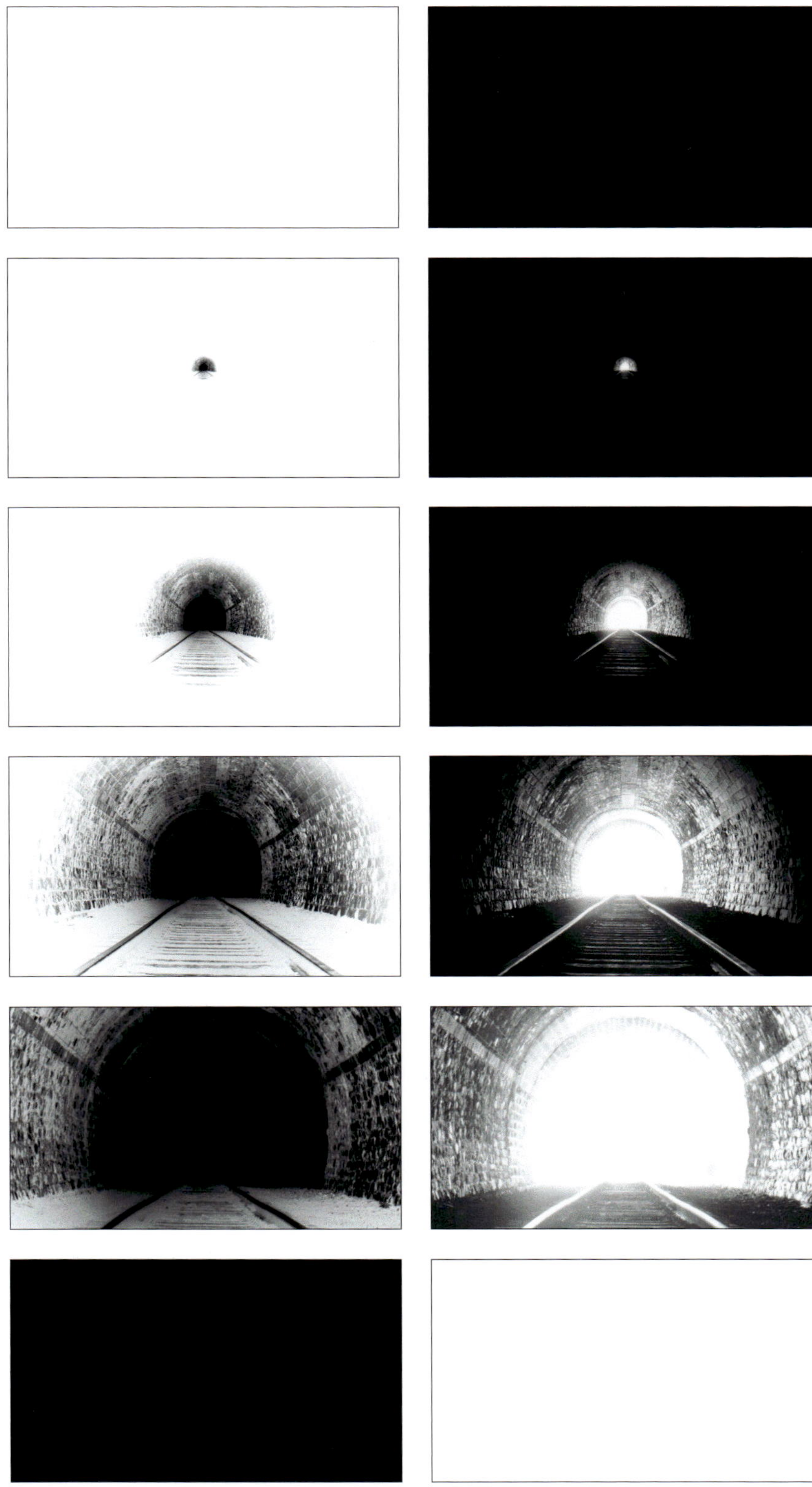

A friend told me about a new East German aphorism that was going around. People were saying that they could see a tunnel, at the end of the light.

John Smith

Steve Hates Fish

2015, HD video, seamless loop, 5 minutes cycle

Some years ago I became fascinated by *Word Lens*, a newly developed language translator app for smartphones. When the phone's camera was pointed at a piece of text the app would attempt to translate the text into a chosen language and graphically represent the translated text as part of the image on the phone's screen. The app was surprisingly efficient, but it interested me most when it got things wrong.

Steve Hates Fish was commissioned for a film programme that was screened in the window of Tintype gallery in North London and viewed from the street after dark, both by deliberate visitors and casual passers-by. Filming directly from the screen of my smartphone, I told *Word Lens* to translate from French into English, deliberately confusing the software by pointing my camera at the English shop signs in Essex Road, the busy shopping street in which the gallery was situated. In an environment overloaded with information the signs ran riot, as the restless software did its best to fulfil its task, looking for French words to translate in places where there were none.

J.S.

Steve Hates Fish is a prime example of John Smith's talent for eliciting a smile from his viewers by coupling a single clever idea with the most limited of means and an uncomplicated post-production process. As is typical of Smith's work, the outward humour is also based on a more complex background. With the ever-accelerating progress of technological developments, the voices admonishing us to beware of the algorithms that are increasingly intervening in our everyday lives have also become more vehement. At regular intervals, Hollywood films prophesy artificial intelligences' looming seizure of power from humans. Watching Smith's video this danger still seems very distant, and the AI seems almost sympathetically human in its flawed and obsessive attempts to find translations: Smith has filmed a series of shop signs in central London and used a smartphone app to ask this artificial intelligence for a translation from French to English. The AI then attempted to find a (preprogrammed) meaning in what was presented to it. The app simply could not accept the fact that it seemed unable to discover any French words in the cityscape and that it could just read the lettering which was already in English as it was. This human characteristic is also known as *confirmation bias* in the field of psychology. *Steve Hates Fish* thus visualises in the most literal sense that to err is not just human.

D.B.

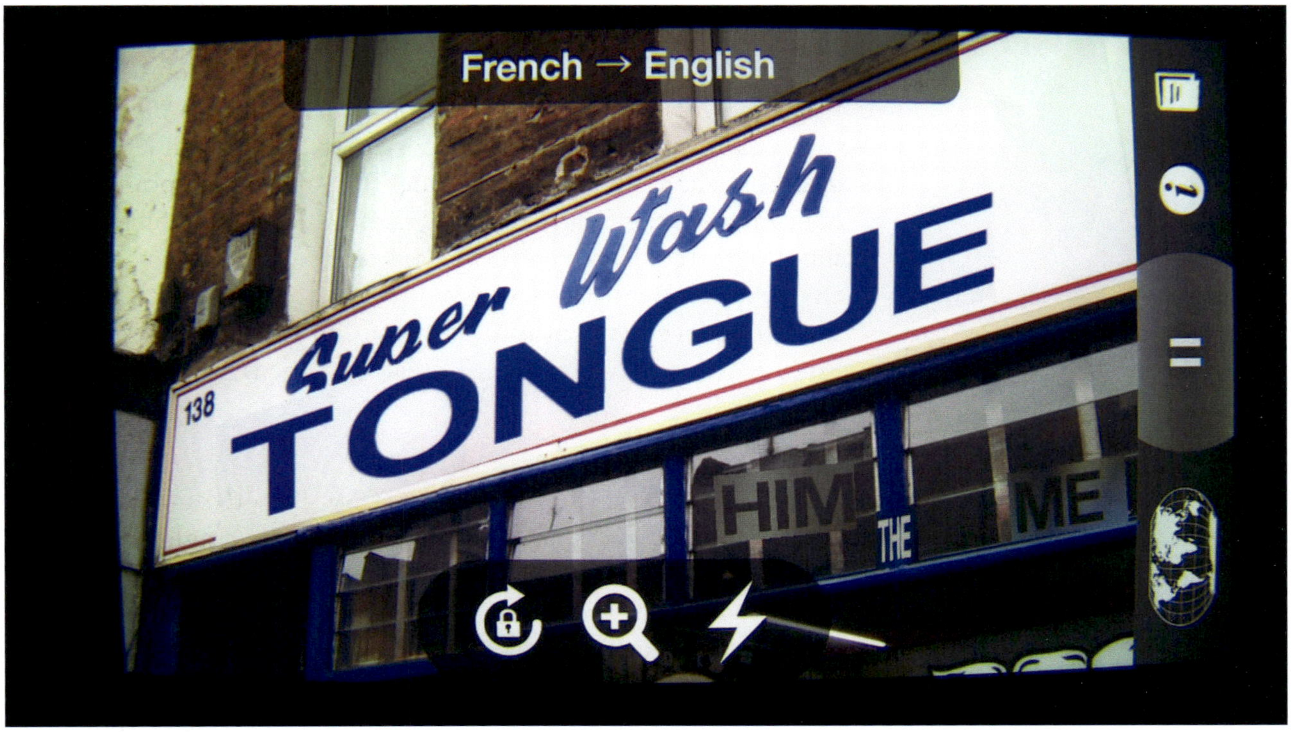
French → English
Super Wash
TONGUE
138
HIM
THE
ME

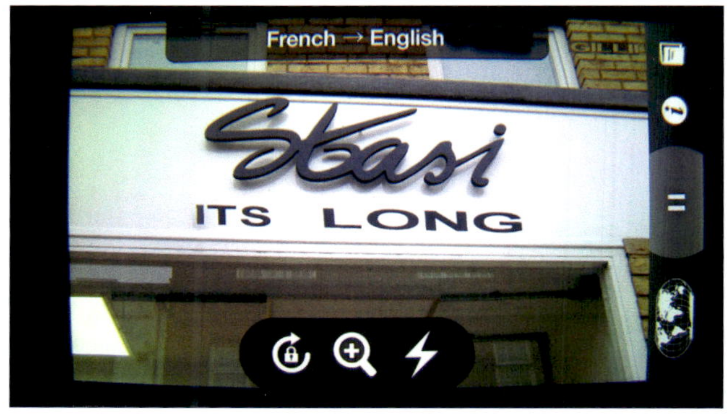
French → English
Stasi
ITS LONG

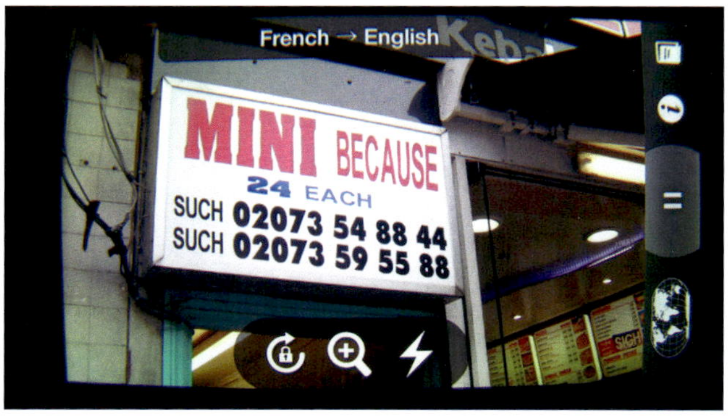
French → English
MINI BECAUSE
24 EACH
SUCH 02073 54 88 44
SUCH 02073 59 55 88

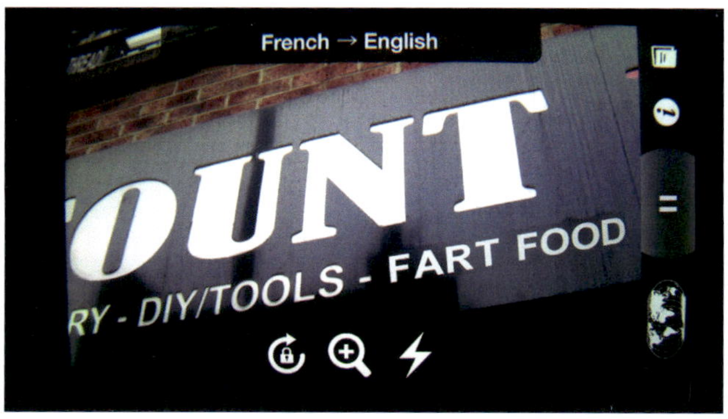
French → English
OUNT
RY - DIY/TOOLS - FART FOOD

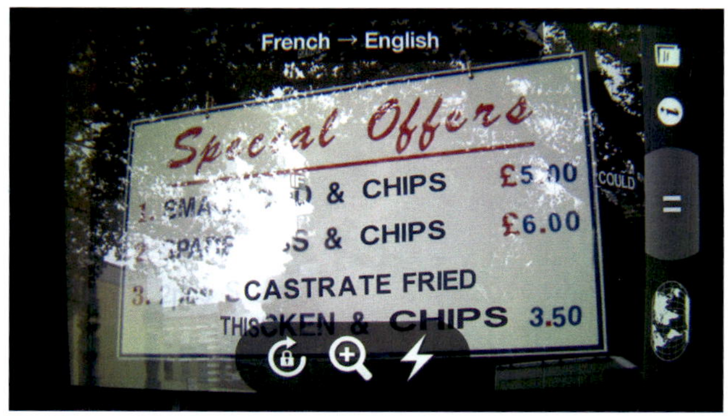
French → English
Special Offers
& CHIPS £5.00
& CHIPS £6.00
CASTRATE FRIED
CHIPS 3.50
COULD

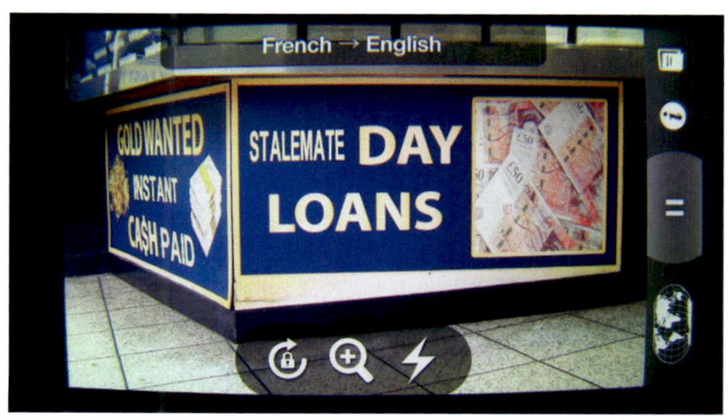
French → English
GOLD WANTED
INSTANT
CASH PAID
STALEMATE DAY
LOANS

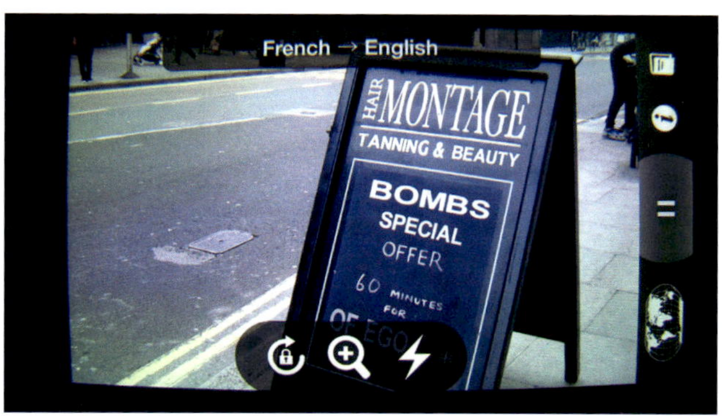
French → English
HAIR MONTAGE
TANNING & BEAUTY
BOMBS
SPECIAL
OFFER
60 MINUTES FOR

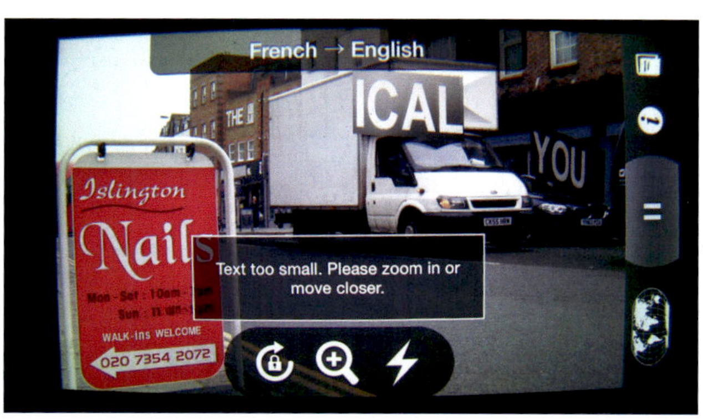
French → English
ICAL
YOU
Islington
Nails
WALK-INS WELCOME
020 7354 2072
Text too small. Please zoom in or move closer.

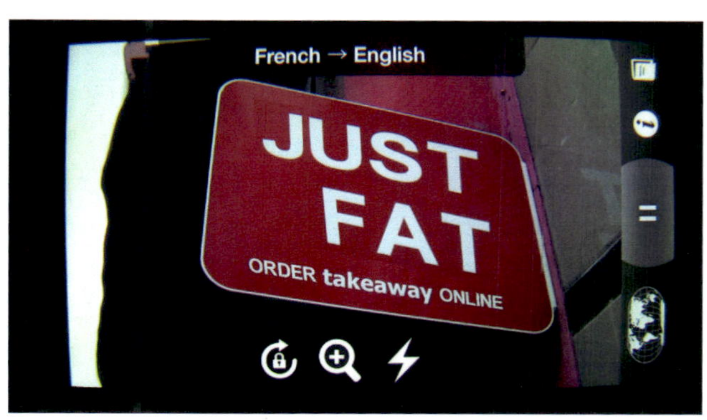
French → English
JUST
FAT
ORDER takeaway ONLINE

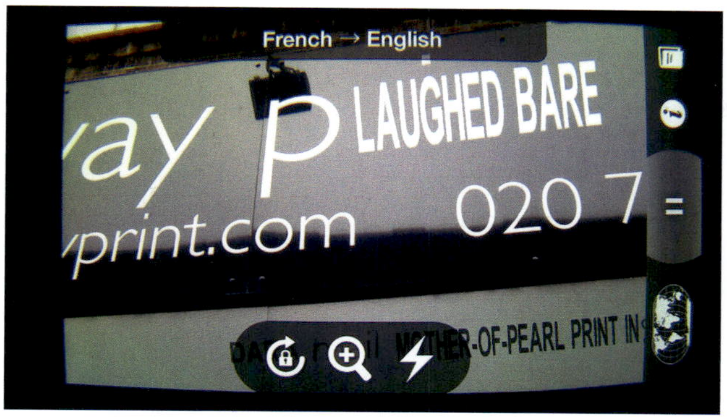
French → English
ay p LAUGHED BARE
print.com 020 7
MOTHER-OF-PEARL PRINT IN

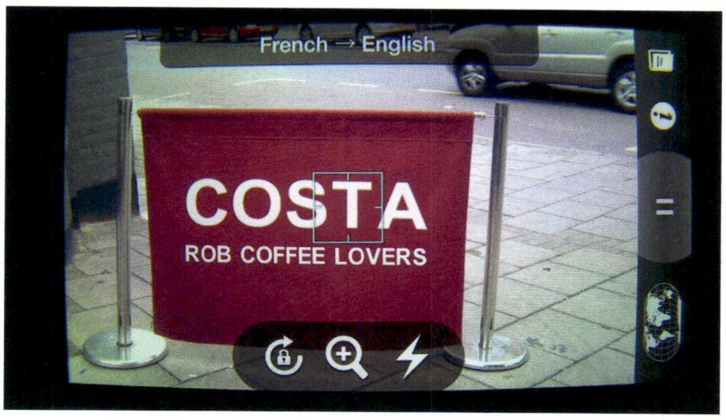
French → English
COSTA
ROB COFFEE LOVERS

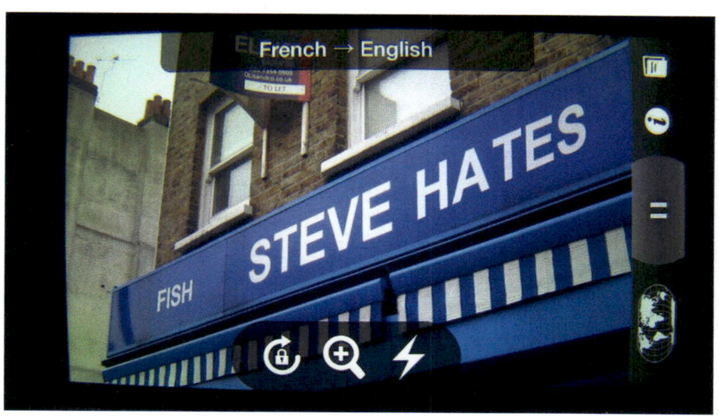
French → English
STEVE HATES
FISH

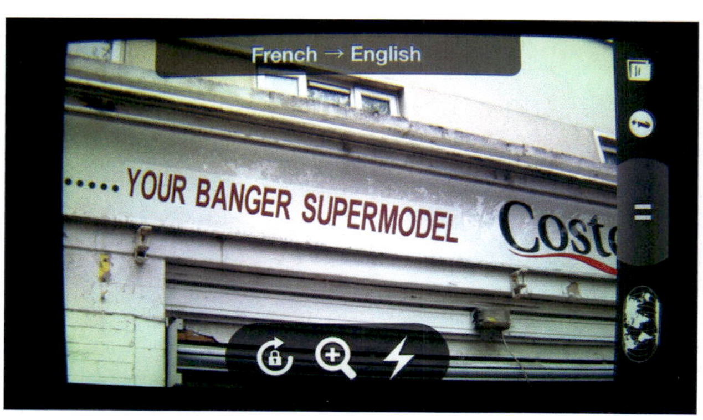
French → English
YOUR BANGER SUPERMODEL

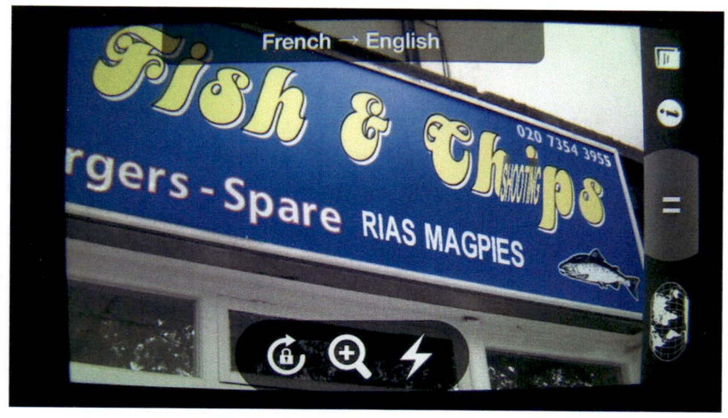
French → English
Fish & Chips
020 7354 3955
rgers - Spare RIAS MAGPIES

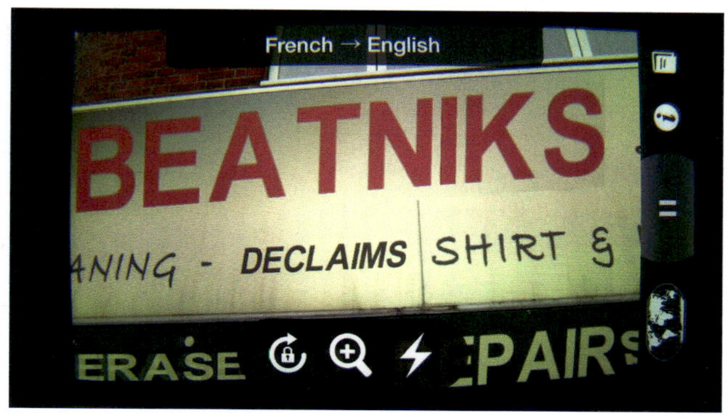
French → English
BEATNIKS
NING - DECLAIMS SHIRT &
ERASE EPAIRS

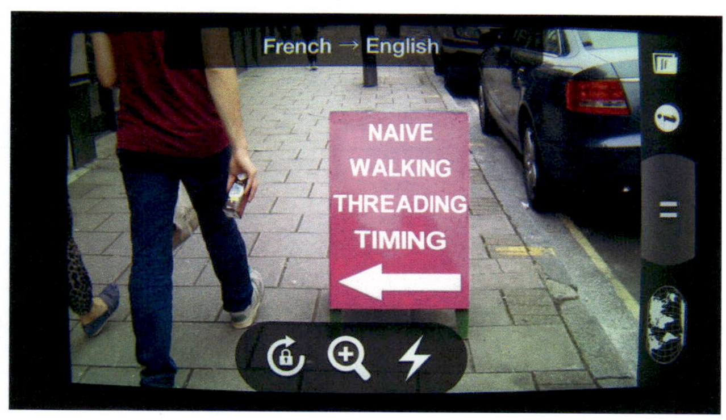
French → English
NAIVE
WALKING
THREADING
TIMING

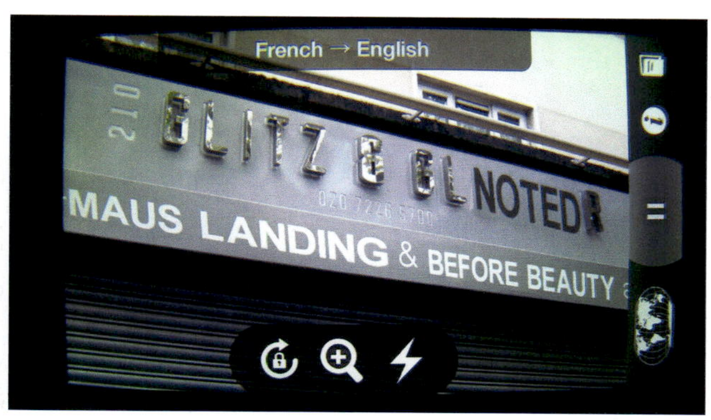
French → English
210
GLITZ & GL NOTED
MAUS LANDING & BEFORE BEAUTY

John Smith

Steve Hates Fish

2015, HD-Video, Endlosschleife, 5-minütiger Zyklus

Vor einigen Jahren war ich fasziniert von *Word Lens*, einer neu entwickelten Übersetzer-App für Smartphones. Wenn man die Kamera des Telefons auf einen Text richtete, versuchte die App, ihn in die gewählte Sprache zu übersetzen und den übersetzten Text in das Bild integriert grafisch auf dem Bildschirm des Telefons darzustellen. Die App war erstaunlich leistungsfähig, aber am meisten interessierte es mich, wenn sie etwas falsch machte.

Steve Hates Fish ist ein Auftragswerk für ein Filmprogramm, das im Schaufenster der Galerie Tintype in Nord-London gezeigt wurde. Nach Einbruch der Dunkelheit sahen es von der Straße aus sowohl Besucher, die ganz gezielt dorthin gekommen waren, als auch zufällig vorbeigehende Passanten. Während ich den Bildschirm meines Smartphones filmte, forderte ich *Word Lens* auf, vom Französischen ins Englische zu übersetzen und verwirrte die Software absichtlich, indem ich die Kamera auf die englischsprachigen Ladenschilder in der Essex Road richtete, die belebte Einkaufsstraße, in der sich die Galerie befand. In dieser mit Informationen überladenen Umgebung wucherten überall Schilder, und die rastlose Software tat ihr Bestes, um ihre Aufgabe zu erfüllen, indem sie für ihre Übersetzung nach französischen Wörtern suchte, wo es keine gab.

J.S.

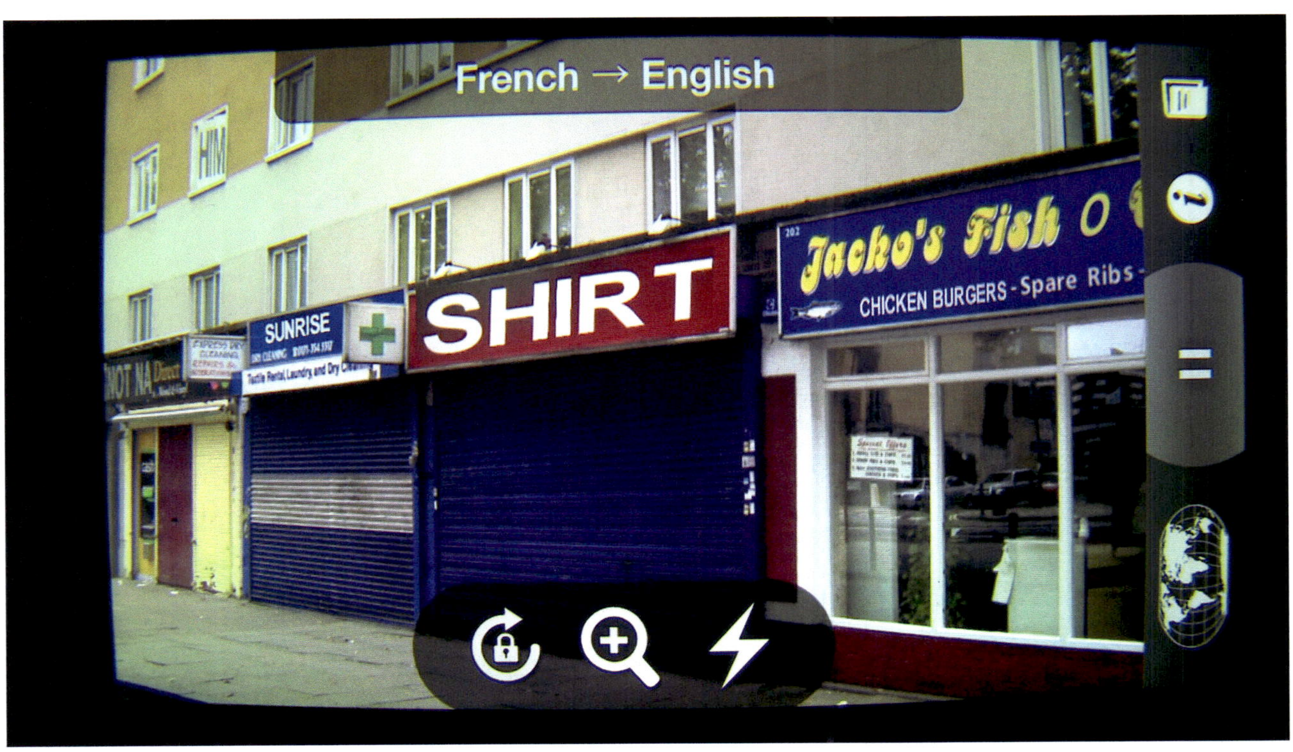

Steve Hates Fish

Steve Hates Fish ist ein Paradebeispiel für John Smiths Talent, die Zuschauer*innen mit geringsten Mitteln und unaufwendiger Postproduktion, aber einer einzigen klugen Idee zum Schmunzeln zu bringen. Wie für Smith üblich, beruht auch der vordergründige Humor dieser Arbeit wieder auf einem komplexeren Hintergrund. Mit dem immer schnelleren Voranschreiten technologischer Entwicklungen werden ebenfalls die mahnenden Stimmen in Bezug auf Algorithmen, die im zunehmenden Maß in unser alltägliches Leben eingreifen, vehementer. Hollywood-Filme prophezeien in regelmäßigen Abständen eine bevorstehende Machtübernahme von Künstlichen Intelligenzen über die Menschheit. Bei der Betrachtung von John Smiths Video scheint diese Gefahr noch in weiter Ferne und die K.I. mit ihrem fehlerhaften und zwanghaften Versuch, Übersetzungen zu finden, fast schon sympathisch human: Smith filmt eine Reihe von Ladenschildern inmitten von London und verlangt von der Künstlichen Intelligenz in Form einer Smartphone-App eine Übersetzung aus dem Französischen ins Englische. Diese versucht nun in dem Vorgefundenen einen (vorprogrammierten) Sinn zu finden. Die App kann sich einfach nicht damit abfinden, dass sie scheinbar keine französischen Wörter im Stadtbild entdecken kann und die Beschriftungen in der bereits vorhandenen englischen Sprache einfach gelesen werden könnten wie sie sind. Eine menschliche Eigenschaft, welche man in der Psychologie auch als *confirmation bias* bezeichnet. *Steve Hates Fish* verbildlicht damit im wahrsten Sinne des Wortes, dass Irren nicht nur menschlich ist.

D.B.

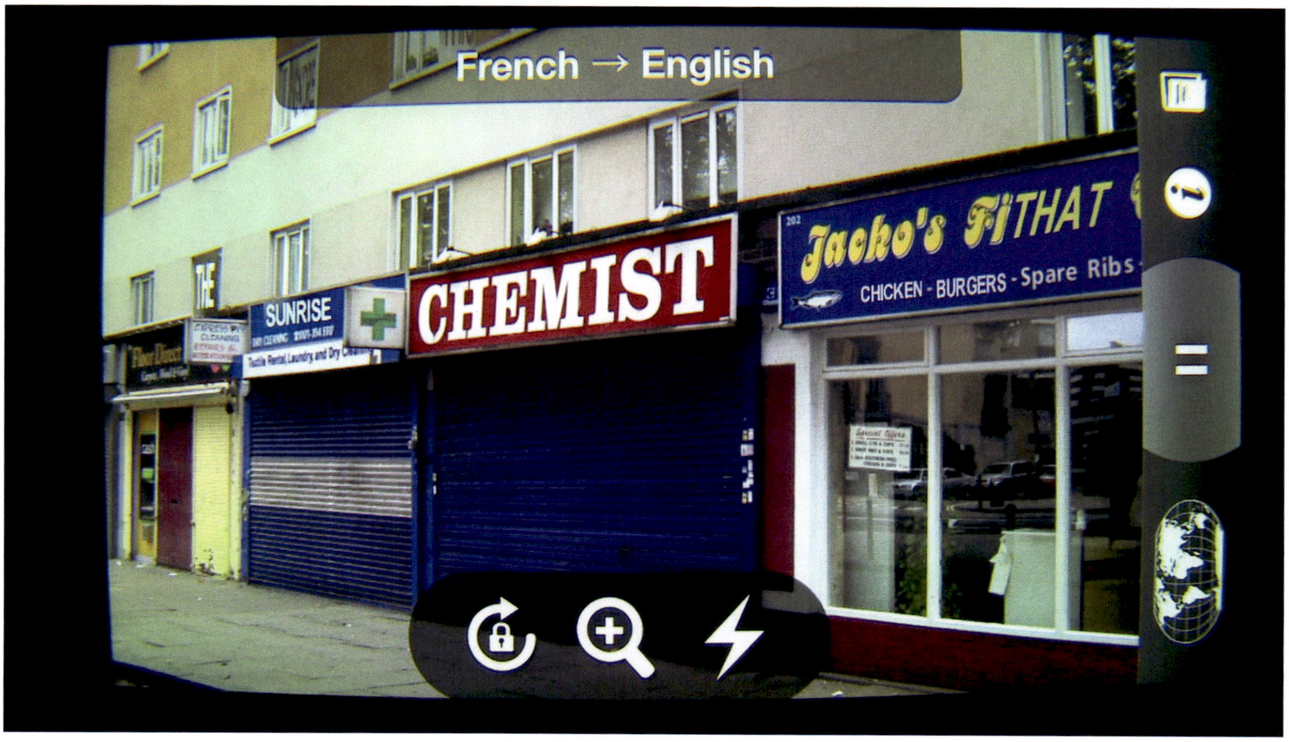

John Smith

Who Are We?

2016, HD video, 4 minutes

In the months leading up to the UK's referendum on EU membership, the acute divisions in British society became more and more evident. Watching BBC Television's topical debate programme *Question Time* four weeks before the referendum, I was dismayed by the extent of the crude nationalism and outright xenophobia displayed by many members of the audience and the panel of experts. Why were they so angry, and so certain that leaving the EU would resolve the nation's problems? When the programme's presenter pointed to someone at the back of the room and invited a question from 'You sir, up there, on the far right' I knew that I had to make a video work from this material.

J.S.

Who Are We? initially appears to be a clip summarising an episode of the BBC's political debate programme *Question Time*, which could have been posted on a platform like YouTube. John Smith has condensed the television show, which features panels of experts and integrates audience members into its discussions, from its actual length of one hour to just under four minutes. However, the editing has not been carried out with the aim of presenting its content in concentrated form. When presenter David Dimbleby repeatedly responds to the thunderous applause in reaction to a comment from the audience by inviting a person to speak with the identical words – 'You sir, up there, on the far right.' – it becomes clear that Smith has intervened more substantially through his editing. The artist has converted the show, which is recorded live and is otherwise broadcast in its full length after its post-production process, into the exact opposite. With the repetition of 'far right', originally actually used to describe a location, Smith additionally evokes an association with the political position known under that name by combining it with a deliberately chosen selection of clips. The actual debate, which was supposed to deal with the Brexit vote that would be carried out four weeks later, tended to become fixated on the issue of immigration from the very beginning. In combination with the affirmative applause, the statements of the men emphatically pleading their case for Brexit – one from the audience and one from the panel of experts – seem to reinforce one another in an echo chamber shortly before the end, until they finally remain stuck like a broken record. As at the beginning of the film, Smith finally once again uses the *Who Are We?* of the work's title, a question supposedly answered constantly throughout the programme but actually continuously avoided, to challenge us to occupy ourselves not just with the political situation in the United Kingdom, but more universally with the definition of a national identity.

D.B.

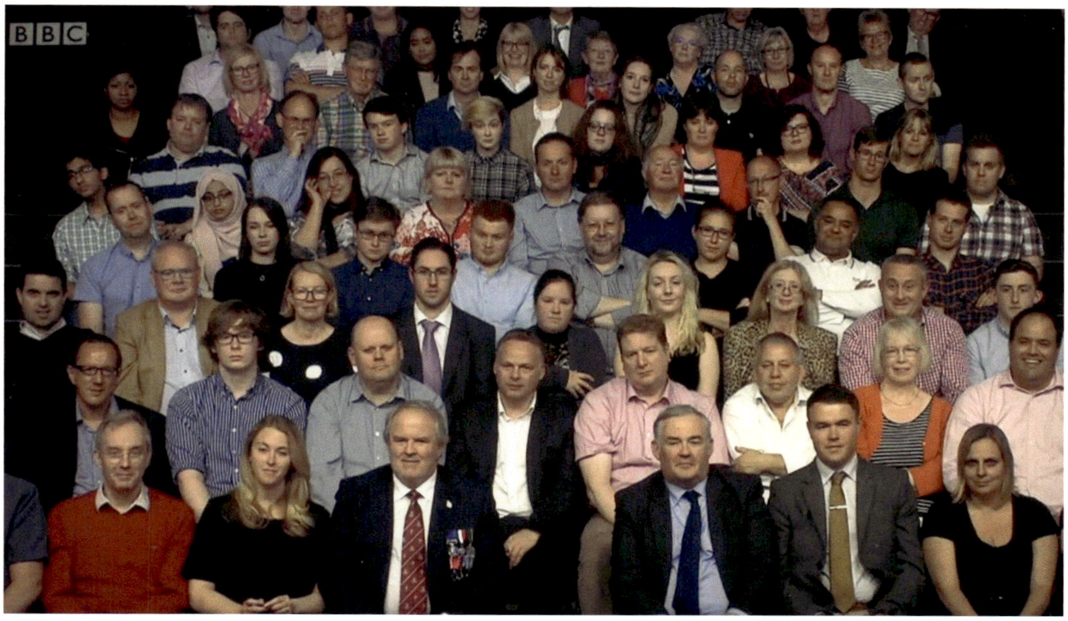
BBC

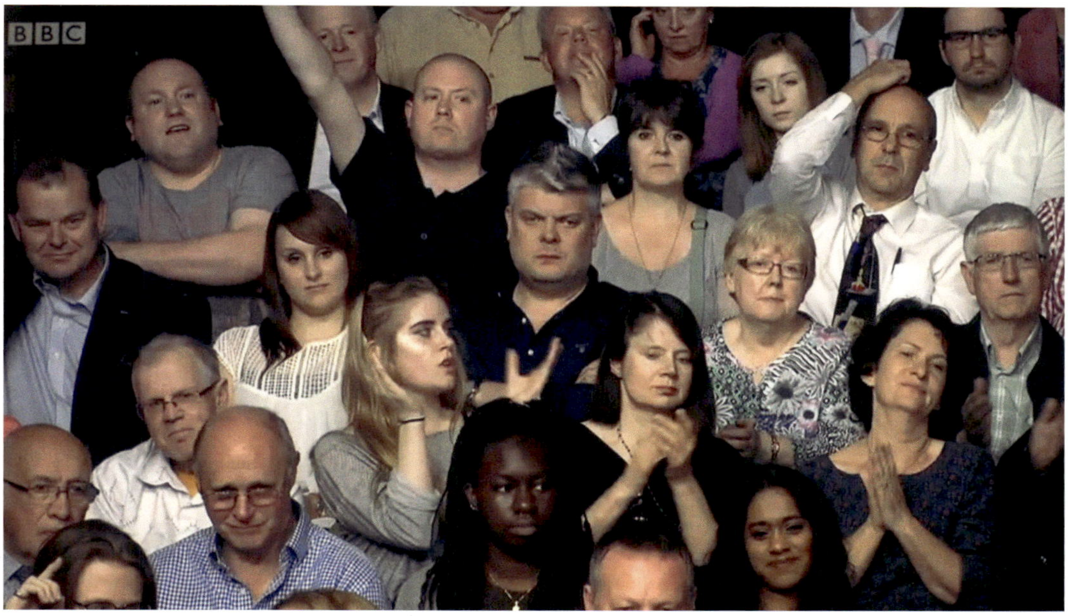
BBC

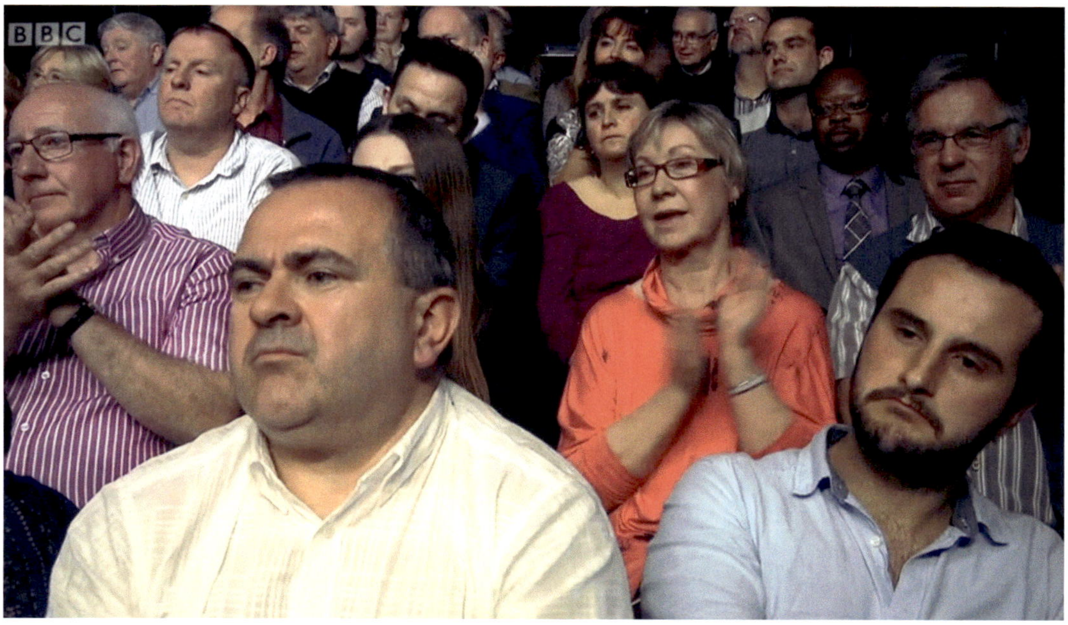
BBC

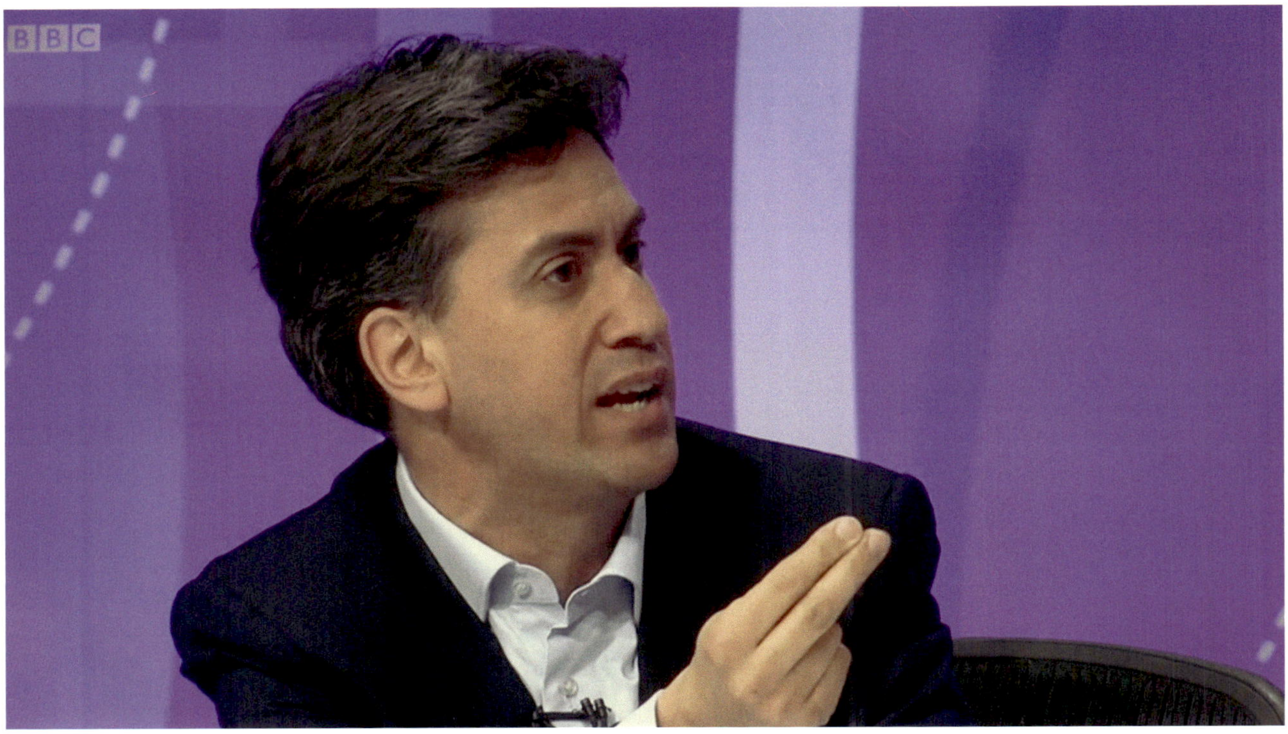

You can't actually tell us the country we're going to be like. Which country would it be like? Just tell us the country. Canada, Albania, Norway, Switzerland?

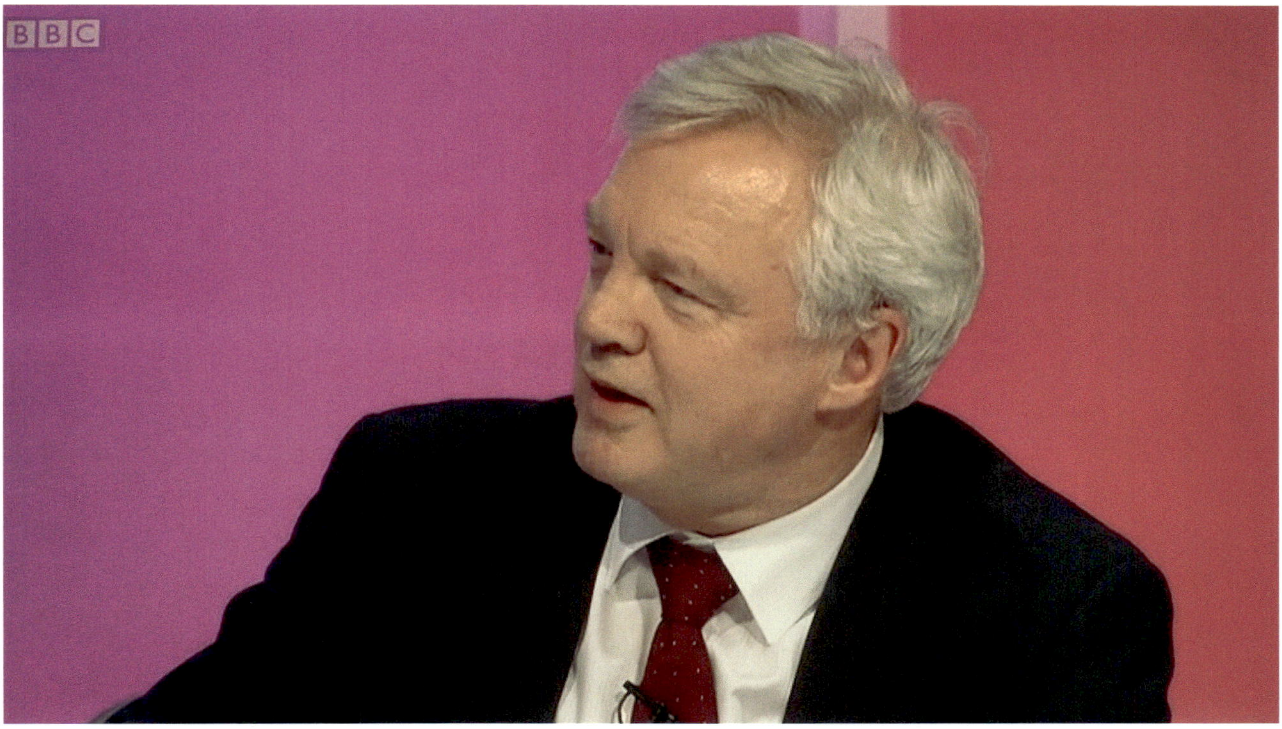

The country that we're going to be like is Great Britain.

John Smith

Who Are We?

2016, HD-Video, 4 Minuten

In den Monaten vor dem Referendum über die EU-Mitgliedschaft des Vereinigten Königreichs wurden die akuten Spaltungen in der britischen Gesellschaft immer deutlicher. Als ich vier Wochen vor dem Referendum die aktuelle Diskussionssendung *Question Time* im BBC-Fernsehen verfolgte, war ich bestürzt über das Ausmaß des plumpen Nationalismus und der unverhohlenen Fremdenfeindlichkeit, die viele Zuschauer*innen und Mitglieder des Expert*innengremiums an den Tag legten. Warum waren sie so wütend und so sicher, dass ein Austritt aus der EU die Probleme der Nation lösen würde? Als der Moderator der Sendung auf jemanden im hinteren Teil des Raums zeigte und ihn aufforderte, seine Frage zu stellen, indem er sagte, „Bitte, der Herr dort oben, ganz rechts außen“, da wusste ich, dass ich aus diesem Material eine Videoarbeit machen musste.

J.S.

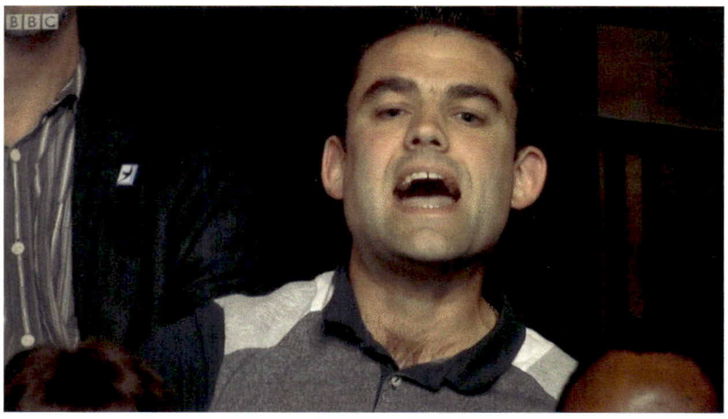

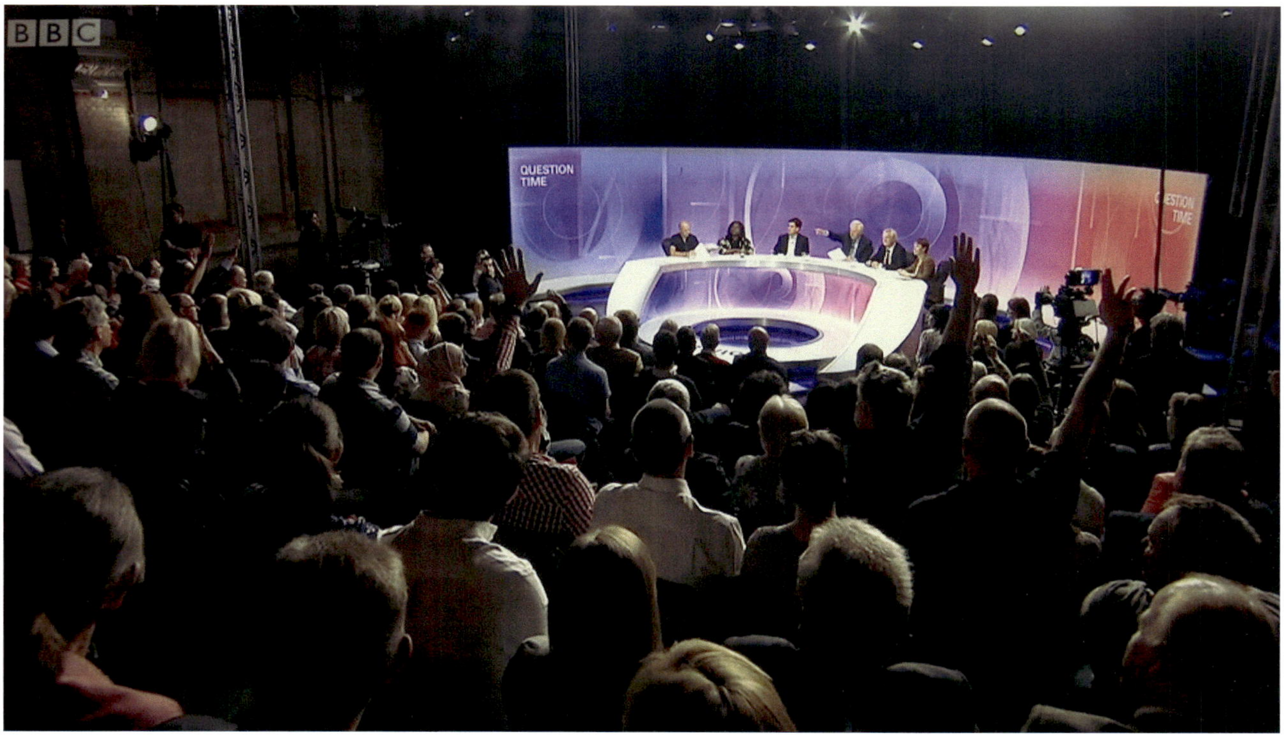

Who Are We?

Zu Beginn wirkt *Who Are We?* wie ein zusammenfassender Clip der politischen Diskussionsrunde *Question Time* des britischen Senders BBC, der so auch auf einer Plattform wie YouTube zur Verfügung gestellt worden sein könnte. John Smith verdichtet hier die tatsächlich einstündige Fernsehsendung mit einer Expert*innenrunde und in die Diskussion involvierten Zuschauer*innen auf knappe vier Minuten. Es handelt sich dabei aber nicht um einen Zusammenschnitt mit dem Ziel einer inhaltlichen Konzentration: Als der Moderator David Dimbleby nach tosendem Applaus als Reaktion auf einen Publikumskommentar wiederholt mit dem gleichen Satz: „Bitte, der Herr dort oben, ganz rechts außen", eine Person auffordert sich zu äußern, wird deutlich, dass Smith bei der Bearbeitung bedeutend mehr eingegriffen hat. Die in Echtzeit aufgenommene und sonst in der Postproduktion ungekürzt gesendete Show konstruiert der Künstler in das genaue Gegenteil um. Mit der Wiederholung „Far right", die ursprünglich eigentlich als eine verortende Deskription gemeint ist, ruft John Smith, im Zusammenspiel mit gezielt ausgewählten Schnipseln, zusätzlich die Assoziation mit der gleichlautenden politischen Haltung hervor. Die eigentliche Diskussionsrunde, die sich mit der Entscheidung des Brexits, die vier Wochen später konkret folgen wird, auseinandersetzen soll, tendiert von Beginn an stark dazu sich auf die Thematik der Immigration zu versteifen. Die ausdrücklich für den Brexit plädierenden Aussagen der Männer, einmal aus dem Publikum und einmal aus der Expert*innenrunde, scheinen sich mit zustimmendem Beifall in Smiths Version kurz vor Ende gegenseitig hochzuschaukeln, bis sie dann wie eine springende Schallplatte hängenbleiben. Wie zum Einstieg des Films fordert Smith uns mit der titelgebenden Frage *Who Are We?* – die in der Sendung nur vermeintlich ständig beantwortet, aber eigentlich permanent umschifft wird – zuletzt noch einmal auf, sich nicht nur mit der politischen Lage in Großbritannien, sondern sich universell mit der Definition einer nationalen Identität auseinanderzusetzen.

D.B.

John Smith

Jour de Fête

2017, HD video, seamless loop, 1 minute cycle

During the last week of July the village of Serviès-en-Val in the South of France celebrates its annual fête. A stage is erected in the main square and fairground attractions are installed, sometimes in surprising locations.

J.S.

At the beginning we see a crucifix. This image is accompanied by a pop-like droning and the sound of heavy impacts that are reminiscent of a whip's lashes and evoke an association with the Passion story.

As the framing of the scene expands, we see that a girl and a boy are each hitting a boxing machine at a fair while a little girl and a woman watch them. The girl evidently achieves the highest possible number of points, eliciting a pained groan of 'aaaahhhr' from the device. However, she has apparently also hurt herself hitting it, although she just laughs this off.

Here Smith seems to be bringing the story of Christ's suffering – the point of reference for Christianity's highest holidays – into the present. And within this approximately one-minute sequence, which repeats in a loop, he raises every question of faith that we could ask ourselves, particularly in connection with the church. The vertical format alone, which is unusual for video works, already establishes a close connection with altar paintings, which are only rarely to be found in horizontal formats within sacred spaces. The combination of the crucifix and an annual fair can be seen as a humorous and clever questioning of Christian holidays and the way we celebrate them today – more like a funfair than an occasion for devotion. Why do we celebrate suffering? The figure of Christ on the cross is turned towards us and the fair's visitors the entire time, though, interestingly, he is looking neither at us nor the people at his feet but towards the heavens. And the fundamental question is raised: what do we believe in? What does this Christian tradition and the institution of the church still have to do with the present and the lives of us people today?

T.I.

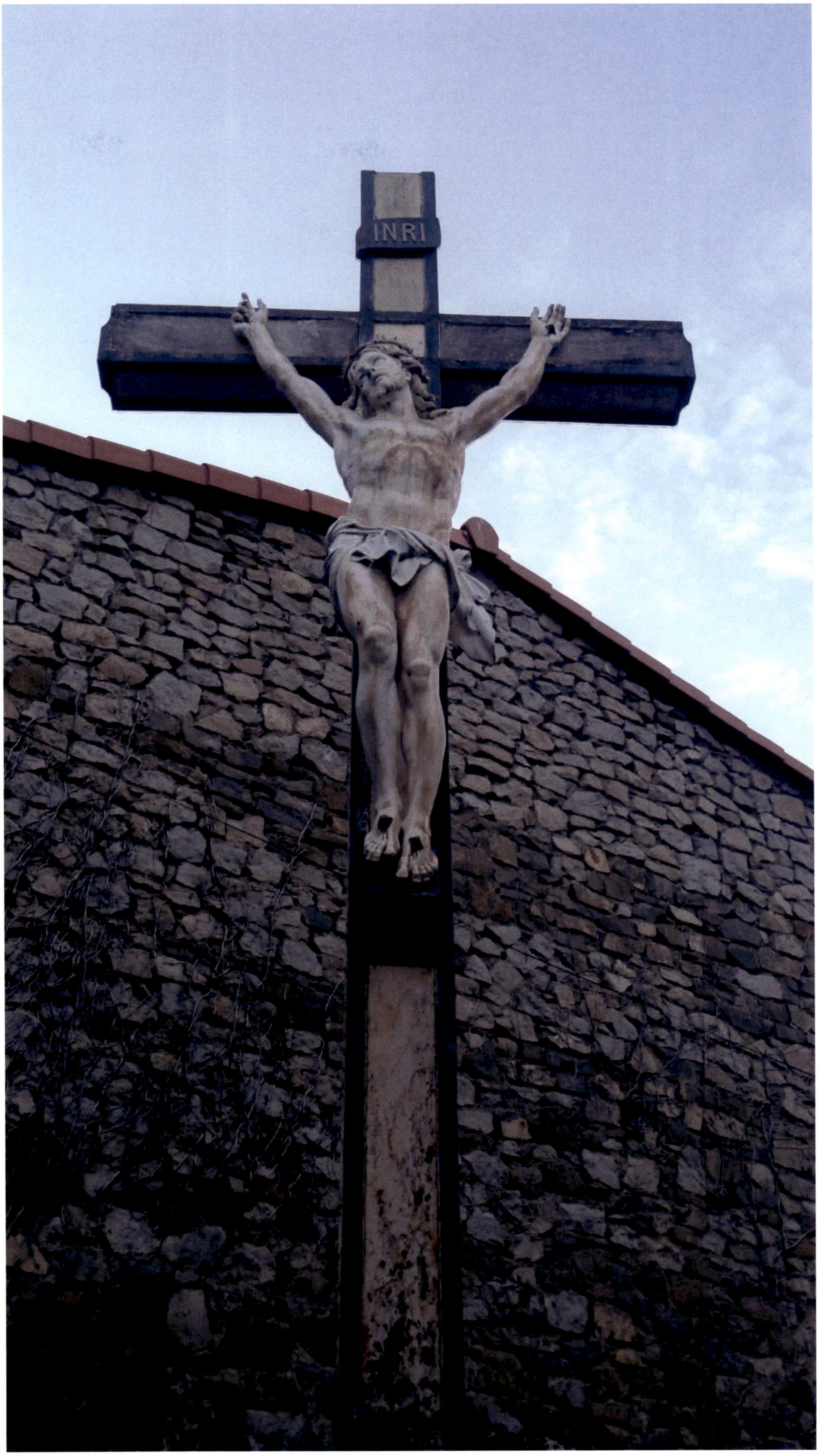
INRI

John Smith

Jour de Fête

2017, HD-Video, Endlosschleife, 1-minütiger Zyklus

Am letzten Wochenende im Juli feiert das südfranzösische Dorf Serviès-en-Val jedes Jahr sein Dorffest. Auf dem größten Platz gibt es eine Bühne und es werden Jahrmarktsattraktionen aufgestellt – manchmal an überraschenden Orten.

J.S.

Zu Beginn sehen wir ein Kruzifix. Dieses Bild wird begleitet von poppigem Gedudel und dem Geräusch satter Schläge, die an Peitschenhiebe erinnern und eine Assoziation zur Passionsgeschichte hervorrufen.

Mit Vergrößerung des Bildausschnitts können wir sehen, dass auf einem Jahrmarkt ein Mädchen und ein Junge jeweils auf einen Boxautomaten einschlagen, ein kleines Mädchen und eine Frau schauen ihnen dabei zu. Das Mädchen erreicht offenbar die Höchstpunktzahl und entlockt dem Gerät ein schmerzstöhnendes „Aaaahhhr". Allerdings hat sie sich wohl selbst bei dem Schlag wehgetan, lacht jedoch nur darüber.

Smith scheint hier die Leidensgeschichte Christi – Bezugspunkt der höchsten christlichen Festtage – in die Gegenwart zu bringen. Und wirft in dieser etwa einminütigen Sequenz, die sich im Loop wiederholt, sämtliche Glaubensfragen, die man sich stellen kann, insbesondere in Bezug auf die Kirche, auf. Allein das für Videoarbeiten untypische Hochformat stellt eine enge Verknüpfung zu Altarbilder her, die im sakralen Raum nur selten im Querformat zu finden sind. Die Kombination von Kruzifix und Jahrmarkt kann als humorvolle und kluge Hinterfragung christlicher Feiertage und die Art, wie wir sie heute begehen, angesehen werden. Eher mit Rummel, als mit Andacht. Warum feiern wir das Leiden? Der Christus am Kruzifix ist uns und den Jahrmarktbesucher*innen die ganze Zeit zugewandt, doch schaut er interessanterweise nicht uns oder die Menschen zu seinen Füßen an, sondern in den Himmel. Und es stellt sich die Grundsatzfrage: Woran glauben wir? Was hat diese christliche Tradition und Institution Kirche noch mit der Gegenwart und dem Leben von uns Menschen heute zu tun?

T.I.

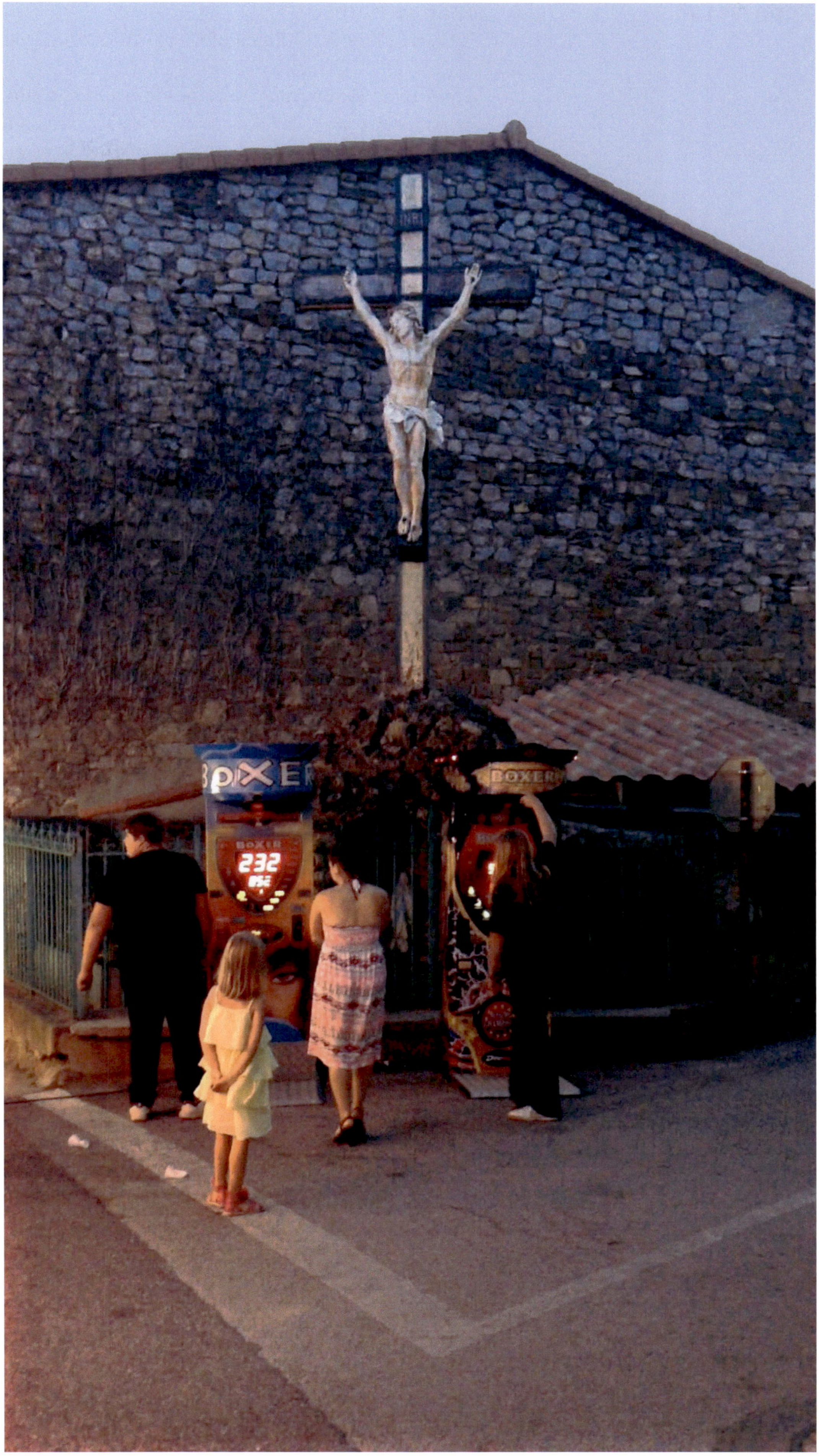
BOXER
232
BOXER

John Smith

A State of Grace

2019, HD video, 3 minutes

As a frequent flyer with a well-known budget airline I became very familiar with the company's safety instructions, which were displayed prominently on the back of every seat. Confused about the intended significance of the enigmatic diagrams, I started to ascribe them with my own invented meanings. I decided to make a film which explored details of the card in close-up and spent several years trying to photograph it whenever I took a flight. Unfortunately something always went wrong. Eventually I gave up, but was later surprised to discover that an identical safety card was available for sale on eBay, enabling me to photograph its bizarre diagrams in detail and tell my own story about the perils of flying.

J.S.

At first we suddenly hear the hum of the turbines from the interior of an airplane and the typical 'ding dong' signal that tells us to put on our seat belts. After that, the film cuts to the visuals on the safety cards found in every seat pocket. The images are accompanied by John Smith's voice. He tells us about his first trip by plane to Ireland, during which he still paid close attention to the safety warnings. Because, according to Smith, Ireland is a country where Christianity and particularly the Catholic Church are very important, he read the little images on the safety card as a form of religious instruction presented by the Catholic Church. The depiction of the male figure who is wearing a life jacket and whose head is bowed slightly becomes, in a sense, the symbol of the narrator, because the figure's facial expression and pose seem to reflect the inner states of Smith. Above the clouds, the images inspire him to begin contemplating his sins, and this causes him to feel very uneasy.

This reinterpretation of the safety card is reminiscent of the stories in children's books. However, the illustrations of the narrative which Smith creates out of his experience have nothing to do with the images' actual function. Within our culture, their content is subject to a specifically defined interpretation as safety instructions; individual interpretations actually ought to be ruled out. Nonetheless, Smith overturns this predetermined reading. By embedding them within a new context, he transforms the universal, visualised instructions for what to do in an emergency into individualised depictions of his personal world of inner feelings. In doing so he illustrates the fact that even specifically defined pictorial content can be deconstructed. Accordingly there is no unambiguous and absolute link between image and message. Pursuing this line of thought further, we arrive at the essence of the interpretation of images, which is ultimately subjective.

T.I.

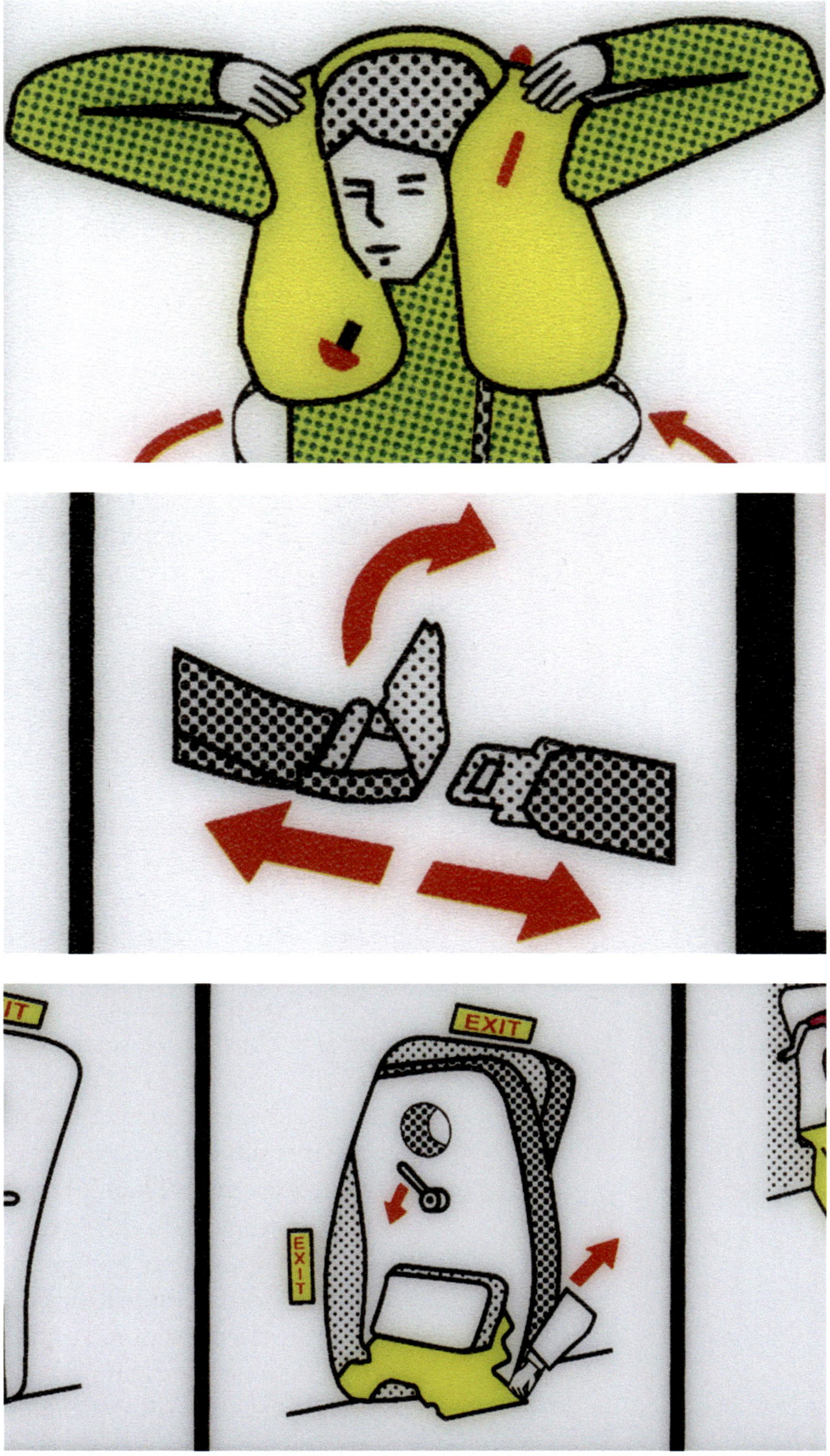

There was no way out. I started to panic. My stomach was in knots. Now I was hearing voices, why were they tempting me so with their perfumes and their duty-free spirits – how could I shut them out? The ways of the world were truly wicked.

John Smith

A State of Grace

2019, HD-Video, 3 Minuten

Als Vielflieger bei einer bekannten Billigfluglinie war ich mit den Sicherheitshinweisen des Unternehmens sehr gut vertraut. Sie waren deutlich sichtbar auf der Rückseite jedes Sitzes angebracht. Verwirrt darüber, was die rätselhaften Diagramme wohl bedeuten mochten, begann ich, ihnen meine eigenen, erfundenen Bedeutungen zuzuschreiben. Ich entschied mich, einen Film zu machen, der die Details dieser Tafel in Nahaufnahmen behandeln sollte und versuchte über mehrere Jahre, jedes Mal, wenn ich im Flugzeug saß, sie abzufilmen. Leider ist immer etwas schiefgegangen. Schließlich gab ich auf, entdeckte später aber zu meiner Überraschung, dass eine identische Sicherheitstafel bei eBay angeboten wurde, was es mir ermöglichte, Detailaufnahmen von den bizarren Diagrammen zu machen und meine eigene Geschichte von den Gefahren des Fliegens zu erzählen.

J.S.

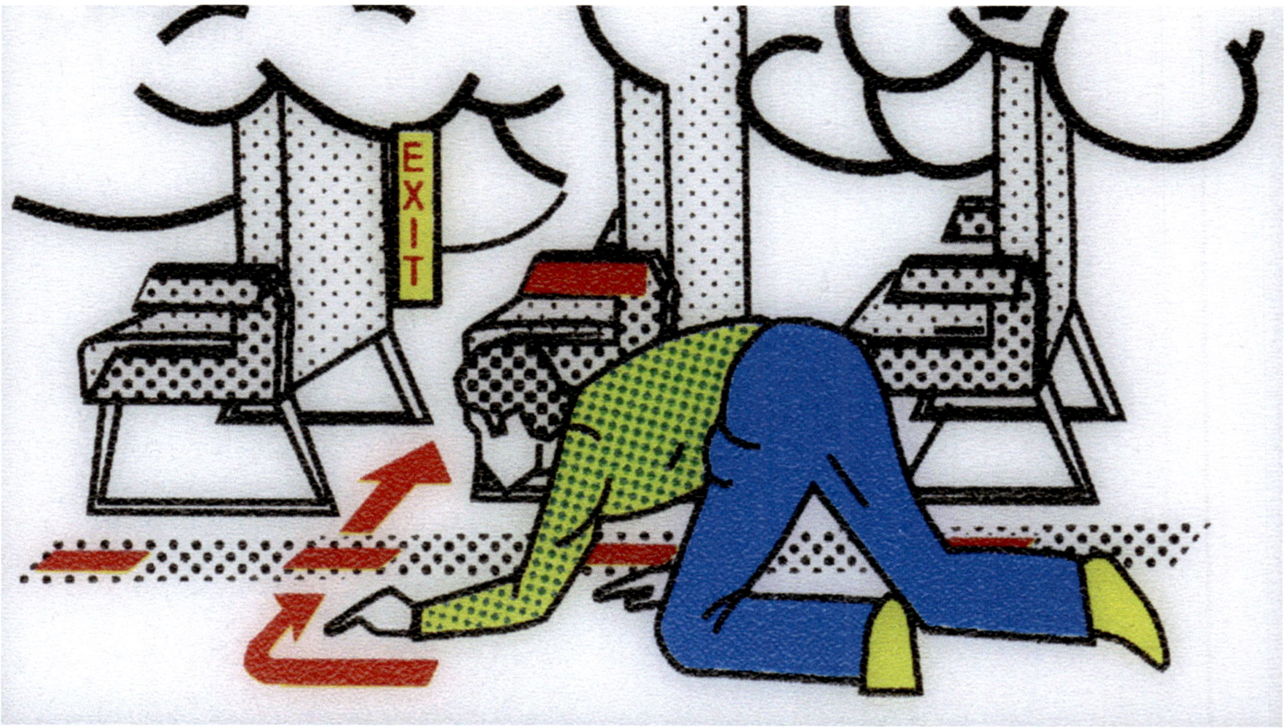

Too late to repent now, I was a miserable crawling degenerate destined to burn in hell.

A State of Grace

Zunächst hören wir unvermittelt das dröhnende Geräusch der Turbinen in einem Flugzeuginnenraum und das typische „Ding Dong"-Signal, das die Anschnallpflicht anzeigt. Im Folgenden werden bildliche Darstellungen der Safety Cards eingeblendet, die sich in jeder Sitztasche befinden. Begleitet werden die Bilder von der Stimme John Smiths. Er erzählt von seiner ersten Flugreise nach Irland, auf der er den Sicherheitshinweisen noch hohe Aufmerksamkeit schenkte. Da, so Smith, Irland ein Land ist, in dem das Christentum und die katholische Kirche im Besonderen sehr wichtig sind, liest er die Bildchen der Safety Card als eine Form religiöser Instruktionen der katholischen Kirche. Die Darstellung der männlichen Person mit Rettungsweste, die ihr Gesicht etwas nach unten neigt, wird gleichsam zum Symbol des Sprechers, da Gesichtsausdruck und Körperhaltung des Bildes die inneren Zustände Smiths widerzuspiegeln scheinen. Über den Wolken beginnt er – angeregt von den Abbildungen – über seine Sünden nachzudenken und fühlt sich dabei sehr unwohl.

Diese Uminterpretation der Safety Card erinnert an Geschichten in einem Kinderbuch. Doch haben die Illustrationen der Erzählung, die John Smith aus seinem Erlebnis macht, nichts mit der eigentlichen Funktion der Bilder zu tun. Diese erfahren innerhalb unseres Kulturkreises eine bestimmte zugewiesene inhaltliche Lesart als Sicherheitsinstruktionen; individuelle Auslegungen sollen eigentlich ausgeschlossen werden. Smith hebelt die festgelegte Deutung dennoch aus. Er verwandelt mittels des neuen Kontextes, in den er sie einbettet, die universellen, verbildlichten Anweisungen für Notfälle in besondere Abbildungen seiner individuellen inneren Gefühlswelten. Somit verdeutlicht er, dass selbst konkret definierte Bildinhalte dekonstruiert werden können. Es gibt folgerichtig keine eindeutige, absolute Verknüpfung von Bild und Botschaft. Verfolgt man diesen Gedanken weiter, stößt man auf den Kern der Deutung von Bildern, die letztlich subjektiv ist.

T.I.

John Smith

Covid Messages

2020, HD video, 22 minutes

In March 2020, as the Covid-19 pandemic started to claim its first lives in Britain, Prime Minister Boris Johnson held a televised press conference. In order to avoid infection, he advised the public to carry on with daily life as normal, but to regularly wash their hands with soap and water for as long as it took to sing *Happy Birthday* twice. This seemed to me to be a strange proposition – if it was concerned with washing for a specific duration, why hadn't he chosen a longer song that you only needed to sing once? And why choose an upbeat tune like *Happy Birthday*, surely a more sombre refrain would be more appropriate to the situation? This bizarre choice of music seemed to me like a magic spell, an incantation designed to keep the virus at bay. As a critique of the government's handling of the pandemic, *Covid Messages* builds upon this observation to create an imaginary scenario where the supernatural progressively takes hold.

J.S.

Rituals are standard features of magical actions and ways of thinking, and they are also recommended by psychologists for stressed workers. In a situation like the Corona pandemic, which represents an exceptional state of society, the conditions are good for resorting to behaviours like these.

With his special sense for the semantic diversity of the seemingly ordinary, John Smith has discovered this magical aspect in the British prime minister's press conferences and developed it into a story featuring uncanny and absurd events. The song *Happy Birthday* forms his point of departure. Smith has set it to music as a mix of Frédéric Chopin's 'Funeral March' (Piano Sonata No. 2 in B-flat minor, Op. 35) and a medieval chant. However, the magic does not work. The virus spreads.

The government's repeated misjudgements finally call the dead on to the scene, and they intervene after a new way of calculating the number of victims leads to a significant reduction in their number. The government thus appears to be in a position to bring the dead back to life, so to speak. This leads to even greater outrage among the spirits, whose interventions in the events of the press conferences become increasingly intense.

Smith has once again subverted medial reality in this film. He uses a few classic editing techniques to sketch a scenario that allows the drama of what is going on in society – which we have to picture to ourselves in terms of a dramaturgical background – to break through into the staged objectivity and routine of the press conferences.

U.F.

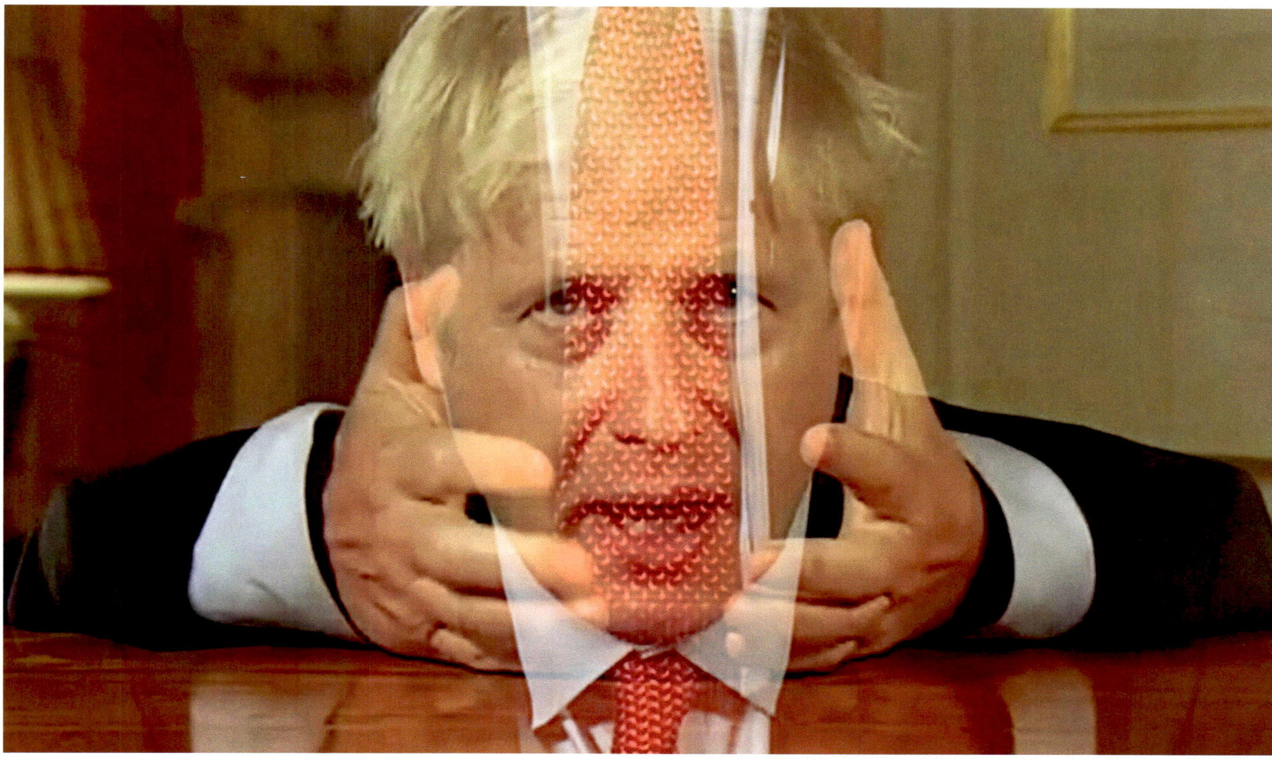

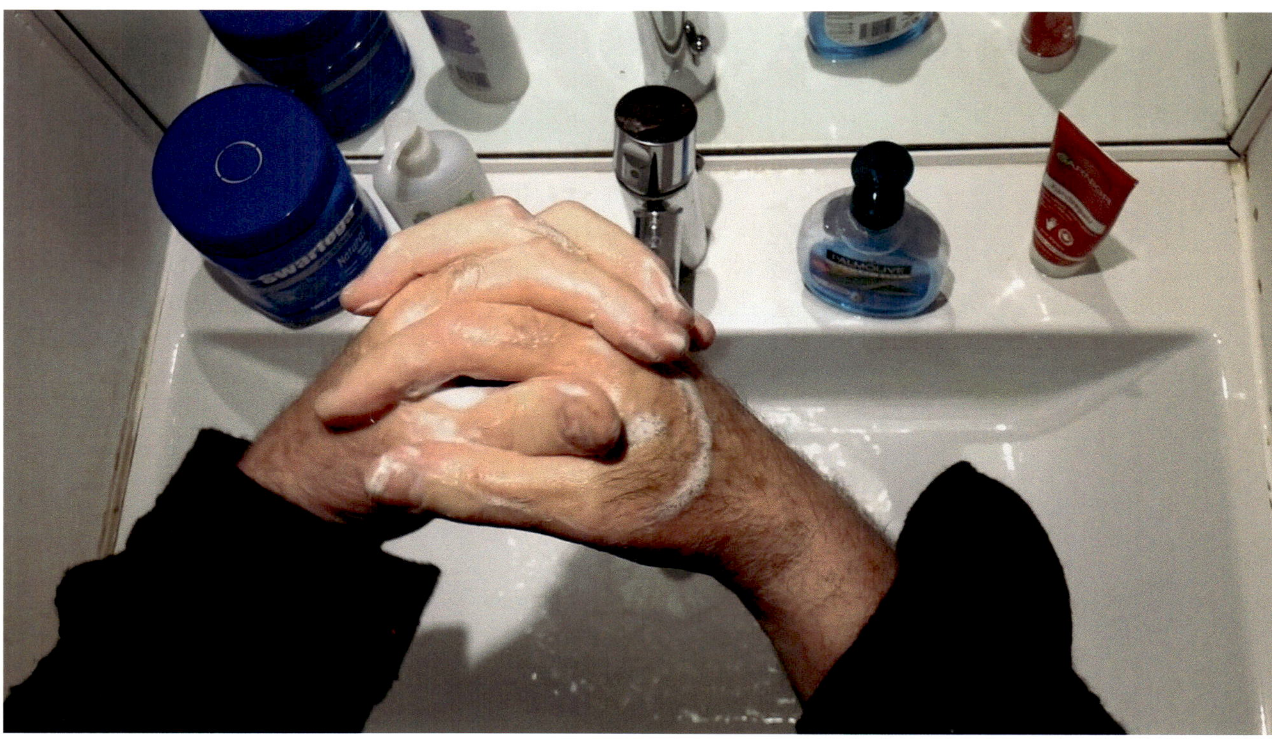

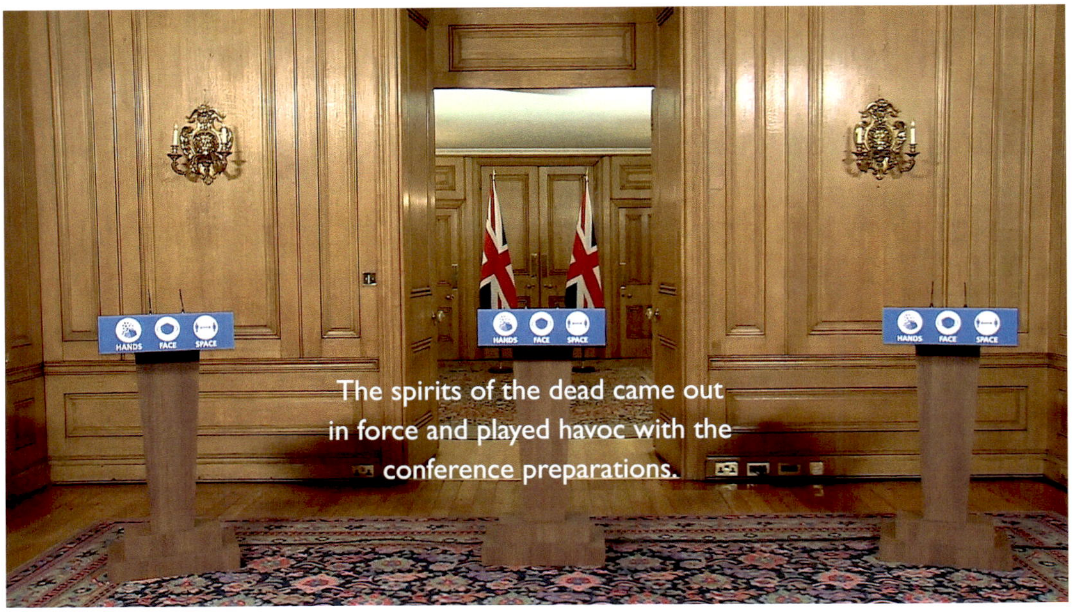
The spirits of the dead came out in force and played havoc with the conference preparations.

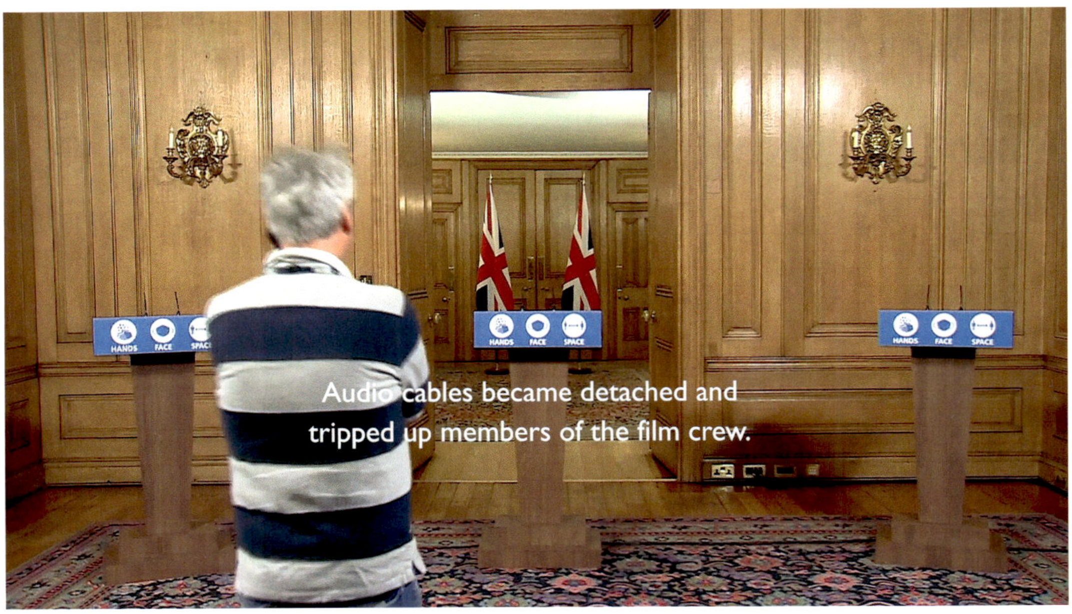
Audio cables became detached and tripped up members of the film crew.

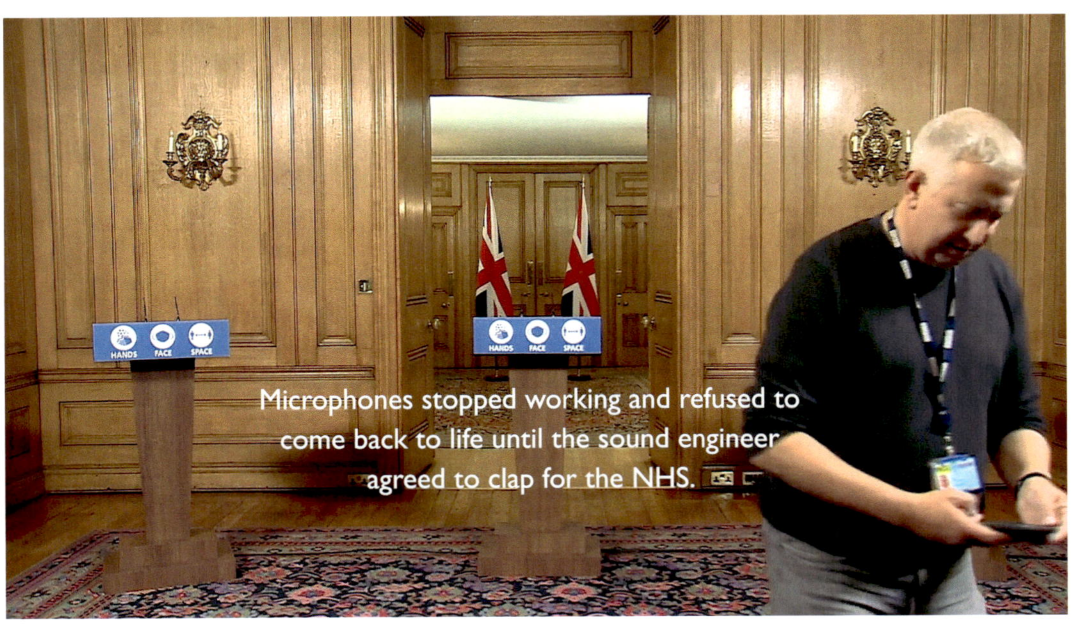
Microphones stopped working and refused to come back to life until the sound engineer agreed to clap for the NHS.

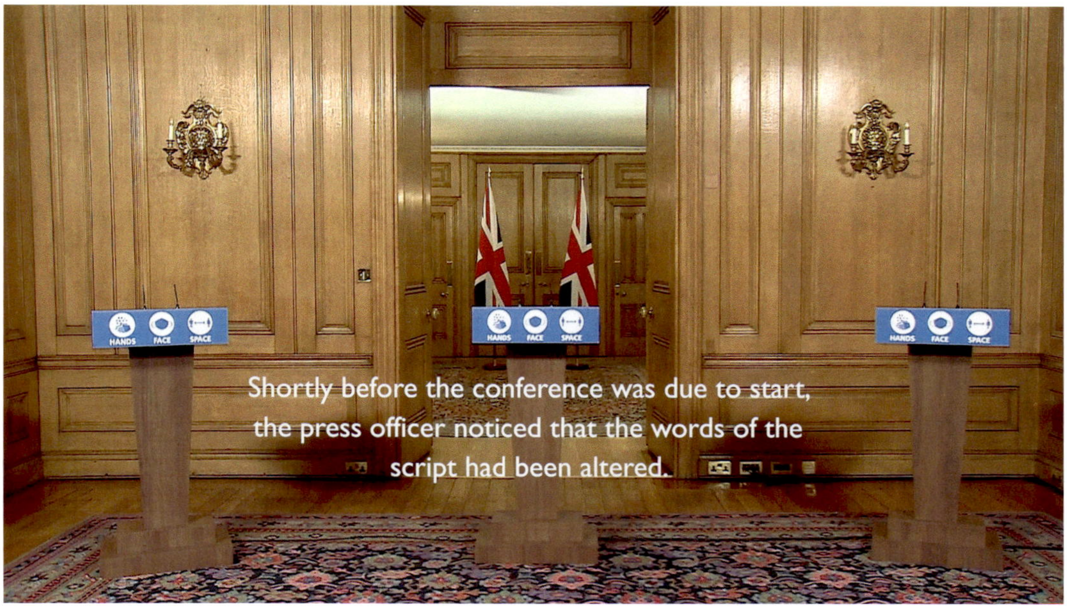
Shortly before the conference was due to start,
the press officer noticed that the words of the
script had been altered.

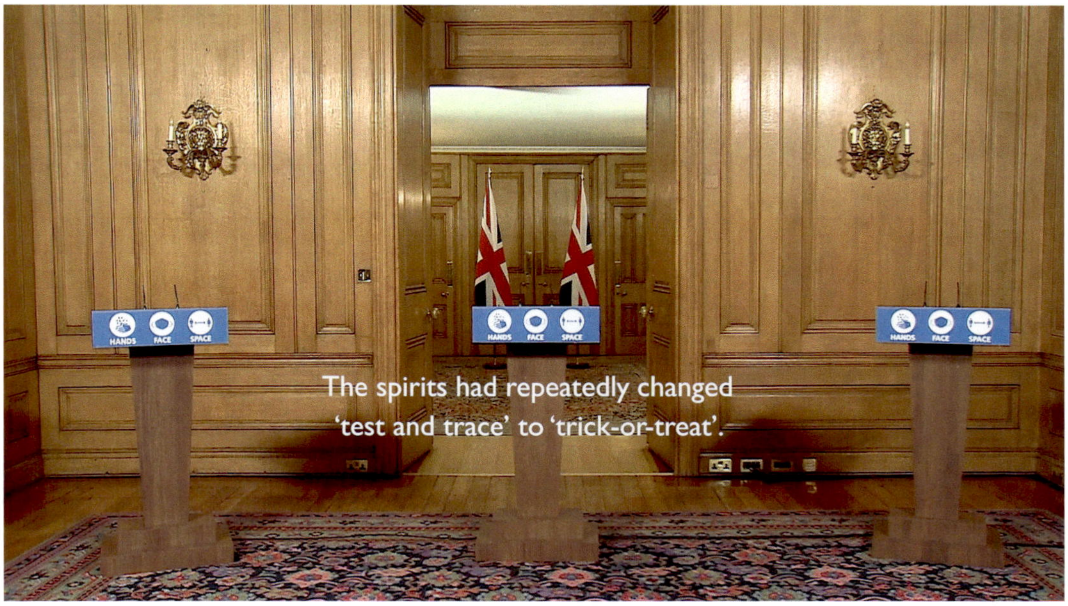
The spirits had repeatedly changed
'test and trace' to 'trick-or-treat'.

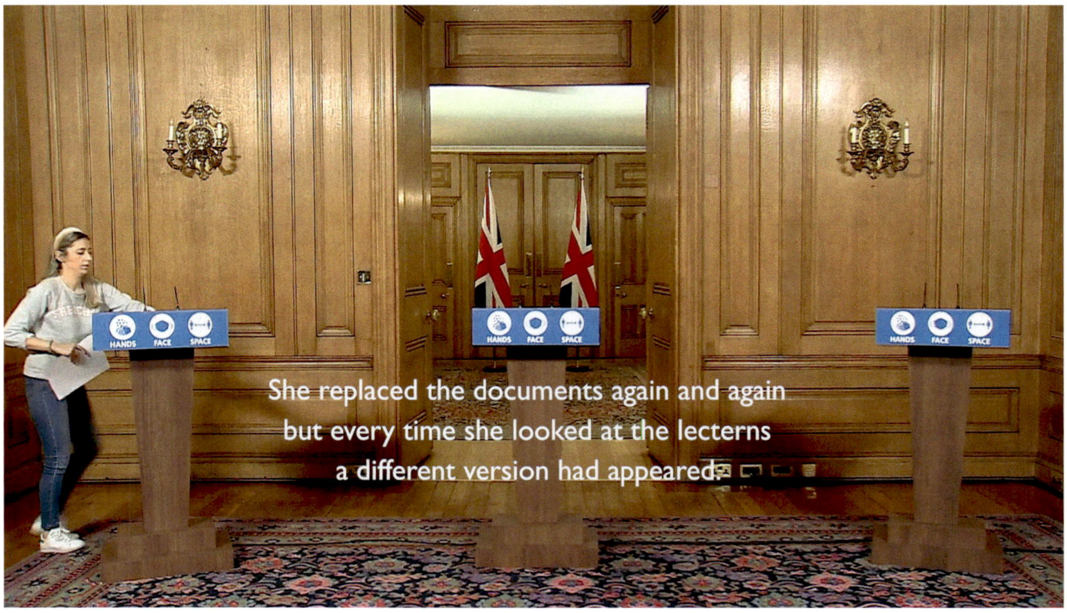
She replaced the documents again and again
but every time she looked at the lecterns
a different version had appeared.

John Smith

Covid Messages

2020, HD-Video, 22 Minuten

Als die Covid-19-Pandemie im März 2020 ihre ersten Opfer in Großbritannien forderte, hielt Premierminister Boris Johnson eine Fernseh-Pressekonferenz. Um Ansteckungen zu verhindern, so sagte er der Öffentlichkeit, solle man das tägliche Leben wie gewohnt fortsetzen, sich aber regelmäßig die Hände mit Wasser und Seife waschen, und zwar so lange, wie es dauert, zweimal *Happy Birthday* zu singen. Dieser Vorschlag wirkte seltsam. Wenn es um das Zeitmessen ging, warum hatte die Regierung dann nicht ein längeres Lied gewählt, dass man nur einmal singen müsste? Und warum war die Wahl auf eine fröhliche Melodie wie *Happy Birthday* gefallen, wo doch sicherlich ein düsterer Refrain der Situation viel eher angemessen wäre? Die Wasch- und Gesangsroutine war so bizarr, dass sie schon wie ein Zauberritual wirkte, eine Beschwörung, um das Virus in Schach zu halten. Als Kritik am Umgang der Regierung mit der Pandemie beruht *Covid Messages* auf dieser Beobachtung und entwirft ein Szenario, in welchem Zauberei und das Übernatürliche allmählich Einzug halten.

J.S.

Rituale sind feste Bestandteile magischer Handlungen und Denkweisen oder werden von Psychologen für gestresste Arbeitende empfohlen. In einer Situation wie der Corona-Pandemie, die einen Ausnahmezustand darstellt, sind die Voraussetzungen gut, auf solche Verhaltensweisen zurückzugreifen.

Mit seiner besonderen Sensibilität für die Bedeutungsvielfalt des scheinbar Alltäglichen hat John Smith in den Pressekonferenzen des britischen Premierministers diesen magischen Moment entdeckt und daraus eine Geschichte entwickelt, in der Unheimliches und Absurdes geschieht. Den Ausgangspunkt bildet das Lied *Happy Birthday*. John Smith intoniert es als Mix aus dem Trauermarsch von Frédéric Chopin (Klaviersonate Nr. 2 b-Moll op. 35) und einem mittelalterlichen Choral. Doch der Zauber wirkt nicht. Das Virus breitet sich aus.

Die wiederholten Fehleinschätzungen der Regierung rufen letztlich die Toten auf den Plan, die eingreifen, nachdem sich, durch eine Änderung der Berechnung der Opferzahlen, deren Höhe deutlich reduziert hat. Damit schien die Regierung in der Lage zu sein, Tote sozusagen ins Leben zurückzuholen. Das führt zu noch größerer Empörung der Geister, die immer intensiver in das Geschehen der Pressekonferenzen eingreifen.

Einmal mehr unterwandert John Smith in diesem Film die mediale Wirklichkeit. Mit wenigen klassischen Mitteln der Filmbearbeitung entwirft er ein Szenario, das die Dramatik des Geschehens in der Gesellschaft – das man sich als dramaturgischen Hintergrund vorstellen muss – in die inszenierte Sachlichkeit und Routine der Presstermine durchbrechen lässt.

U.F.

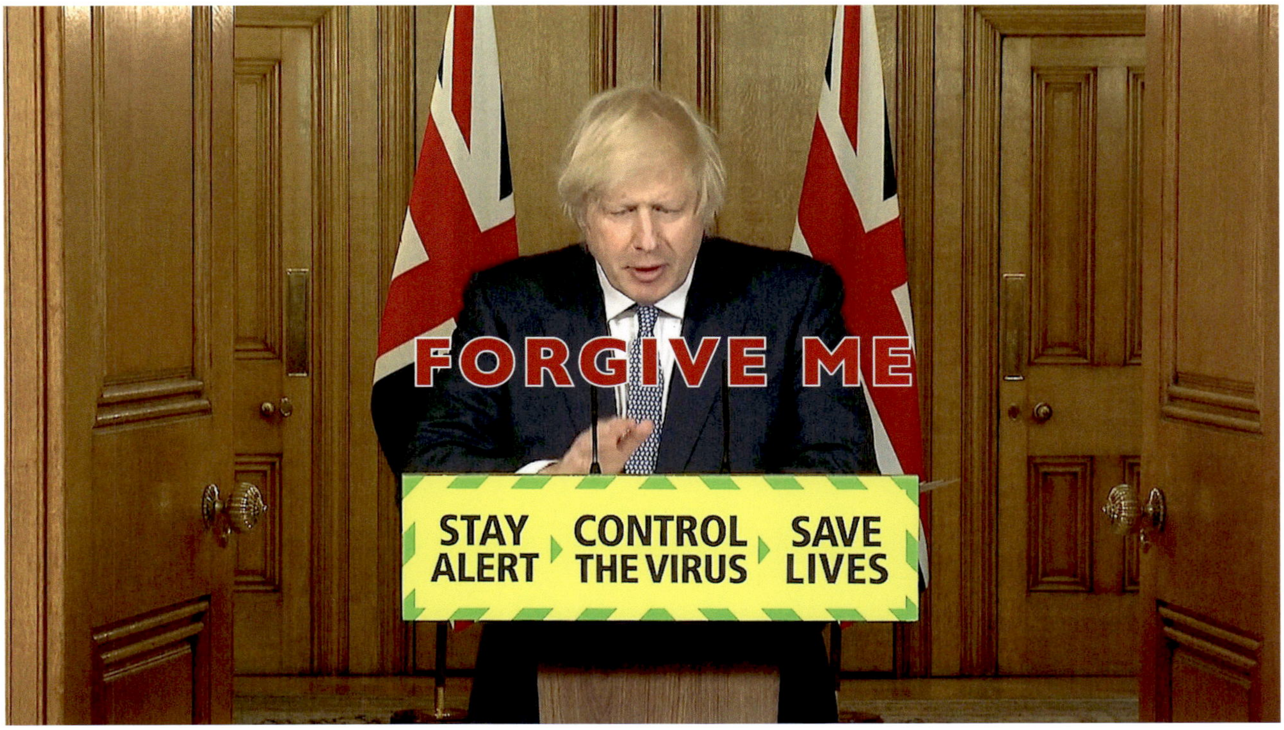
FORGIVE ME
STAY ALERT
CONTROL THE VIRUS
SAVE LIVES

John Smith

Record

2021, HD video, 1 minute

Record, featuring a visit to the University of East London by Prince Philip, the Duke of Edinburgh, was filmed on May 9th 2002 and edited on April 9th 2021. In addition to the probable record that the film describes, it also holds two personal records, both as my shortest film and the one that took the longest time to complete.

J.S.

John Smith's film *Record* causes us to experience an unbelievable range of emotions in just 60 seconds: from the grief of anticipating a tribute to Prince Philip, who died in the spring of 2021, to merriment and amusement when the video elicits a grin from us by taking an entirely unexpected turn.

In 2002 the prince visited the University of East London, where Smith was teaching. Smith organised security clearance and a press pass for himself to be able to film him. Smith refers to Philip's death in the film's subtitles – and, shortly thereafter, to the fact that he succeeded in capturing what is surely the closest close-up of His Royal Highness's ear. This humorous and nonetheless reverent handling of the Duke of Edinburgh's death would presumably have been entirely to the liking of Prince Philip, who was known for his progressive thinking and actions as well as his humour.

T.I.

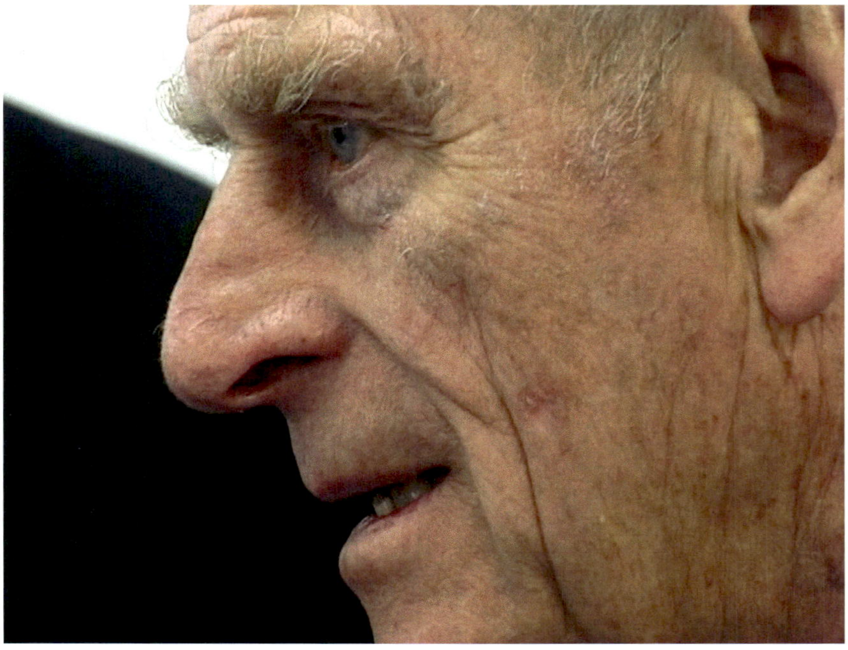

John Smith

Record

2021, HD-Video, 1 Minute

Record, ein Film, bei dem der Besuch von Prinz Philip, dem Duke of Edinburgh, in der University of East London im Mittelpunkt steht, wurde am 9. Mai 2002 gefilmt und an seinem Todestag, dem 9. April 2021, geschnitten. Nebst dem darin beschriebenen, wahrscheinlichen Rekord, stellt der Film auch zwei persönliche Rekorde auf. Zum einen ist er mein kürzester Film und zum anderen derjenige, dessen Fertigstellung am längsten gedauert hat.

J.S.

Der Film *Record* von John Smith lässt uns in nur etwa 60 Sekunden eine unglaubliche Bandbreite an Emotionen durchleben: Von Wehmut, aufgrund eines zu erwartenden Nachrufs auf den im Frühling 2021 verstorbenen Prinzen Philip, bis hin zur Heiterkeit und Amüsement, wenn das Video eine völlig überraschende Wendung nimmt und uns damit ein Schmunzeln entlockt.

Der Prinz besuchte 2002 die University of East London, an der Smith lehrt. Um ihn filmen zu können, besorgt er sich die Sicherheitsfreigabe und einen Pressepass. In den Untertiteln des Films verweist Smith auf den Tod Philips – und kurz darauf, dass ihm die wohl größte Nahaufnahme des Ohrs seiner Königlichen Hoheit gelungen war. Dieser humorvolle und dennoch ehrerbietige Umgang mit dem Tod des Duke of Edinburgh wäre vermutlich ganz im Sinne Prinz Philips gewesen, der für sein fortschrittliches Denken und Handeln ebenso wie für seinen Humor bekannt war.

T.I.

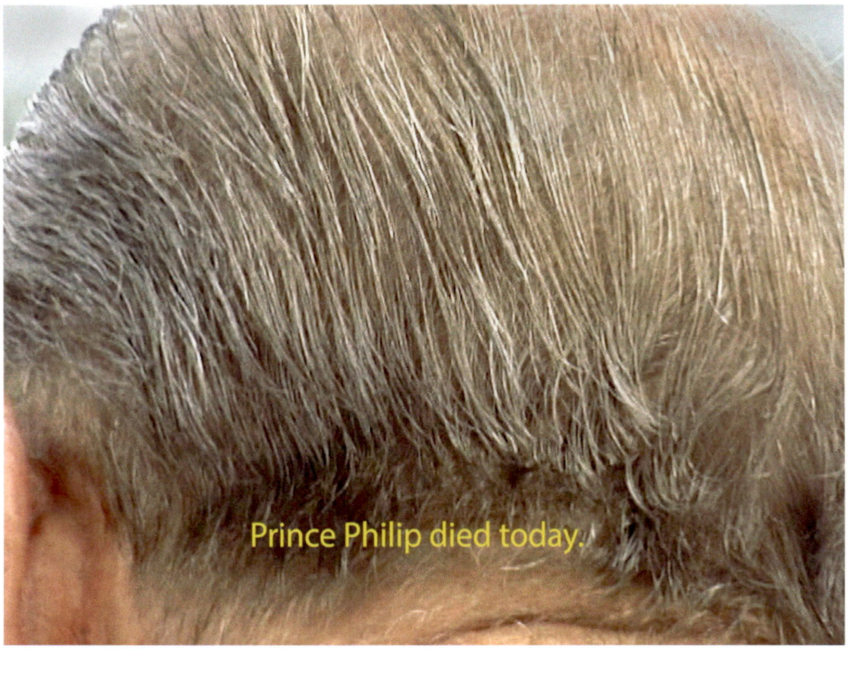

John Smith

Biography

John Smith was born in Walthamstow, London in 1952. He studied at North-East London Polytechnic and the Royal College of Art, after which he became an active member of the London Filmmakers' Co-op. Inspired in his formative years by conceptual art and structural film, but also fascinated by the immersive power of narrative and the spoken word, he has developed a diverse body of work that subverts the perceived boundaries between documentary, fiction, representation and abstraction.

Since 1972 Smith has made over sixty film, video and installation works that have been shown in independent cinemas, art galleries and on television around the world. His films have been awarded major prizes at international film festivals in Oberhausen, Leipzig, Hamburg, Stuttgart, Graz, Geneva, Uppsala, Pamplona, Bordeaux, Lucca, Palermo, Split, Cork, Seoul, Ann Arbor and Chicago. He received a Paul Hamlyn Foundation *Award for Artists* in 2011, and in 2013 he was the winner of Film London's *Jarman Award*.

John Smith lives and works in London.
www.johnsmithfilms.com

Biografie

John Smith wurde 1952 in Walthamstow, London, geboren. Er studierte an der North-East London Polytechnic und dem Royal College of Art, wurde anschließend aktives Mitglied der London Filmmakers' Co-op. In den Anfangsjahren inspiriert von der Konzeptkunst und dem Strukturellen Film, zudem interessiert an der einnehmenden Wirkung des Erzählens und des gesprochenen Wortes, kann er inzwischen auf ein breites Œuvre verweisen. Es unterwandert die gewohnten Grenzen zwischen Dokumentarischem, Fiktion, Repräsentation und Abstraktion.

Seit 1972 hat Smith über 60 Film-, Video- und Installationsarbeiten produziert, welche in unabhängigen Programmkinos, Kunstgalerien und im Fernsehen weltweit gezeigt worden sind. Er erhielt für seine Filme bedeutende Preise auf internationalen Filmfestivals in Oberhausen, Leipzig, Hamburg, Stuttgart, Graz, Genf, Uppsala, Pamplona, Bordeaux, Lucca, Palermo, Split, Cork, Seoul, Ann Arbor und Chicago. Ihm wurde 2011 der Paul Hamlyn Foundation *Award for Artists* verliehen, und er gewann 2013 den Film London *Jarman Award*.

John Smith lebt und arbeitet in London.
www.johnsmithfilms.com

John Smith

Complete Filmography
Vollständige Filmografie

Triangles, 1972, 3 mins, 16mm, colour, sound
Someone Moving, 1972, 5 mins, 16mm, colour, sound
The Hut, 1973, 5 mins, 16mm, colour, sound
Words, 1973, 7 mins, 16mm, colour, sound. Collaboration with Lis Rhodes
Out the Back, 1974, 5 mins, Super 8mm, colour, silent
William and the Cows, 1974, 6 mins, 16mm, colour, silent
Faces 1, 1974, 11 mins, 16mm, B/W, silent
Faces 2, 1974, 3 mins, 16mm, B/W, silent
Associations, 1975, 7 mins, 16mm, colour, sound
Leading Light, 1975, 11 mins, 16mm, colour, sound
Nine Short Stories, 1975, 3 mins, 16mm, B/W, silent
Subjective Tick-Tocks, 1975, 11 mins, 16mm, B/W, sound
The Girl Chewing Gum, 1976, 12 mins, 16mm, B/W, sound
Summer Diary, 1976–77, 30 mins, 16mm, colour, sound
Gardner, 1977, 6 mins, SD video from 16mm, colour, sound
Hackney Marshes – November 4th 1977, 1977, 15 mins, 16mm, colour, silent
Hackney Marshes (TV version), 1978, 30 mins, HD video from 16mm, colour, sound
7P, 1978, 7 mins, 16mm, colour, sound
Blue Bathroom, 1978–79, 25 mins, 16mm, colour, sound
Celestial Navigation, 1980, 10 mins, 16mm, colour, sound
Spring Tree, 1980, 3 mins, 16mm, colour, silent
Shine So Hard, 1981, 32 mins, 16mm, colour, sound
Light Sleep, 1981, 6 mins, 16mm, colour, sound
Shepherd's Delight, 1980–84, 35 mins, 16mm, colour, sound
Om, 1986, 4 mins, 16mm, colour, sound
The Black Tower, 1985–87, 24 mins, 16mm, colour, sound
Dungeness, 1987, 12 mins, 16mm, colour, silent. 3 films for theatre production by Graeme Miller
Slow Glass, 1988–91, 40 mins, 16mm, colour, sound
Gargantuan, 1992, 1 min, 16mm, colour, sound
Home Suite, 1993–94, 96 mins, SD video, colour, sound
Blight, 1994–96, 14 mins, HD video from 16mm, colour, sound. Collaboration with Jocelyn Pook
The Kiss, 1999, 5 mins, HD video from 16mm, colour, sound. Collaboration with Ian Bourn
The Waste Land, 1999, 5 mins, SD video, colour, sound
Regression, 1999, 17 mins, SD video, colour, sound
Lost Sound, 1998–2001, 28 mins, SD video, colour, sound. Collaboration with Graeme Miller
Worst Case Scenario, 2001–03, 18 mins, SD video from 35mm, colour & B/W, sound
Frozen War (Hotel Diaries 1), 2001, 11 mins, SD video, colour, sound
Museum Piece (Hotel Diaries 2), 2004, 12 mins, SD video, colour, sound
Throwing Stones (Hotel Diaries 3), 2004, 11 mins, SD video, colour, sound
B & B (Hotel Diaries 4), 2005, 6 mins, SD video, colour, sound
Pyramids/Skunk (Hotel Diaries 5), 2006–07, 17 mins, SD video, colour, sound
Dirty Pictures (Hotel Diaries 6), 2007, 14 mins, SD video, colour, sound
Six Years Later (Hotel Diaries 7), 2007, 9 mins, SD video, colour, sound
Flag Mountain, 2010, 8 mins, HD video, colour, sound
Demo Tape, 2010, 5 mins, SD video, colour, sound
unusual Red cardigan, 2011, 12 mins, SD video, colour, sound
The Man Phoning Mum, 2011, 12 mins, HD video, colour, sound
Horizon (Five Pounds a Belgian), 2012, 18 mins, HD video, colour, sound
Soft Work, 2012, 37 mins, HD video, colour, sound
Dad's Stick, 2012, 5 mins, HD video, colour, sound
Dark Light, 2014, 4 mins, HD video, B/W, sound

John Smith

White Hole, 2014, 7 mins, HD video, B/W, sound
Steve Hates Fish, 2015, 5 mins, HD video, colour, sound
Who Are We?, 2016, 4 mins, HD video, colour, sound
Song for Europe, 2017, 4 mins, HD video, colour, sound
Jour de Fête, 2017, 1 min, HD video, colour, sound
The Last Word, 2018, 8 mins, HD video, colour, sound. Collaboration with Marcia Farquhar
The Camera, The Actor, 2019, 5 mins, HD video, colour, sound
A State of Grace, 2019, 3 mins, HD video, colour, sound
Citadel, 2020, 16 mins, HD video, colour, sound
Covid Messages, 2020, 22 mins, HD video, colour, sound
Time and Motion, 2021, 2 mins, HD video, colour, sound
Record, 2021, 1 min, HD video, colour, sound

Selected Solo Exhibitions
Einzelausstellungen (Auswahl)

Kunstmuseum Magdeburg (2022, 2005)
CAST, Cornwall (2020)
Kate MacGarry, London (2020, 2016)
Fine Arts, Sydney (2019)
Tanya Leighton, Berlin (2017, 2015, 2013, 2012, 2010)
Alma Zevi, Venice (2017)
Wolverhampton Art Gallery (2016)
Galerie für Zeitgenössische Kunst, Leipzig (2015)
Centre d'Art Contemporain de Noisy-le-Sec, Paris (2014)
The Gallery, Tyneside Cinema, Newcastle upon Tyne (2014)
Figge von Rosen, Cologne (2013)
Kestnergesellschaft, Hannover (2012)
Turner Contemporary, Margate (2012)
Weserburg Museum für Moderne Kunst, Bremen (2012)
Uppsala Konstmuseum, Sweden (2011)
PEER Gallery, London (2011)
Pallas Projects, Dublin (2011)
Royal College of Art Galleries, London (2010)
Sala Diaz Gallery, Texas (2010)
Ikon Gallery, Birmingham (2006)
Open Eye Gallery, Liverpool (2003)
Pearl Gallery, London (2002)

Selected Group Exhibitions
Gruppenausstellungen (Auswahl)

Instantly! Street Photography in Vienna, Museen der Stadt Vienna (2022)
Biennale für Freiburg, Museum für Neue Kunst, Freiburg (2021)
Atlas of Modernity, Muzeum Sztuki, Łodz (2021)
Tourism, Stadtgalerie, Bern (2021)
Le Cours des Choses, CAPC Musée d'Art Contemporain de Bordeaux (2020)
Migrating Worlds: The Art of the Moving Image in Britain, Yale Centre for British Art, Connecticut (2019)
Face It!, Kunstmuseum Ravensburg (2019)
As Seen on Screen, Walker Art Gallery, Liverpool (2019)
Double Takes, Museum of Contemporary At, Cleveland, Ohio (2019)
Journeys with The Waste Land, Turner Contemporary, Margate (2018)
Age of Terror: Art Since 9/11, Imperial War Museum, London (2017)
Between Film and Photography, FOMU Museum, Antwerp (2017)
After the Fact: Propaganda in the 21st Century, Städtische Galerie im Lenbachhaus, Munich (2017)
The Image of War, Bonniers Konsthall, Stockholm (2017)

Moscow Biennial (2017)
Biennale für aktuelle Fotografie, Heidelberg (2017)
Found, Foundling Museum, London (2016)
Double Act: Art and Comedy, MAC, Belfast (2016)
Historicode: Scarcity and Supply, Baijia Lake Museum, Nanjing (2016)
Invocable Reality, Museu d'Art Contemporani de Barcelona (2014)
The Reluctant Narrator, Museu Coleção Berardo, Lisbon (2014)
Le Corbeau et le Renard: Revolt of Language with Marcel Broodthaers, Museum für Gegenwartskunst, Basel (2014)
The Surface of the World, Museum of Contemporary Art, Manila (2014)
Constellations, Tate Liverpool (2013)
Image Counter Image, Haus der Kunst, Munich (2012)
Descriptive Acts, San Francisco Museum of Modern Art (2012)
Has The Film Already Started?, Tate Britain (2011)
Locus Solus: Impressions of Raymond Roussel, Museo Reina Sofía, Madrid (2011)
Berlin Biennale (2010)
The Talent Show, Walker Art Center, Minneapolis and MoMA PS1, New York (2010)
Venice Biennale (2007)
A Century of Artists' Film in Britain, Tate Britain (2004)
Live in Your Head: Concept and Experiment in Britain 1965–75, Whitechapel Gallery, London (2000)
The British Art Show, United Kingdom touring exhibition (1984)

Retrospectives at Film Festivals
Retrospektiven auf Filmfestivals

Oberhausen Short Film Festival, Germany
États Généraux du Film Documentaire, Lussas, France
DOK Leipzig Festival for Documentary and Animated Film, Germany
Dokufest Documentary and Short Film Festival, Prizren, Kosovo
Cork Film Festival, Ireland
Uppsala Short Film Festival, Sweden
Pravo Ludski Film Festival, Sarajevo, Bosnia
Hamburg Short Film Festival, Germany
Tampere Film Festival, Finland
Message to Man Film Festival, St Petersburg, Russia
Underdox Film Festival, Munich, Germany
La Rochelle Film Festival, France
Stuttgart Filmwinter, Germany
Brief Encounters Short Film Festival, Bristol, UK
Regensburg Short Film Week, Germany
Vilnius Short Film Festival, Lithuania
Open City Documentary Festival, London, UK
Avant Film Festival, Karlstad, Sweden
Winterthur Short Film Festival, Switzerland

Selected Collections
Sammlungen (Auswahl)

Tate Gallery, London
Arts Council England
Museum of Modern Art, New York
Muzeum Sztuki, Łodz
FRAC Île de France, Paris
Ella Fontanals-Cisneros, Miami
Kunstmuseum Magdeburg, Magdeburg
Ferens Art Gallery, Hull
Wolverhampton Art Gallery, Wolverhampton

John Smith

Selected Publications

Publikationen (Auswahl)

William Raban and John Smith, *Made in London*, in *Film Talks: 15 Conversations on Experimental Cinema*, eds. Simon Payne and Andrew Vallance, Contact, UK (2021)

A.L. Rees, *Fields of View: Film, Art and Spectatorship*, ed. Simon Payne, British Film Institute, UK (2020)

Johanna Gosse, *Broken English: Allegories of Media Ruin in the Digital Age*; John Smith, *Artist's Statement*, in *Artists' Moving Image in Britain since 1989*, eds. Erika Balsom, Lucy Reynolds, Sarah Perks, Yale University Press, USA (2019)

Mark Prince, *Waiting Game*, in *Talking Art 2: Art Monthly interviews with artists since 2007*, ed. Patricia Bickers, Ridinghouse and Art Monthly, UK (2018)

Andy Birtwistle, *Meaning and Musicality: Sound-Image Relations in the Films of John Smith*, in *The Music and Sound of Experimental Film*, eds. Holly Rogers and Jeremy Barham, Oxford University Press, USA (2017)

Lili Reynaud-Dewar, *I am John Smith (You are also John Smith, we are John Smith, here's how to be John Smith)*, in *John Smith: Le Baiser* (cat.), La Galerie, Noisy-le Sec, France (2014)

Martin Herbert, *Mediate the Immediate: On John Smith*; Kathrin Meyer, *John Smith's The Black Tower: Close-up Views of What Cannot Be Shown*; Ethan de Seife, *John Smith and his Gargantuan Newt*; Ian Christie, *English Eccentric*, in *John Smith*, eds. Tanya Leighton and Kathrin Meyer, Mousse Publishing, Italy and Sternberg Press, Germany (2013)

Tom Holert, *Visual Antagonisms and a Critique of the Frame*, in *Image Counter Image* (cat.) Haus Der Kunst, Munich, Walther König, Germany (2012)

Gemma Lloyd and Gareth Bell-Jones, *John Smith Returns*; Thomas Cuckle, *A Pause for Reflection; John Smith in Conversation with RCA Students*, in *John Smith: Solo Show* (cat.), Royal College of Art, London, UK (2010)

Andy Birtwistle, *Cinesonica: Sounding Film and Video*, Manchester University Press, UK (2010)

David Curtis, *A History of Artists' Film and Video in Britain, 1897–2004*, British Film Institute, UK (2007)

Joe Moran, *Reading the Everyday*, Routledge, UK (2005)

Nicky Hamlyn, *Film Art Phenomena*, British Film Institute, UK (2003)

Cornelia Parker, *John Smith's Body*; A.L. Rees, *Associations: John Smith and the Artists' Film in the UK*; Ian Bourn, *The Sound of Loss*; Nicky Hamlyn, *John Smith's Local Locations*; Cate Elwes, *Trespassing Beyond the Frame* (interview), in *John Smith – Film and Video Works 1972–2002*, Picture This Moving Image/Watershed Media Centre, UK (2002)

Michael Maziere, *John Smith's Films: Reading the Visible*, in *The Undercut Reader – Critical Writings on Artists' Film and Video*, Wallflower Press, UK (2002)

A.L. Rees, *A History of Experimental Film and Video*, British Film Institute, UK (1999)

A Directory of British Film & Video Artists, Arts Council/University of Luton Press, UK (1995)

The Elusive Sign – British Avant-Garde Film & Video 1977–87 (cat.), Arts Council/British Council, UK (1988)

The British Art Show (cat.), Orbis/Arts Council, UK (1984)

A Perspective on English Avant-Garde Film (cat.), Arts Council/British Council, UK (1978)

Colophon

This catalogue has been published on the occasion of the exhibition:
Die Publikation erscheint anlässlich der Ausstellung:

John Smith

Waldeinsamkeit
Films from the 21st Century

Kunstmuseum Magdeburg
8 March – 6 June 2022 / 8. März – 6. Juni 2022

Editors / Herausgeber*innen
Annegret Laabs, Uwe Gellner

Texts / Texte
Erika Balsom, Annegret Laabs

Short texts by Kunstmuseum Magdeburg staff / Kurztexte der Mitarbeiter*innen des Kunstmuseums Magdeburg
Dana Margarete Adele Bulic (D.B.), Uwe Förster (U.F.), Uwe Gellner (U.G.), Theresia Ilchmann (T.I.)

Editing / Redaktion
Uwe Gellner, Dana Margarete Adele Bulic

Copy Editing and Assistance / Lektorat und Mitarbeit
Friederike Börngen, Magdalena Burkhardt, Uwe Förster, Theresia Ilchmann, Loana Aepler

Translation into German / Übersetzung ins Deutsche
Logan Kennedy & Leonhard Unglaub, Lunenburg, Nova Scotia, Canada (Text E. Balsom, Texts J. Smith)
adrem, Stadt Südliches Anhalt (Texts J. Smith)

Translation into English / Übersetzung ins Englische
Michael Wetzel, Berlin (Text A. Laabs, Short texts)

Book Design / Gestaltung
Fraser Muggeridge studio, London

Printing and Binding / Druck und Bindung
Grafisches Centrum Cuno, Calbe

Exhibition / Ausstellung

Concept / Konzept
John Smith, Uwe Gellner

Scientific Assistance / Wissenschaftliche Assistenz
Dana Margarete Adele Bulic

Museums Education / Museumspädagogik
Uwe Förster

Public Relations / Öffentlichkeitsarbeit
Magdalena Burkhardt

Assistance / Mitarbeit
Theresia Ilchmann, Uwe Förster

Administration / Verwaltung
Cornelia Sewitz

Film Technicial Support / Filmtechnik
ephemer.art: Daniel Schulz, Robert Rehnig

Colophon

Technical Crew / Techniker
Michael Daniel, Roland Killinger, Klaus Pfeiffer

Visitor Service / Besucher*innenservice
Ulrike Kropp, Sibylle Reichelt-Höfer

Bibliographic information published by the Deutsche Nationalbibliothek: The Deutsche Nationalbibliothek lists this publication in the Deutsche Nationalbibliografie; detailed bibliographic data is available in the Internet at dnb.de.

Bibliografische Information der Deutschen Nationalbibliothek: Die Deutsche Nationalbibliothek verzeichnet diese Publikation in der Deutschen Nationalbibliografie; detaillierte bibliografische Daten sind im Internet über dnb.de abrufbar.

Published by / Erschienen im:
VfmK Verlag für moderne Kunst GmbH
Schwedenplatz 2/24
A-1010 Wien / Vienna
hello@vfmk.org
www.vfmk.org

Kunstmuseum Kloster Unser Lieben Frauen Magdeburg
Regierungsstraße 4–6
D-39104 Magdeburg
www.kunstmuseum-magdeburg.de

Distribution / Vertrieb
Europe / Europa: LKG, www.lkg-va.de
UK: Cornerhouse Publications, www.cornerhousepublications.org
USA: D.A.P., www.artbook.com

ISBN 978-3-903572-94-2

Printed in Germany / Gedruckt in Deutschland

KUNSTMUSEUM MAGDEBURG KLOSTER UNSER LIEBEN FRAUEN KMd
KLOSTER BERGESCHE STIFTUNG
SACHSEN-ANHALT
VF MK